Means of Grace,
Hope of Glory

Raymond Chapman is Emeritus Professor of English Literature in the University of London and a non-stipendiary priest in the Diocese of Southwark. For many years he was Deputy Chairman of the Prayer Book Society.

Means of Grace, Hope of Glory

Five hundred years of
Anglican thought

Compiled by
Raymond Chapman

CANTERBURY
PRESS
Norwich

Compilation and commentary © Raymond Chapman 2005

First published in 2005 by the Canterbury Press Norwich
(a publishing imprint of Hymns Ancient & Modern Limited,
a registered charity)
St Mary's Works, St Mary's Plain, Norwich, Norfolk, NR3 3BH

www.scm-canterburypress.co.uk

British Library Cataloguing in Publication data

A catalogue record for this book is available
from the British Library

ISBN 1-85311-651-3

Typeset by Regent Typesetting, London
Printed and bound in Great Britain by
William Clowes Ltd, Beccles, Suffolk

Contents

Acknowledgements

Permission to include extracts from the following copyright material is gratefully acknowledged. Attempts have been made to trace all copyright holders. Any errors or omissions, if notified, will be corrected in any future edition.

Affairs of State. Reprinted by kind permission of the Ven. George Austin.

After the Deluge and *Christian Proficiency.* Reprinted by kind permission of SPCK.

The Church of England in Crisis. Reprinted by kind permission of the Very Revd Trevor Beeson.

Thomas Cranmer after Five Hundred Years. Reprinted by kind permission of the Revd Dr Roger Beckwith.

The Ultimate Mystery. Reprinted by kind permission of Mrs Elaine Bishop and the John Bishop Charitable Trust.

Not Angels but Anglicans. Reprinted by kind permission of the Very Revd David Edwards.

A Church for the Twenty-first Century. Reprinted by kind permission of the Revd Professor Robert Hannaford.

'The Odour of Anglicanism'. Reprinted by kind permission of Lady Phyllis James.

Fathers and Anglicans, The Peculiar Character of Anglicanism and *Loving Learning and Desiring God.* Reprinted by kind permission of the Revd Canon Arthur Middleton.

The Priest and the World. Reprinted by kind permission of the Revd Canon W. J. Milligan.

The Real Common Worship. Reprinted by kind permission of the Revd Dr Peter Mullen.

Church and State in Britain since 1820 . Reprinted by kind permission of Mrs Gillian Nicholls.

Celebrate the Christian Story. Reprinted by kind permission of the Right Revd Michael Perham.

Love's Redeeming Work. Reprinted by kind permission of the Right Revd Geoffrey Rowell.

'Towards a theology of a local ordained ministry'. Reprinted by kind permission of the Ven. John Tiller.

Neither Archaic nor Obsolete. Reprinted by kind permission of the Revd Dr Peter Toon.

One Church, One Lord. Reprinted by kind permission of John Whale Esq.

Anglican Identities. Reprinted by kind permission of the Rt. Hon. and Most Revd Rowan Williams.

Extracts from the Book of Common Prayer, the rights of which are vested in the Crown, are reproduced by permission of the Crown's Patentee, Cambridge University Press.

Editorial Notes

The usage of authors in spelling and punctuation has been treated liberally rather than with absolute consistency. It has mostly been accepted, but changed wherever it was likely to cause difficulty or misunderstanding to the modern reader. The original use of capital letters within sentences, which may give a distinctive emphasis, has generally been retained.

[ ] denotes editorial additions or comments within extracts.

[. . .] denotes editorial omissions from the original text.

< > denotes expansion of initials or abbreviations in the text.

The numbers at the end of each extract refer to pages in the edition cited in the list of sources.

In the Sources section, the date of first publication of a text is given in parentheses after the title, where it differs from that of the edition used. Extracts from well-known poems and novels which have appeared in many editions are usually referenced only by title and chapter or lines.

The title of the book is taken from the splendid General Thanksgiving, added to the Book of Common Prayer in 1662. The sub-headings of chapters are from the same book, including the Prefaces, Ordinal and Articles.

Introduction

The settled continuance of the Doctrine and Discipline of the Church of England

How can one define, explain, even accept as credible, an institution like the Church of England? It is a Church which claims to be both Catholic and Protestant, though some of its members disown one or the other name and claim that their party alone maintains continuity with apostolic tradition. It is acknowledged to be a Church of the Reformation, yet asserts its continuity with the medieval *ecclesia anglicana,* the English part of Western Christendom. It is a Church established by law and having an official role in many State functions yet it is not financed by the State, and its clergy are not State employees. It attaches importance to a set liturgy and uniform practice yet offers a wide choice of services and tolerates a good deal of individual enterprise in conducting public worship. It is a Church whose authority runs only through two provinces in a small country, yet it has been the mother of a world-wide communion of independent provinces.

The first English reformers had to create a new order from a twofold change. One was a repudiation of papal authority with the assertion that the Monarch was the Supreme Governor of the Church of England and that no other seat of authority had any jurisdiction over it. The other was the tide of change in doctrine and liturgy which was sweeping across Europe. The two were related but not identical, and tension between departure and continuity would be the cause of long-lasting discussion and controversy. The new leaders had to find a distinctive ecclesiology and liturgy, while still keeping the link with the past and not becoming one of the more radical and independent churches emerging from the Reformation. The English Reformation was in fact the most conservative of the sixteenth-century breaks from Rome. In keeping episcopacy and the forms of church government, and in producing a liturgy which derived much of its content and structure from medieval church and monastic worship, it had a strong case for the continuity which it claimed.

The break with Rome was made by an aggressive king who wavered between conservatism and change in matters of doctrine. He was followed by a boy whose minority was controlled by two successive Protectors who moved the Church in a more Protestant direction, and then by a Queen who returned England for five years to the Roman obedience. After the storms and violence of the early Tudor period had subsided, the Church of England found more peace and stability under Elizabeth I and began to define its identity. There were still threats from without and dissension from within, but it became possible to look at what had been done and consider where it was going to lead. Richard Hooker is perhaps as near as any man to being a founding father of the Church of England, but he was not its creator. He built on the situation, giving it a rationale and authority; and there were other notable thinkers to balance and extend his work. John Jewel in the late sixteenth century and Lancelot Andrewes in the early seventeenth were the most prominent among many divines who defended their Church as Reformed but not heretical, independent of any outside authority but well ordered and governed. Any examination of sources must draw much of its material from this formative period when controversy moved to settlement. When the Church of England came again to dominate the religion of the country after its suppression under the Commonwealth, there was already a tradition to be upheld and developed. There was also an unresolved question. What were the distinguishing marks of this Church which was declared to be autonomous but also part of the universal Catholic Church? Was there anything in doctrine, liturgy or government that could be regarded as distinctively Anglican? To justify the claim to catholicity and continuity, the early apologists generally denied that she had done anything innovative, but had purged the English Church of errors and corruption, producing a national Church of Apostolic purity. Since the evidence about the New Testament Church is, to put it mildly, lacking in close detail, it was useful to find another source of justifying authority. The early Fathers of the Church were reckoned to be untainted by later schisms and papal claims. The study of patristics and the concomitant appeal to early teaching and practice became an enduring feature of Anglican scholarship.

In the chapters which follow we can discern the development of principles and attitudes characteristic of this Church but always appealing to the great Christian tradition and denying novelty. The process has been gradual, sometimes tentative, and never identifying a radical point of departure. There is no foundation document like the Westminster Confession, though the Book of Common Prayer may be regarded as its most authoritative written source. There is no theologian to give his name in the way that Lutheran and Calvinist have become defining titles. There is no word of doctrine or organisation equivalent to such collective names as Baptist and Congregationalist The Church of England is rather like England herself, a country which has moved on through many changes without a single point of national emergence like unification or a declaration of independence.

However, the identification of the Church of England with Englishness has not always been felicitous. It could, and sometimes did, tend to erastianism: the superior influence of the State over the Church in matters ecclesiastical. Henry VIII declared himself to be 'The only supreme head of the Church of England'. Elizabeth I, under a new Act of Supremacy in 1559, was declared to be 'The only supreme governor of this realm, and of all other her highness's dominions and countries, as well as all spiritual or ecclesiastical things or causes as temporal'. As a national Church claiming the loyalty of all citizens, it was able to have the support of Parliament in making and enforcing rules of worship and belief. Such rules were too often applied without regard to individual freedom of conscience. The Church was also subject to the effect of political events, caught up in the antagonisms of the Civil War, suppressed under the Commonwealth and emerging with greater subsequent authoritarianism and distrust of extremes.

It was for a long time fashionable to regard the Laudian Church as the golden age of the Church of England, the foundation of her later strength. The piety and lasting influence of the great Caroline divines and poets cannot be questioned, but it must not be forgotten that there were many other parties and opinions in the Church before the Civil War which also affected future developments. It was similarly supposed that the eighteenth century was a period when the Church was slack in practice, indifferent in matters of doctrine and generally conformist to the political climate. The upheavals of the previous century did bring a desire for peace in matters of religion and a rational rather than emotional faith, with a consequent distrust of religious fervour which was stigmatised as 'enthusiasm'. The desire to be comprehensive and avoid extremes could become lukewarm and lose strong believers, as it lost Wesley, who nevertheless did not cease to regard himself as a presbyter in the Church of England. But it is a travesty to write off the Church in those years, which saw the great Evangelical Revival as strongly in the Established Church as in Nonconformity, the pastoral devotion of many parish clergy, and the quest of many, clergy and lay, for personal holiness. Extracts from eighteenth-century writers will testify to these truths.

There followed new challenges and new strengths. The Evangelicals were influential throughout the nineteenth century. The Oxford Movement emphasised again the sacramental faith and practice which had emerged in the early seventeenth century, and the place of Anglican clergy as priests in the Apostolic Succession. They looked to the Laudian writers and also to the Fathers, for proof that their Church was an ongoing part of the universal Catholic Church. They took their stand on the Church of England as a *via media*, a middle way between what they regarded as 'Popery' and 'Dissent'; and this too had precedent in George Herbert and some of his contemporaries. The restoration of ceremonial practices and private confession aroused opposition from other members of the Church, leading to much fierce polemic on both sides, legislation to control ritual, and consequent prosecution of some determined priests. This *odium theologicum*, theological hatred, did no good to the reputation of the Church and produced a regrettable 'party spirit'.

At the same time, the privileged position of the Church of England was eroded, first by legislation passed by Parliament after the Reform Act of 1832 allowed members of the House of Commons not to subscribe to the Thirty-nine Articles. The mainstream Nonconformist churches grew in strength, opposed the imposition of tithes and church rates, and took an increasing part in education. University College, London was founded in 1827 to challenge the Anglican monopoly over the universities. Other local universities followed, and the Test Acts at Oxford and Cambridge were repealed in 1871. All the Christian churches had to meet attacks from sceptics and agnostics fuelled by scientific discoveries and new biblical criticism. The Church of England suffered a crisis of identity in the nineteenth century and has never returned to the complacent certainty of earlier years.

The twentieth century brought further loss and gain. All the churches experienced a decline in attendance at services and a spirit of secularism grew across British society. In the face of common problems, the party spirit grew less divisive, though it has still not totally disappeared. Relations with other churches improved on a scale and at a rate that would have seemed impossible a century earlier. At the same time, many Anglican theologians were keen to define what was distinctive about their own Church. After revisions to the Book of Common Prayer failed to get Parliamentary approval in 1927 and 1928, there was increasing dissatisfaction with some aspects of establishment. In 1975 the Worship and Doctrine Measure gave the Church of England freedom to develop new liturgies by the approval of its own General Synod. By the end of the century, the Church was facing the problems which affected the whole of the nation and beyond, after two world wars, the end of empires and the virtual disappearance of the old social class structure. There were ethical questions raised by medical advances, new thinking about sexuality, and many others for which traditional moral theology had no set answers.

So to return to our opening question: is it possible to say anything coherent about this unique Church? The chapters which follow try to show that it is possible, that she has developed her own practice and ethos while remaining within the great catholic tradition which her first apologists were so anxious to assert. Through examining what has been written about various aspects of her development over four and a half centuries, we may hope to find at least some things which are peculiar, in both senses of the word, to the Church of England. She has been fortunate in many ways, notably in the allegiance of saints to lead her into holiness, scholars to give her intellectual integrity and millions of ordinary people who have found their faith best expressed though her services and formularies. She was fortunate also in the early years when, despite acts of bigotry and persecution, England escaped the bitter wars of religion which ravaged much of Europe.

She has become the Mother Church of a world-wide communion, but what is represented in this book is confined to the Church of England in its literal sense. To range further would make a book either unmanageably large or too diffuse, but despite great cultural and racial differences across the globe, there is a way in which what developed in a small island has spread its influence. I have used the word 'Anglican' freely to avoid continual repetition of 'Church of England', while recognising that it was first recorded in 1635 and was not in common use until later. Equally, I have used 'Protestant' as a convenient general term, subsuming but not ignoring the Lutheran and Calvinist directions, both of which worked within the Church of England in her formative years and later. All the writers presented were members of the Church of England, including some like Wesley and Newman whom she lost by her own shortcomings, and by whose loss she perhaps learned some wisdom. The vast amount of writing concerning the Church of England must make any selection only a small fraction of the whole. It is quite intimidating to contemplate the rows of shelves in a library, with their volumes of works polemical, apologetic, devotional, liturgical, exegetical and historical. Further, it must be remembered that Anglican writers, being fallible and sometimes inconsistent like the rest of us, do not always pursue the same line through all their writing. What follows is not intended to nail anyone to a single position, but to offer a selection which represents the principal, and sometimes conflicting, Anglican views. It is part of the oddity of this Church, with both positive and negative consequences, to be able to contain differing views on many things.

If it were necessary to pick out one feature as most distinctive, it would probably be a desire for moderation, avoiding extremes, seeking to accommodate different views, respecting reason and experience as powerful elements in individual faith. As well as the *via media* between papal and non-episcopal structures, there has been a love of the *mediocritas firma* recommended by Nicholas Bacon when the Elizabethan Settlement was being debated in Parliament in 1559. The call was not for mediocrity in the modern sense, but for a temperate avoidance of excess, an expression of the classical 'golden mean'. These very things have sometimes been her weakness, encouraging slack doctrine and muting the prophetic voice. They have also been her strength, holding her members together in difficult times. In the sad complexities which still divide the Christian Churches, it may be that she has been granted such traits as gifts towards the coming of the Kingdom.

2

The Church

The blessed company of all faithful people

The question of what constitutes the true Church has been asked through all the Christian centuries, starting from the warnings of the New Testament writers against heretics and schismatics who were defiling the pure gospel which had been received. The Fathers and Councils of the early Church argued, and sometimes fought, over what was in and who was out. Growing tensions between the Eastern and Western Churches culminated in a schism in 1054. The Reformation period aroused more thinking and disputing about the nature of the Church than there had been for many centuries before. All the Reformers and their followers were vigorous in claiming that they had not broken away but had rather, as their name implied, reformed errors and abuses and by so doing had restored the real Church of Christ which had been corrupted.

From the beginning, the apologists for the Church of England maintained that there was no departure or schism. Faith in the 'Catholic and Apostolic Church' of the Nicene Creed was affirmed. The unbroken line of Apostolic Succession through episcopal hands was claimed for the ordained clergy, though the emphasis was at least as much on the continuity of Apostolic teaching and tradition as on the act of ordination. Like the other Reformers, they believed that they had purified and corrected errors, returning the nation to a tradition which had been marred by additions and false claims. The emphasis was on the Church Militant, for the right worship and ordering of life in this world, looking to the Church Triumphant and 'everlasting life' but modifying the cult of saints, drastically reducing the number of their commemorations and discouraging prayers for the dead. These and similar usages would return later, more strongly in some sections of the Church than in others, but the Church of England has always maintained a pragmatic concern for time and place, for the needs of human society and the good ordering of daily life.

After Henry VIII repudiated papal authority over his realm, the matter of jurisdiction was a major issue. No foreign power was to control the English Church, or any part of the national life. Number Thirty-seven of the Thirty-nine Articles promulgated in 1571 decreed that 'The Bishop of Rome, hath no jurisdiction in the Realm of England'. The English Sovereign was now the 'Supreme Governor' of both Church and State. The harsher consequences, the years of persecution and civil disability of Roman Catholics stand as the least happy part of our history. Yet the idea of the Godly Prince, the national ruler ordering and protecting the religious as well as the secular life of the people, was a feature of the Reformation in other countries and caused some tensions with Rome even in those which continued to accept papal jurisdiction. The new emphasis was on national Churches with power to command obedience and attendance at worship. As the words of Hooker given below make clear, the English position in this matter was Lutheran rather than Calvinist: the sovereign was head of both Church and State rather than civil affairs being subject to a theocracy. In England, as elsewhere, Church membership and conformity were seen as a necessary part of national citizenship. To defy the settlement could count as sedition and treason. It was assumed that all loyal subjects were part of the Church and that those who separated themselves from it for reasons of conscience were a danger to the state and not to be tolerated. The sentiments which Henry Fielding gives to Parson Thwackum in *Tom Jones* (1749) are satirical, but not far from what many people believed:

'When I mention religion, I mean the Christian religion; and not only the Christian religion, but the Protestant religion; and not only the Protestant religion, but the Church of England.'

The Oxford Movement revived attention to the nature of the universal Church and the place of the Church of England within it. Supporters of the Movement were cool towards the first Reformers, claimed Hooker as one himself, and drew on both the early and the Laudian Church for their support. They were sometimes too eclectic in compiling their catenae of proof texts, but they brought the doctrine and the ecclesiology of their Church back into a prominence which had for some time been lacking. The 'Branch Theory' became popular: it underlies many of the defences made by earlier Anglican theologians but was now more clearly defined. Although the Church may have suffered schism and loss of universal communion, retention of the traditional faith and the Apostolic Succession were held to provide an invisible unity. The Tractarians maintained that the Roman Catholic, Orthodox and Anglican churches fulfilled these conditions and could therefore be accepted as 'branches' of the true Church. Most Anglican thinkers today would accept this definition, though being less inclined to exclude the non-episcopal churches from the fold.

It may be said today that the Church of England is still the national Church, in so far as everyone in the country is a member of a parish and has certain rights and expectations without necessarily being a regular church attender. It no longer claims leadership in all matters of religion. Official services and commemorations are regularly ecumenical, and increasingly with the participation of other faith communities on some occasions. Most people who do not follow another faith or conscientiously hold a humanist or atheist position will put themselves down as 'Church of England' if pressed for a religious affiliation. The matter of residual attachment, and the 'folk religion' which draws people into a church for rare personal or communal reasons, is a challenge to the clergy. Does it offer opportunity for mission and the reawakening of faith, or should the Church of England take a position as a church ministering to those who choose to be confirmed and communicating members? Many believe that the two are complementary rather than polarised.

The extracts which follow give some of the arguments and assertions on the matter from the sixteenth to the twenty-first century.

John Jewel (1522–71), Bishop of Salisbury from 1560, was one of the first and strongest defenders of the Anglican position against both Roman Catholic and Puritan objections, particularly in his Apologia Ecclesiae Anglicanae, *1562.*

We believe, that there is one church of God, and that not confined, as it was heretofore, to the Jewish people, in one angle or kingdom, but that it is CATHOLIC and UNIVERSAL, and so diffused or spread over the face of the whole earth, that there is no nation which can justly complain that it is excluded and cannot be admitted into the church and people of God. That this church is the kingdom, the body, and spouse of Christ; that Christ is the only prince of this kingdom; that there are in the church divers orders of ministers; that there are some who are deacons, others who are presbyters, and others who are bishops, to whom the instruction of the people, and the care and management of religion are committed. And yet that there neither is, nor is it possible there should be, any one man who has the care of this whole catholic church, for Christ is ever present with his church, and needs not a vicar, or sole and perfect successor; and that no mortal man can in his mind contain all the body of the universal church, that is, all the parts of the earth; much less can he reduce them into an exact order, and rightly and prudently administer its affairs.

John Jewel, *Apology* (1562), Religious Tract Society, no date, page 303

The arguments of Jewel and others were undergirded by legal sanctions, a less happy feature of the early Church of England, as in the Canons set out in 1604.

Whosoever shall hereafter affirm That, the Church of England, by law established under the King's Majesty, is not a true and Apostolical Church, teaching and maintaining the doctrine of the Apostles; let him be excommunicated *ipso facto* and not restored, but only by the Archbishop, after his repentance, and public revocation of this his wicked error.

Canon III

Richard Hooker (c. 1554–1600) was a Fellow of Corpus Christi College, Oxford and later Master of the Temple Church in London. He wrote the first systematic defence of the Church of England in his Treatise on the Laws of Ecclesiastical Polity. *He opposed the Puritans who would accept nothing which was not specifically supported by Scripture, and equally con-*

demned what he saw as the corruption of the Roman Church. He has been claimed as a forefather of Anglo-Catholicism, but shows a good deal of the spirit of moderate Calvinism. Much of what he wrote was not so much a specific defence of the Church of England as it stood in his time but rather an attempt to set out the marks of an ideal Reformed Church in the Catholic tradition. Ultimately, he is not a refuge for any party in the Church of England, but is certainly one of her greatest and most influential thinkers. He was of his time in holding the belief that membership of the Church and of the nation went together, and that the two jurisdictions could not be totally separated.

We hold, that seeing there is not any man of the Church of England but the same man is also a member of the Commonwealth, nor any member of the Commonwealth which is not also of the Church of England, therefore as in a figure triangle the base doth differ from the sides thereof, and yet one and the self-same line is both a base and also a side; a side simply, a base if it chance to be the bottom and underlie the rest: so albeit properties and actions of one do cause the name of a Commonwealth, qualities and functions of another sort, the name of the Church to be given to a multitude, yet one and the self-same multitude may in such sort be both. Nay, it is so with us, that no person appertaining to the one can be denied also to be of the other: contrariwise, unless they against us should hold, that the Church and the Commonwealth are two, both distinct and separate societies; of which two one comprehendeth always persons not belonging to the other, (that which they do,) they could not conclude out of the difference between the Church and the Commonwealth, namely, that the Bishops may not meddle with the affairs of the Commonwealth, because they are governors of another corporation, which is the Church; nor kings, with making laws for the Church, because they have government, not of this corporation, but of another divided from it, the Commonwealth; and the walls of separation between these two must for ever be upheld: they hold the necessity of personal separation, which clean excludeth the power of one man's dealing with both; we of natural, but that one and the same person may in both bear principal sway.

The Works of Richard Hooker, Clarendon Press, 1820, vol. 3, pages 288–9 (Book 8, 1)

John Donne (1571–1631) moved from his Roman Catholic upbringing to the Church of England and became Dean of St Paul's in 1621. As well as his more famous devotional satirical and erotic poetry, he composed some memorable sermons (p. 34). In this poem he expresses the uncertainty about religious allegiance which troubled many in his own time and afterwards. Is true faith to be found in the Roman Catholic or the Lutheran Church? Has the Church of England achieved her goal or is she still seeking?

Show me dear Christ, thy spouse, so bright and clear.
What! is it she, which on the other shore
Goes richly painted? or which robbed and tore
Laments and mourns in Germany and here?
Sleeps she a thousand, then peeps up one year?
Is she self truth and errs? now new, now outwore?
Doth she, and did she, and shall she evermore
On one, on seven, or on no hill appear?
Dwells she with us, or like adventuring knights
First travail we to seek and then make Love?
Betray, kind husband, thy spouse to our sight
And let mine amorous soul court thy mild Dove,
Who is most true, and pleasing to thee, then
When she's embraced and open to most men.

John Donne, *Poetical Works*, Oxford University Press, 1979,
'Divine Poems' XVIII

Sir Thomas Browne (1605–82) was a physician and a scholar. His firm but independent loyalty to his Church was moderate in an age of fierce religious controversy.

There is no church wherein every point so squares unto my conscience, whose articles, constitutions and customs seem so consonant unto reason, and as it were framed to my particular devotion, as this whereof I hold my belief; the Church of England, to whose faith I am a sworn subject, and therefore in a double obligation subscribe unto her articles, and endeavour to observe her constitutions. No man shall reach my faith unto another article, or command my obedience to a canon more: whatsoever is beyond, as points indifferent, I observe according to the rules of my private reason or the humour and fashion of my devotion; neither believing this because Luther affirmed it, or disapproving that because Calvin hath disavouched it. I condemn not all things in the Council of Trent, nor approve all in the Synod of Dort. In brief, where the Scripture is silent, the Church is my text; where that speaks, 'tis but my comment; where there is a joint silence of both, I borrow not the rules of my religion from Rome or Geneva, but the dictates of my own reason. It is an unjust scandal of our adversaries and a gross error in ourselves to compute the nativity of our religion from Henry VIII, who, though he rejected the Pope, refused not the faith of Rome; and effected no more but what his own predecessors desired and assayed in ages past, and was conceived the State of Venice would have attempted in our days. It is as uncharitable a point in us to fall upon those popular scurrilities and opprobrious scoffs of the Bishop of Rome, whom as a temporal prince we owe the duty of good language. I confess there is cause of passion between us. By his sentence I stand excommunicate, and my posterity: 'heretic' is the best language he affords me, yet can no ear witness I ever returned to him the name of Antichrist, Man of Sin, or Whore of Babylon. It is the method of charity to suffer without reaction: those usual satires and invectives of the pulpit may chance produce a good effect on the vulgar, whose ears are opener to rhetoric than logic; yet do they in no wise confirm the faith of wiser believers, who know that a good cause needs not to be patroned by a passion, but can sustain itself upon a temperate dispute.

Religio Medici and Other Writings of Sir Thomas Browne, Dent, 1925, pages 6–7

Henry Hammond (1605–60), Canon of Christ Church, Oxford, and a chaplain to Charles I, defends the Church of England against Roman Catholic charges of schism during the Commonwealth when public Anglican worship was prohibited.

As yet, blessed be God, the Church of England is not invisible; it is still preserved in bishops and presbyters rightly ordained, and multitudes rightly baptized, none of which have fallen off from their profession; and the only thing imaginable to be objected in this point being this, that the schism hath so far been extended by the force, that many, if not most Churches parochial are filled by those who have set up a new, or a no-form of worship, and so that many men cannot any otherwise than in private families serve God after the Church-way, that sure will be of little weight, when the Romanists are remembered to be the objectors, who cannot but know that this is the only way that they have had of serving God in this kingdom these many years, and that the night meetings of the primitive Christians in dens and caves are as pertinent to the justify-ing of our condition as they can be of any, and when it is certain that 'the forsaking of the assemblies' is not 'our wilful fault', but only our un-happy lot, who are forced either not to frequent the assemblies, or else to encourage, and incur the scandal of seeming to approve, the practices of those that have departed from the Church. That we do not decline order or public communion, and consequently are not to be charged for not enjoying those benefits of it which we vehemently thirst after, is evident by the extensive nature of our persecution, the same tempest having with us thrown out all order, and form, bishops, and liturgy together, and to that cursedness of theirs, and not to any obstinateness or unrec-oncilableness of ours, which alone were the guilt of non-communion, is all that unhappiness of the constant sons of the present English Church to be imputed, in which alone this whole objection is founded.

The Miscellaneous Theological Works of Henry Hammond, Parker, 1849, vol. 2, page 290

John Bramhall (1594–1663), Archbishop of Armagh, argues the claim of the Church of England to be a true part of the Catholic and Apostolic Church.

Whosoever doth preserve his obedience entire to the universal Church, and its representative a general Council, and to all his superiors in their due order, so far as by law he is obliged; who holds an internal com-munion with all Christians, and an external communion so far as he can with a good conscience; who approves no reformation but that which is made by lawful authority, upon sufficient grounds, with due moderation; who derives his Christianity by the uninterrupted line of Apostolical succession; who contents himself with his proper place in the ecclesiastical body; who disbelieves nothing contained in Holy Scripture, and if he hold any errors unwittingly and unwillingly, doth implicitly renounce them by his fuller and more firm adherence to that infallible rule; who believeth and practiseth all those *credenda* and *agenda* which the universal Church spread over the face of the earth doth unanimously believe and practise as necessary to salvation, without condemning or censuring others of different judgement from himself in inferior questions, without obtruding his own opinions upon others as articles of Faith; who is implicitly prepared to believe and do all other speculative and practical truths, when they shall be revealed to him; and, in sum, 'that prefers not a subtlety or an imaginary truth before the bond of peace'; he may securely say, 'My name is Christian, my surname is Catholic'.

From hence it appeareth plainly, by the rule of contraries, who are schismatics; whosoever doth uncharitably make ruptures in the mystical Body of Christ, or 'sets up altar against altar' in His Church, or withdraws his obedience from the Catholic Church, or its representative a general Council, or from any lawful superiors, without just grounds; whosoever doth limit the Catholic Church unto his own sect, excluding all the rest of the Christian world, by new doctrines, or erroneous censures, or tyrannical impositions; whosoever holds not internal communion with all Christians, and external also so far as they continue in a Catholic constitution; whosoever, not contenting himself with his due place in the Church, doth attempt to usurp an higher place, to the disorder and disturbance of the whole body; whosoever takes upon him to reform without just authority and good grounds; and, lastly, whosoever doth wilfully break the line of Apostolical succession, which is the very nerves and sinews of ecclesiastical unity and communion, both with the present Church, and with the Catholic Symbolical Church of all successive ages; he is a schismatic, whether he be guilty of heretical pravity or not.

John Bramhall, *A Just Vindication of the Church of England* (1654), Parker, 1842, vol. 1, pages 111–12

William Wilberforce ((1759–1833) is largely remembered today for his passionate work as a Member of Parliament towards the abolition of the slave trade. He was one of the Evangelical 'Clapham sect' and his writing established him as the leader of the influential Evangelical party in the Church of England.

Christianity in its best days (for the credit of our representations let this be remembered, by those who object to our statement as austere and contracted) was such as it has been delineated in the present work. This was the religion of the most eminent Reformers, of those bright ornaments of our country who suffered martyrdom under Queen Mary; of their successors in the times of Elizabeth; in short, of all the pillars of our Protestant church; of many of its highest dignitaries; of Davenant, of Jewel, of Hall, of Reynolds, of Beveridge, of Hooker, of Andrews, of Smith, of Leighton, of Usher, of Hopkins, of Baxter and of many others of scarcely inferior note. In their pages the peculiar doctrines of Christianity were everywhere visible, and on the deep and solid basis of these doctrinal truths were laid the foundations of a superstructure of morals proportionably broad and exalted. Of this fact their writings still extant are a decisive proof: and they who may want leisure, or opportunity, or inclination, for the perusal of these valuable records, may satisfy themselves of the truth of the assertion, that, such as we have stated it, was the Christianity of those times by consulting our Articles and Homilies, or even by carefully examining our excellent Liturgy. But from that tendency to deterioration lately noticed, these great fundamental truths began to he somewhat less prominent in the compositions of many of the leading divines before the time of the civil wars. During that period, however, the peculiar doctrines of Christianity were grievously abused by many of the sectaries, who were foremost in the commotions of those unhappy days; who, while they talked copiously of the free grace of Christ, and the operations of the Holy Spirit, were by their lives an open scandal to the name of Christian.

William Wilberforce, *A Practical View of the Prevailing Religious System etc.* (1797),
SCM Press, 1958, pages 113–14

John Henry Newman (1801–90) was the leading figure of the Oxford Movement until he entered the Roman Catholic Church in 1845, where he later became a Cardinal. While he was still in the Church of England, he wrote a strong defence of the Via Media, *the 'middle way' which she held between Rome and the non-episcopal Churches. Although the Tractarians made a great deal of the* Via Media, *it should be noted that the term had been previously used for many years. 'Clericus', speaking for Newman himself, replies to the question from 'Laicus': 'You separate your creed and cause from that of the Reformed Churches of the Continent?'*

Not altogether; but I protest against being brought into that close alliance with them which the world now-a-days would force upon us. The glory of the English Church is, that it has taken the VIA MEDIA, as it has been called. It lies *between* the (so called) Reformers and the Romanists; whereas there are religious circles, and influential too, where it is thought enough to prove an English Clergyman unfaithful to his Church, if he preaches anything at variance with the opinions of the Diet of Augsburg, or the Confessions of the Waldenses.

J. H. Newman, *The Via Media of the Anglican Church*, Longmans, 1845, vol. 2, pages 87–8

William Gresley (1801–76), a Prebendary of Lichfield, wrote in both polemic and fiction to support the ideals of the Oxford Movement. Three hundred years after Hooker and Jewel, he returns to the classical Anglican defence that the English Reformation was not a break from the past but a continuation of the true tradition.

Yes, our national character, in all its strength and nobleness, is the emanation of our national Church. The Church is the mould in which it has been cast; and no wonder that God's true Church should sanctify and elevate the people amongst whom it abides. The character of a people evidently depends on the moral principles in which they are trained; and the distinctive genius of the English is clearly traceable to their Church. There is a peculiarity in the Anglican Church which distinguishes it from all other Protestant communities. When God opened men's eyes to discern the errors of Romanism, the English reformers did not, like their continental brethren, cast aside the authority of ages, and reconstruct a Church for themselves; they simply repaired and cleansed their ancient temples: for, though neglected and dilapidated, the framework was entire, the plan was perfect. They subjected her doctrine and discipline to the test of Scripture. What was contrary to Scripture, they at once discarded; what was agreeable to it, they retained and reverenced as a sacred legacy from the Apostolic ages. Her outward form and structure, her threefold ministry, her dioceses and parishes, her Apostolic ordination, her creeds, her very services, which had been handed down from age to age – all these they retained; only they removed from them whatsoever was contrary to the word of God; and the Church stood forth to the world fresh in the beauty of her intrinsic holiness, the exact model, nay, rather the continued identification, of the one Catholic and Apostolic Church.

William Gresley, Portrait of an English Churchman, Rivington, 1840, pages 75–6

W. F. Hook (1798–1875), Dean of Chichester, sympathised with the Tractarians but fell out with Pusey over later developments. He defended the continuity of the Church of England but had no doubt that the Reformation was real and necessary, as he here robustly declares in terms of which Bishop Jewel would have approved.

You see, then – and in these days it is particularly necessary to bear the fact in mind – that ours is the Old Catholic Church of England; a Church which traces its origin to the Apostles and our Lord; a Church which in the dark ages laboured under abuses and corruptions, which were removed under the Episcopates of Archbishop Cranmer and Archbishop Parker. Nothing can be more mistaken than to speak of these great men as the founders of our Church. One only is our founder, and that is Christ. And as well might we say of a man when he has washed his face that he is not the same man as he was before his ablution, as to say of the Church of England that she is a different Church since the Reformation from what she was before.

W. F. Hook, The Church and its Ordinances, Bentley, 1876, page 109

The growth of the Anglican Communion overseas called for definition of relationship to the mother Church. The 'Lambeth Quadrilateral' was formulated as Resolution 11 of the Lambeth Conference in 1888 as a basis for agreement.

(a) The Holy Scriptures of the Old and New Testaments, as containing all things necessary to salvation, and as being the rule and ultimate standard of faith.

(b) The Apostles' Creed, as the Baptismal Symbol; and the Nicene Creed, as the sufficient statement of the Christian faith.

(c) The two Sacraments ordained by Christ Himself – Baptism and the Supper of the Lord – ministered with unfailing use of Christ's words of Institution, and of the elements ordained by Him.

(d) The Historic Episcopate, locally adapted in the methods of its administration to the varying needs of the nations and peoples called of God into the Unity of His Church.

Charles Gore (1853–1932), Bishop successively of Worcester, Birmingham and Oxford, was a leading Anglo-Catholic who accepted much of the new biblical criticism and pressed for a Christian approach to social issues. He argues for the abiding catholicity of the Church of England in spite of some Calvinistic tendencies in her early formularies. His approach to the Thirty-nine Articles is similar to that taken by Newman in Tract 90, but less extreme in its claims.

On some central points the Church of England possesses [. . .] definite and explicit dogmas; but with regard to many matters which were in controversy at the period of the Reformation, on points which belonged respectively to the Calvinistic, Lutheran and Tridentine positions, you find that, as a matter of fact, the Articles appear to have been intended not as definite solutions but rather as 'articles of peace'; they aim at shelving rather than defining questions. You have quite definitely Calvinistic articles formulated at the period of the Reformation and Lutheran articles and Tridentine decrees, but the Articles of the Church of England on points then in controversy lack the definiteness of the Lutheran, or Calvinistic, or Tridentine decisions. And we may be thankful the Church of England did not commit herself. Indefinite *formulae*, are not indeed satisfactory. They may appear to say much and in fact say little. This is, I think, the case with many of our articles. But none of greater definiteness drawn up at that moment could have failed to commit us to what, in the great issue, would have imperilled our position. The moment was one of transition and movement. It is very untrue to call it a moment of settlement. This is apparent in retrospect. What has become of definite Calvinism and definite Lutheranism all over Europe? Has Rome stopped at the Tridentine position? Had the sixteenth century the materials at its disposal which are necessary for understanding the early history of Christian doctrine? However unsatisfactory then the articles are positively as statements of truth they are satisfactory in what they are not. It is the very fact that the Church of England at the Reformation did not commit herself to any one of the three then dominant tendencies, which leaves us now at the present moment in a unique position of hopefulness among the Churches of Europe. We are left standing firm on the Creeds, the Sacraments, the apostolic succession of the ministry; and on that basis we are to rise with the help of the clearer knowledge we now have, to the full apprehension and presentation of the ancient faith.

Charles Gore, *The Mission of the Church*, John Murray, 1892, pages 48–50

N. P. Williams (1883–1943), Lady Margaret Professor of Divinity at Oxford, followed the Anglo-Catholic line a generation after Gore. He offers similar arguments, prompted by the general uncertainty and questioning which troubled many aspects of life after the Great War.

At the present time [1926], it is possible to look back too apprehensively to the perils which beset the English Church at the Reformation and to the risks which she has subsequently encountered. By identifying ourselves too closely with her past anxieties and controversies, we may lose our sense of perspective. These things cannot be overlooked by the historian, but a sound judgement will regard them as dangers incident to the growth of a living organism which has survived them and gathered from them strength to meet and overcome the trials of the present and the future. Throughout her post-Reformation history, the Church of England has given proof of a steadfastness of purpose and a power of recovery amid such perils which we may well review with thankfulness and confidence. The path on which she entered in the sixteenth century was new and untried, and its beginnings were dark and uncertain; but no one who watches her progress along it can doubt that she was guided by the Spirit of God, acquiring stores of spiritual energy which have revived her in periods of faintness and have quickened her to fresh and accumulated effort. Under this guidance, she has achieved successes which were beyond the dreams of the medieval Church. She has prosecuted her apostolic mission and planted apostolic faith and order in regions outside the hope and imagination of the most sanguine of Crusaders. Without novel or sensational experiments, adhering closely to traditional lines of doctrine and practice, she has made her influence felt as a permanent element in the life of the Christian Church, fostering in her sons a devotion and a temper of mind which have added no small strength and supplied new impetus to the spiritual activities of the modern world. From the protestantism of her early reformers she has found her way to a positive assertion of her claim to an abiding place in the Catholic community from which she has never separated herself by any action or declaration.

N. P. Williams, 'The Origin of the Sacraments', in E. G. Selwyn (ed.), *Essays Catholic and Critical*, SPCK, 1926, pages 365–6

Alwyn Williams, Bishop of Durham from 1939 to 1952, finds a distinctively Anglican ethos continuing from the sixteenth century to the twentieth.

It is hardly possible to write about Anglicanism without at least mentioning the famous phrase '*via media*' so often used to describe it. And the phrase, of course, has genuine meaning and usefulness. None the less it suggests an intention of compromise which is easily misleading. It is true that the English temper has through most of English history seemed to have a genius for the refusal of extremes, for readiness to accept the complications of real life and of human nature as a warning against attempts to shape rigid lines of action or theory in its practical concerns. It is equally true that the Church of England is in a hundred ways characteristically English both in strength and weakness, in its curious anomalies and in the puzzles it offers to the systematic mind. But all this is far from proving that Anglicanism in early days or later set itself to a middle course by means of a conscious avoidance of extremes. There was a positive sense of direction in its best and leading minds. There were certain guiding lines to follow: they were not altogether distinct from those which Rome had followed, but there came decisive points at which Rome must be left: they were not altogether distinct from those followed by Luther or Calvin or Zwingli, but there came decisive points at which those great men too must be left, despite the binding power of Scriptural allegiance. Anglicanism followed a line of its own not because the attempt was made to keep at something like equal distance from certain extremes judged to be false, but because its main principles, as they were gradually formulated and expressed, disclosed a particular character and directed a particular growth. Those principles have been variously balanced and their weight at one period or another variously judged, but in the main they have been consistently held.

A. T. P. Williams, The Anglican Tradition in the Life of England, SCM Press, 1947,
pages 20–1

The Church of England has always claimed the possession of 'sound learning', with an intellectual as well as a spiritual approach to faith. Mandell Creighton (1843–1901), Bishop of Peterborough and then of London, believed that the Church had come through the Reformation with her powers of scholarship unscathed by controversy. He praises the Book of Common Prayer, of which more is said in Chapter 6, below.

Reforming efforts ended in a sense of hopeless weariness; but one truth became apparent, that reform was only possible by returning to the principles of sound learning. It was just this principle that was applied in the changes made in the English Church in the sixteenth century. It was not that England alone possessed the necessary learning; that learning and its conclusions had long been the common property of serious and thoughtful men. But England had the unique opportunity of applying it calmly and dispassionately. In foreign countries the Reformation movement was inextricably mingled with grave political disturbances. It wore a revolutionary aspect. It needed popular leaders whose opinions were necessarily coloured by the conflict in which they were engaged. The new theology had to be adapted to the purpose of attack and defence. This was not the case in England. There was no great leader whose personality impressed itself upon the changes that were made. There was no motive to attend to anything save the long record of the aspirations of sound learning. Our Prayer Book is the standing record of the result of this process. It is sometimes said that the Prayer Book is unduly exalted and extolled. This only means that while individually we might suggest additions or alterations in points of detail, there is no advance of learning which modifies the general principles, with reference to which its work, as a whole, was done. There is no body of opinion which could, on the grounds of knowledge, suggest any material alterations.

Mandell Creighton, *The Church and the Nation*, Longmans, 1901, pages 252–3

Michael Ramsey (1904–88) was one of the most notable theologians to have been Archbishop of Canterbury, the position to which he was appointed in 1961. He did much to improve relations which the Roman Catholic and Orthodox Churches while maintaining, as this passage shows, belief in the continuing catholicity of his own Church. The 'angelic doctor' is St Thomas Aquinas.

The Anglican use, method and direction discovered themselves in reaction from the pressure of Luther, Calvin and Trent; and it is possible that in the reaction against misleading systems there was a missing of certain valuable elements which those systems contained. Thus, though the Anglican method led to a balanced use of Scripture as interpreted by tradition and to an escape from the lopsidedness of the Reformed scripturalism, there may yet have been loss through the missing of the more, 'dynamic' use of Scripture known amongst the Reformed. In other words our emphasis (right as it has been) upon the 'Word made flesh' may have led us to miss something of the meaning of the 'Word spoken' as Reformed Christianity values it.

Similarly the reaction against Rome may have led to loss through neglect of the angelic doctor, from whom Hooker himself had learnt not a little. The day of revenge has come. The catastrophic times through which we have been passing have exposed the contemporary weaknesses of the Anglican use. Can it offer the wholeness of system which the Thomist offers? Does it sufficiently understand the notes of crisis and judgement which the Confessional Protestant has been making his own? It has seemed that Anglicanism has had less to say and has said it less powerfully than these two theologies upon its flanks. Its members often look to them rather than to their mother, and ask 'Has she a theology of her own?'

But history may soon repeat itself, and, as in the latter days of the reign of Queen Elizabeth [I], Anglican divinity may soon rediscover itself and, while claiming to say far less than the Schoolman and the

Confessionalist, may speak both *with* a wider authority than they and *to* the whole man rather than to a part of him. [. . .] If these judgements be true the Anglican need not be too diffident or apologetic, though he may need to be more modest, in what he claims to say.

A. M. Ramsey, 'What is Anglican Theology?', *Theology*, vol. 48, 1945, pages 3–4

Stephen Sykes, formerly Bishop of Ely and now Principal of St John's College, Durham, defends the reality and the evolution of Anglican doctrine.

Now it is certainly true that the Anglican reformation lacked the kind of doctrinal definiteness given, for example, to the Lutheran church by Luther and the Lutheran confessional documents; and an explicit part of the seventeenth-century apologia for the Anglican church was that it did not insist on the kind of formulated system of doctrine produced at the Council of Trent. But it would have astonished Cranmer or Hooker to be told that Anglicans had no doctrinal commitment, when the explicit claim which they were making was that the church professed the identical faith of the apostles and of the early church. The point and significance of the Thirty Nine Articles in relation to Anglicanism is also frequently misrepresented. Ambiguous they may be, and related to specific controversies of the sixteenth century. But it is nonsense to say that they are void of doctrinal content, or that they add nothing to the bare confession of the creed. The very reason for omitting in 1865 that phrase from the formula of assent demanding acknowledgement of all and every one of the articles was precisely because this it was found to be too restricting to the consciences of nineteenth-century Anglicans. Similarly, the reason for further loosening the terms of the declaration of assent in 1975 was that even the previous ambiguity no longer corresponded to the real divergence of belief which some modern Anglicans professed from the substance of the Articles. In other words, there has taken place a substantial change in the Anglican requirement for doctrinal commitment among its officially commissioned personnel. It is simply not historically correct to suppose that this has always been the case in the Anglican church, or that the present wide doctrinal freedom has always been characteristic of Anglicanism. The case is rather that in response to the pressures initially of controversy and subsequently (and decisively) of biblical and historical criticism, the Anglican church has progressively shed its distinctive confessional commitment, relatively broad though that always was.

S. W. Sykes, *The Integrity of Anglicanism*, Mowbrays, 1978, pages 42–3

Robert Hannaford, Professor of Theology at St Martin's College, Lancaster, assesses the distinctive qualities of the Church of England as seen at the present time.

Unlike the confessional Churches of the Reformation or the Roman Catholic Church with its established dogmatic tradition, the Church of England does not possess agreed and canonically binding dogmatic interpretations of the Scriptures and Christian tradition. It is perfectly true that this has not prevented the Church of England from publicly endorsing the dogmatic implications of ecumenical documents such as the Agreed Statements of the Anglican–Roman Catholic International Commission, but it is not an easy matter to substantiate these agreements from Anglican historic formularies. Anglican formularies, such as the Book of Common Prayer and the Ordinal, are couched in the language of liturgy and inevitably permit a number of interpretations, a possibility which is deliberately foreclosed by the language of dogmatics. This has led to difficulties over the acceptance of the reports by the Vatican. Anglicans are being asked to support their ecumenical gestures by clearer reference to confessional documents, but it is the absence of these which plays an important part in defining their ecclesial identity. To those possessed of a doctrinal *magisterium* the Church of England, and indeed the Anglican Communion of churches as a whole, appears theologically pragmatic and doctrinally plural.

It is true that Anglican doctrine is not easily identifiable but it is a mere caricature to suggest that the Church of England has none. The fact that a great deal of freedom is granted to Anglican theologians does not mean that the same degree of latitude occurs at every point in the church's life. Anglicans, for example, have been hesitant about joining in certain ecumenical schemes because of their commitment to episcopacy. Although it is not defined dogmatically, Anglican practice presupposes a particular ecclesiology, which is reflected in the dignity and importance accorded to the episcopal office. Then again, Anglican liturgical practice, although more varied in both form and content than the Roman Catholic Church, is nonetheless premised on the centrality of the eucharist. Generally speaking the lesser or pastoral offices are seen as either a preparation for or a response to the eucharistic rite, and this is even clearer in the newer Anglican liturgies. Anglicans may not be publicly committed to a single doctrinal interpretation of the eucharist but their collective life makes the rite central. The compilers of the 1981 report of the Church of England Doctrine Commission, *Believing in the Church*, comment that it is 'more typical of Anglicanism to rely upon custom, ceremonial and, above all, its forms of public prayer, to reveal its doctrine by implication'. The public face of Anglican doctrine resides principally in its liturgy and canons.

Robert Hannaford, *A Church for the Twenty-first Century*, Gracewing, 1998,
pages 293–4

Rowan Williams, Archbishop of Canterbury since 2002, continues the thinking about the Church which has concerned his predecessors back to Thomas Cranmer. He gives a brilliantly succinct statement for our own day.

The word 'Anglican' begs a question at once. I have simply taken it as referring to the sort of Reformed Christian thinking that was done by those (in Britain at first, then far more widely) who were content to settle with a church order grounded in the historic ministry of bishops, priest and deacons, and with the classical early Christian formulations of doctrine about God and Jesus Christ – the Nicene Creed and the Definition of Chalcedon. It is certainly *Reformed* thinking, and we should not let the deep and pervasive echoes of the Middle Ages mislead us: it assumes the governing authority of the Bible, made available in the vernacular, and repudiates the necessity of a central executive authority in the Church's hierarchy. It is committed to a radical criticism of any theology that sanctions the hope that human activity can contribute to the winning of God's favour, and so is suspicious of organised asceticism (as opposed to the free expression of devotion to God which may indeed be profoundly ascetic in its form) and of a theology of the sacraments which appears to bind God too closely to material transactions (as opposed to seeing the freer activity of God sustaining and transforming certain human actions done in Christ's name).

Rowan Williams, *Anglican Identities*, Darton, Longman and Todd, 2004, pages 2–3

After much theological thinking and controversy, we may remember the power of hymns to strengthen and confirm the faithful. This one may stand for the whole of the Christian Church, but it must be allowed that Anglicans sing it with fervour and apply it to their own confession.

Thy hand, O God, has guided
Thy flock, from age to age;
The wondrous tale is written,
Full clear, on every page;
Our fathers owned thy goodness,
And we their deeds record;
And both of this bear witness:
One Church, one Faith, one Lord.

Thy heralds brought glad tidings
To greatest, as to least
They bade men rise, and hasten
To share the great King's feast;
And this was all their teaching,
In every deed and word
To all alike proclaiming
One Church, one Faith, one Lord.

Through many a day of darkness,
Through many a scene of strife,
The faithful few fought bravely
To guard the nation's life.
Their gospel of redemption,
Sin pardoned, man restored,
Was all in this enfolded,
One Church, one Faith, one Lord.

And we, shall we be faithless?
Shall hearts fail, hands hang down?
Shall we evade the conflict,
And cast away our crown?
Not so: in God's deep counsels
Some better thing is stored;
We will maintain, unflinching,
One Church, one Faith, one Lord.

Thy mercy will not fail us,
Nor leave thy work undone;
With thy right hand to help us,
The victory shall be won;
And then, by men and angels,
Thy name shall be adored,
And this shall be their anthem,
One Church, one Faith, one Lord.

Edward Plumptre (1823–91),
New English Hymnal, no. 485

3

Authority

The Doctrine and Sacraments, and the Discipline of Christ

Apart from a few sects and eccentric individuals claiming special revelations and new, inspired documents, all parts of the Christian Church have appealed to Scripture for their rationale and justification. Even before the final formation of the biblical canon, the Old Testament, and the writings out of which the New Testament was being made, were cited as authorities for faith and conduct. 'Whatsoever things were written aforetime were written for our learning' (Romans 15.4). The early formulation of doctrine, and the arguments of those eventually adjudged to be heretical, were both based on interpretation of the sacred books. When a new period of religious controversy began in the sixteenth century, the Reformers claimed a strong biblical foundation for their teaching. They announced that they were not innovating but looking back to a primitive purity which had been abused and could be proved from the Bible. They were literally re-forming the Church in accordance with the earliest authority of the divinely-inspired writings.

The Bible was not only the final court of appeal. It was to be read and followed by all the godly, lay and cleric alike, to be their guide in daily decisions as well as in the ultimates of faith. It was to replace the saints' lives, the pious legends and the special devotions which had been the fare provided by the medieval Church. The watchword of the Reformers was *sola scriptura*, scripture alone. The Bible was translated into the vernacular languages of all the countries where the Reformation took hold. It was placed in the churches, openly sold, read by the literate, discussed even by those who could know it only when it was read aloud. But the Reformation was not a monolithic movement. Lutherans, Calvinists, Zwinglians and their sub-sets all took their stand on *sola scriptura*, but engaged in controversies as bitter as their dispute with the Roman Catholic Church. The vernacular translations were sometimes polemical in their choice of words and in added notes. Confrontational texts were freely exchanged in arguments.

In 1538 it was ordered that every church in England should have a copy of the Bible in English. This version, known as the 'Great Bible', was revised and re-issued in 1540 with a Preface by Thomas Cranmer (see below). It was the ancestor of the 'Authorised' or 'King James' version of 1611, the translation familiar to generations of Anglicans through church services and private reading. The Book of Common Prayer through all its revisions from 1549, is strongly based on the Bible, with more allusions and direct quotations than any other book of services. A fundamentalist approach was generally shared until the nineteenth century. The Bible was regarded as the direct Word of God, not only divinely inspired but also verbally directed. Some writers indeed urged caution in private interpretation, but the view that it was the ultimate authority in matters of faith and conduct generally prevailed. This belief did not mean unanimity and concord. Different and even contrary opinions could be supported by selection and interpretation and this was a problem for the Church of England trying to steer its desired 'mean between the two extremes'. Strict Calvinists held that nothing could be justified which was not explicitly permitted in Scripture; the more moderate were content to accept that which was not clearly forbidden, but even this concession did not always make it easy for the official authorities on doctrine, liturgy and morals.

From the middle of the nineteenth century, the unquestioned literalism of Bible reading was challenged by biblical criticism. Anglican scholars were early and vigorous among those who took up the challenge posed by German critics. In 1860 the liberal views expressed by the seven authors of *Essays and Reviews* were widely condemned elsewhere in the Church but the new criticism was not to be silenced. Westcott and others (see below) followed the trend. Revisionist ideas, ranging from the moderate to the radical, generally prevailed in the Church of England at the expense of absolute fundamentalism, although reverence for the Bible as the supreme source of faith and conduct remained.

However, this does not close the question of the source of authority in the Church. Tradition has from the beginning been regarded as vital in preserving orthodoxy: tradition not in the sense of doing what was done yesterday but of the *paradosis*, the handing on, or handing down, of the faith taught by Christ to the Apostles and promulgated by them. The

Bible itself is the book of the Church, the canon of the New Testament was determined by the Church by the end of the fourth century with the exclusion of some books which had been current among the faithful (see Liddon below). In its first formularies, the Church of England looked to the early Councils and Fathers of the Church as well as to the Bible. This meant some delicate walking between Protestant *sola scriptura* and the claim to be in the Catholic line of observing the teachings of the ancient Church. Distinction was drawn between the tradition of the Apostles and their immediate successors and more recent pronouncements which could be dismissed as 'corrupt'. In some respects the Church of England anticipated and continued to follow the line taken by Newman in his *Essay on the Development of Christian Doctrine* (1845) on the true developments of which the seed could be found in the beginning and corruptions which departed from ancient purity; Newman of course brought his investigation to a different conclusion. Discussion continues about the claims of new insights in changing conditions as distinct from evolved development of the original deposit. In particular, ethical questions posed by new medical and psychological knowledge, and consequently not addressed by traditional moral theology, demand a fresh look at judgements which have been taken for granted in the past.

The Church of England has inherited the belief of her early divines that it is proper to make binding rules for her members so long as these are not plainly contrary to Scripture. In general they took the moderate Calvinist view – that the Bible was a guide to what was permitted and not an inflexible code by which everything must be proved. There was a further problem: how should the Church of England relate to the decisions of General Councils? The Conciliar movement had been developing in previous centuries, urging that the supreme authority of the Church lay in its General Councils rather than in sole papal power. This was very convenient for a Church asserting that the pope had no power in England, but some of the later medieval Councils had made rulings which were less acceptable. Article 21 (see below) addressed this dilemma.

The third plank in the Anglican platform is Reason, a criterion shared with the Roman Catholic Church, and, in varying degrees of lesser intensity, with many of the Free Churches. It is a word which causes disquiet in some quarters, partly because of the appropriation of 'Rationalism' as a militant word for sundry forms of atheism, agnosticism and humanism. But there has always been a feeling among some Christian thinkers that Reason has no part in the mystery of faith. Tertullian in the early third century AD wrote, 'I believe because it is absurd.' As against this, some have made a case for the reasonableness of Christianity as a proof of its truth. It was a claim urged strongly in the late seventeenth century by writers like John Locke (1632–1704) and caused some church-men to fear a lapse into Deism. Anglican thought has generally favoured the proper use of Reason, taking the position not of Tertullian but of St Augustine (354–430), 'I believe so that I may understand.' Reason can tell us something about God, but only revelation can lead us to knowing him as he is and as he works. This is the position of St Thomas Aquinas in the thirteenth century and is shared by many recent Anglican theologians, like William Temple and Austin Farrer.

Thomas Cranmer (1498–1556), Archbishop of Canterbury and principal architect of the new Church order and the Book of Common Prayer, declared and expounded the authority of Scripture in a Preface to the revised Great Bible issued in 1540.

In few words to comprehend the largeness and utility of the scripture, how it containeth fruitful instruction and erudition for every man; if any things be necessary to be learned, of the holy scripture we may learn it. If falsehood shall be reproved, thereof we may gather wherewithal. If any thing be to be corrected and amended, if there need any exhortation or consolation, of the scripture we may well learn. In the scriptures be the fat pastures of the soul; therein is no venomous meat, no unwholesome thing; they be the very dainty and pure feeding. He that is ignorant, shall find there what he should learn. He that is a perverse sinner, shall there find his damnation to make him to tremble for fear. He that laboureth to serve God, shall find there his glory, and the promissions [promises] of eternal life, exhorting him more diligently to labour. Herein may princes learn how to govern their subjects; subjects obedience, love and dread to their princes: husbands, how they should behave them unto their wives; how to educate their children and servants: and contrary the wives, children, and servants may know their duty to their husbands, parents and masters. Here may all manner of persons, men, women, young, old, learned, unlearned, rich, poor, priests, laymen, lords, ladies, officers, tenants and mean men, virgins, wives, widows, lawyers, merchants, artificers, husbandmen, and all manner of persons, of what estate or condition soever they be, may in this book learn all things what they ought to believe, what they ought to do, and what they should not do, as well concerning Almighty God, as also concerning themselves and all other. Briefly, to the reading of the scripture none can be enemy, but that either be so sick that they love not to hear of any medicine, or else be so ignorant that they know not scripture to be the most healthful medicine.

The Works of Thomas Cranmer, ed. G. E. Duffield, Sutton Courtenay Press, 1964, page 37

Richard Hooker (p. 10) makes the point that the Bible is the ultimate guide for doctrine but cannot be cited to give textual proof for every detail.

Albeit Scripture do profess to contain in it all things that are necessary unto salvation; yet the meaning cannot be simply of all things which are necessary, but all things that are necessary in some certain kind or form; as all things which are necessary, and either could not at all, or could not easily be known by the light of natural discourse; all things which are necessary to be known that we may he saved; but known with presupposal of knowledge concerning certain principles whereof it receiveth us already persuaded, and then instructeth us in all the residue that are necessary. In the number of these principles, one is the sacred authority of Scripture. Being therefore persuaded by other means that these Scriptures are the Oracles of God, themselves do then teach us the rest, and lay before us all the duties which God requireth at our hands as necessary unto salvation. Further there hath been some doubt likewise, whether *containing in Scripture* do import express setting down in plain terms, or else comprehending in such sort that, by Reason, we may from thence conclude all things which are necessary. Against the former of these two constructions, instances have, sundry ways been given. For our belief in the Trinity, the Co-eternity of the Son of God with his Father, the proceeding of the Spirit from the Father and the Son, the duty – of baptizing infants – these, with such other principal points, the necessity whereof is by none denied, are notwithstanding in Scripture no where to be found by express literal mention, only deduced they are out of Scripture by collection [*inference*]. This kind of comprehension in

Scripture being therefore received, still there is no doubt, how far we are to proceed by collection, before the full and complete measure of things necessary be made up. For let us not think, that as long as the world doth endure, the wit of man shall be able to sound the bottom of that which may be concluded out of the Scripture; especially, if things contained by collection do so far extend, as to draw in whatsoever may be at any time out of Scripture but probably and conjecturally surmised. But let necessary collection be made requisite, and we may boldly deny, that of all those things which at this day are with so great necessity urged upon this Church, under the name of reformed Church-discipline, there is any one which their books hitherto have made manifest to be contained in the Scripture. Let them, if they can, allege but one properly belonging to their cause, and not common to them and us, and shew the deduction thereof out of Scripture to be necessary. It hath been already shewed, how all things necessary unto salvation, in such sort as before we have maintained, must needs be possible for men to know; and that many things are in such sort necessary, the knowledge whereof is by the light of Nature impossible to be attained.

The Works of Richard Hooker, Clarendon Press, 1820, pages 273–4

John Donne (p. 12), preaching on Easter Day 1624 on Revelation 20.6, considers the proper balance of literal and figurative readings of the Bible.

In the first book of Scripture, that of Genesis, there is danger in departing from the letter. In this last book, this of the Revelation, there is as much danger in adhering too close to the letter. The literal sense is always to be preserved; but the literal sense is not always to be discerned: for the literal sense is not always that, which the very Letter and Grammar of the place presents, as where it is literally said, *That Christ is a Vine*, and literally, *That his flesh is bread*, and literally, *That the new Jerusalem is thus situated, thus built, thus furnished*. But the literal sense of every place, is the principal intention of the Holy Ghost, in that place. And his principal intention in many places, is to express things by allegories, by figures; so that in many places of Scripture, a figurative sense is the literal sense, and more in this book than in any other. As then to depart from the literal sense, that sense which the very letter presents, in the book of Genesis, is dangerous, because if we do so there, we have no history of the Creation of the world in any other place to stick to; so to bind ourselves to such a literal sense in this book, will take from us the consolation of many spiritual happinesses, and bury us in the carnal things of this world.

John Donne, Selected Prose, ed. E. Simpson, Clarendon Press, 1967, pages 231–2

Henry Vaughan (1622–95), a Welshman and a loyal supporter of Charles I, was a poet who was influenced by George Herbert, and who later influenced William Wordsworth. His poetry and meditations express the fervent piety of the best in the Church of his time. He shows a reverence for the Bible no less earnest than that of the contemporary Puritans.

Welcome, dear book, Soul's joy and food! The feast
Of Spirits; Heaven extracted lies in thee.
Thou art life's Charter, The Dove's spotless nest
Where souls are hatched unto Eternity
In thee the hidden stone, the Manna lies;
Thou art the great Elixir, rare and choice;
The Key that opens to all Mysteries,
The *Word* in Characters, God in the *Voice*.

O that I had deep cut in my hard heart
Each line in thee! Then would I plead in groans
Of my Lord's penning, and by sweetest Art
Return upon himself the *Law*, and Stones.
Read here, my faults are thine. This Book and I
Will tell thee so; *Sweet Saviour thou didst die!*

H. F. Lyte (ed.), Vaughan's Sacred Poems, Bell, 1890,
pages 87–8, 'Holy Scriptures'

Thomas Traherne (c. 1636–74) makes a noble trio with Herbert and Vaughan, each distinctive in style but all giving poetic expression to the principles of the Church of England in their time. Little of his work was

*known until it was rediscovered early in the twentieth century. He strikes
a more cautious note concerning Bible reading: it is open to all believers,
but we must not trust too implicitly in the personal interpretation of its
mysteries.*

When Thou dost take
This sacred Book into thy hand;
Think not that Thou
Th' included sense dost understand.

It is a sign
Thou wantest sound Intelligence;
If that Thou think
Thyself to understand the Sense,

Be not deceived
Thou then on it in vain mayst gaze
The way is intricate
That leads into a Maze.

Here's nought but what's Mysterious
To an Understanding Eye:
Where Reverence alone stands Ope,
And Sense stands By.

> Thomas Traherne, *Poems, Centuries and
> Three Thanksgivings*, ed. A. Ridler,
> Oxford University Press, 1960, page 159

*Jeremy Taylor (1613–67) was chaplain to Charles I and after the Restoration
became Bishop of Down and Connor. His books* Holy Living *and* Holy
Dying *were for many years among the most widely used Anglican devotional works. Here, in a more substantially theological book, he considers
some difficulties in reading the Bible and disputes the Roman Catholic
claim to receive binding traditions from General Councils.*

But besides these things which are so plainly set down, some for doctrine, as St Paul says, that is, for articles and foundation of faith; some for

instruction, some for reproof some for comfort, that is, in matters practical and speculative, of several tempers and constitutions; there are innumerable places, containing in them great mysteries, but yet either so inwrapped with a cloud, or so darkened with umbrages or heightened with expressions, or so covered with allegories and garments of rhetoric, so profound in the matter, or so altered or made intricate in the manner, in the clothing, and dressing, that God may seem to have left them as trials of our industry, and arguments of our imperfections, and incentives to the longings after heaven and the clearest revelations of eternity, and as occasions and opportunities of our mutual charity and toleration to each other and humility in ourselves, rather than the repositories of faith, and furniture of creeds, and articles of belief.

For wherever the word of God is kept, whether in scripture alone or also in tradition, he that considers that the meaning of the one, and the truth or certainty of the other, are things of great question, will see a necessity in these things which are the subject matter of most of the questions of christendom that men should hope to be excused by an implicit faith in God almighty. For when there are in the explications of scripture so many commentaries, so many senses and interpretations, so many volumes in all ages, and all, like men's faces, exactly none like another, either this difference and inconvenience is absolutely no fault at all, or if it be, it is excusable by a mind prepared to consent in that truth which God intended. [...]

The first ages speak greatest truth, but least pertinently; the next ages, the ages of the four general councils, spake something, not much more pertinently to the present questions, but were not so likely to speak true by reason of their dispositions contrary to the capacity and circumstance of the first ages; and if they speak wisely as doctors, yet not certainly as witnesses of such propositions which the first ages noted not, and yet unless they had noted, could not possibly be traditions. And therefore either of them will be less useless as to our present affairs. For indeed the questions which now are the public trouble were not considered or thought upon for many hundred years, and therefore prime tradition there is none as to our purpose, and it will be an insufficient medium to be used or pretended in the determination; and to dispute concerning the truth or necessity of traditions in the questions of our times, is as if historians, disputing about a question in the English story should fall on wrangling whether Livy or Plutarch were the best writers. And the earnest disputes about traditions are to no better purpose; for no church at this day admits the one half of those things which certainly by the fathers were called traditions apostolical, and no testimony of ancient writers does consign the one half of the present questions to be or not to be traditions. So that they who admit only the doctrine and testimony of the first ages cannot be determined in most of their doubts which now trouble us, because their writings are of matters wholly differing from the present disputes: and they which would bring in after ages to the authority of a competent judge or witness, say the same thing; for they plainly confess that the first ages spake little or nothing to the present question, or at least nothing to their sense of them; for therefore they call in aid from the following ages, and make them suppletory and auxiliary to their designs; and therefore there are no traditions to our purposes. And they who would willingly have it otherwise, yet have taken no course it should be otherwise; for they, when they had opportunity in the councils of the last ages to determine what they had a mind to, yet they never named the number nor expressed the particular traditions which they would fain have the world believe to be apostolical: but they have kept the bridle in their own hands, and made a reserve of their own power, that if need be they may make new pretensions, or not be put to it to justify the old by the engagement of a conciliatory declaration.

The Whole Works of the Right Rev. Jeremy Taylor, ed. C. P. Eden, Longman, 1862, vol. 5, pages 410–11, 439

H. P. Liddon (1829–90), Canon of St Paul's Cathedral, followed Tractarian principles and took a traditionalist view of some of the contemporary tendencies in biblical studies. After explaining that the early Church ruled on the content of Scripture, he defends the right of his own Church to appeal to the Book of Common Prayer for interpretation.

These truths we receive on the authority of the Primitive Christian Church; and if the Church is to be listened to when she says what is Scripture and what Scripture is, she surely may be listened to with advantage if she has anything to tell us as to what Scripture means. In point of fact, when we look closely into the matter, we see that God committed His Revelation of Himself and of His Will, not to one recipient or factor, but to two; not to a book only, not to a society only, but, in different senses, to a book and to a society; to the Bible and to the Christian Church. The Church was to test the claim of any book to be Scripture; she took nearly four centuries before she recognised the claim of the Epistle to the Hebrews. And Scripture in turn was to be the rule of the Church's teaching. History shows that neither Scripture nor Church can be thrown into the background with lasting impunity. If the Church be forgetful of the supreme claims of Scripture, the Book becomes a prey to superstitions and follies which fatally discredit her message to mankind; if Scripture be not interpreted by the original and general sense of the Church, it comes in time to be treated as the plaything of individual fancy, as a purely human literature, as so much material to be torn to shreds by some negative and anti-religious criticism, for the amusement, if not exactly for the improvement or edification, of the world.

To us of the Church of England, the old Primitive Church of Christ, from which we claim lineal descent, still speaks in the language of our Prayer-book: first and most clearly in the three Creeds, and next in all those doctrines of the Faith, which are taken for granted in the Prayers, and especially in the Collects, bequeathed to us by the Christendom of fourteen or fifteen centuries ago, and representative of the mind of still earlier times. The old rule is that *lex supplicandi lex credendi*; [*the law of praying {is} the law of believing*] we must at least believe what we dare to say in prayer to God. This rule makes the whole Prayer-book a rule of faith; and as such it may guide us to the true mind of Scripture.

H. P. Liddon, *Advent in St Paul's*, Longman (1888), 1896, page 480

A more radical view of biblical authority was held by B. F. Westcott (1825–1901). Regius Professor of Divinity at Cambridge, Bishop of Durham, and editor with F. J. A. Hort of a new critical edition of the Greek New Testament, he was writing after the publication of the Revised Version of the Bible, which had aroused some controversy.

I cannot but think that the eager zeal with which English-speaking Christendom has received the effort to make the truth of the New

Testament clearer is not simply a desire for something new, but a proof that we do believe that Holy Scripture has a ruling, trying, quickening power for us, instinct as it were with a personal energy, which answers to our questionings and meets the wants which we acknowledge. And I cannot but think also that the result of the sharp controversies which have already begun will be to drive us to study what the Bible is in its greatest as well as in its minutest features. Such a hope has been the sustaining power of those to whom the work of revision was committed. Without it the labours of more than ten years might have seemed to men already charged with serious duties, little better than literary trifling. And such a hope cannot be wholly unfulfilled. Revising, and using rightly the fruits of revision both bring some disappointments and as we are inclined to think, some losses. But both works stir us to fresh and invigorating inquiries. And who will not rejoice in a call to high effort? No superstition can be more deadening than that by which a man is made to leave his noblest faculties unconsecrated by devout and unceasing exercise. The Bible does not supersede labour, but by its very form proclaims labour to be fruitful. This is a conclusion which we can no longer put out of sight. The Bible does not dispense with thought, but by its last message it lifts thought to sublimer regions. There is no doubt a restless desire in man for some help which may save him from the painful necessity of reflection, comparison, judgement. But the Bible offers no such help. It offers no wisdom to the careless and no security to the indolent. It awakens, nerves, invigorates, but it makes no promise of ease. And by this it responds to the aspirations of our better selves. We cannot – and let me press this truth with the strongest possible emphasis – we cannot by a peremptory and irresponsible decision satisfy ourselves that such and such changes are 'trivial' or 'unmeaning,' or 'pedantic' or 'disastrous'. We know that we are bound to take account of them seriously. The duty may be unwelcome, but we have to face it.

B. F. Westcott, *Lessons from Work*, Macmillan, 1901, pages 148–9

Stephen Sykes (p. 24) makes a clear statement of the regard for the Bible as held by most Anglicans at the present time.

In my view, it belongs inherently to Anglican practice that the Scriptures of the Old and New Testament should be publicly read to the whole Church in the native language of the hearers, as part of the Church's normal worship. It is not, however, part of Anglicanism that the whole Scriptures should be considered to be infallible. Classic Anglicans of the Reformation and later eras did so believe and teach, but in the era of biblical criticism it was discovered that none of the Anglican confessional norms insisted upon verbal inspiration. If there are fundamentals which it is scandalous to challenge, they are not fundamental merely because they are taught in Scripture. Many Anglicans concluded that though there were fundamentals, no one could give an exhaustive list of what they were. This is a position which I consider to be fully defensible today, both theologically and practically. Anglican practice is to read the Scriptures, so that the whole people of God may hear the Gospel for themselves. They hear the Scriptures read, wrapped about by anthems and psalms articulating the praise of God, and crowned by the Creed. In this way is delivered to the Church the setting, the theme, the plot and the resolution of the narrative of God's way with His creation, in highly assimilable form.

But it is also true that every aspect of that narrative, beginning with the very word 'God' itself, is open to question and has been questioned and discussed by theologians within the Church from the very beginning. I would go still further and assert that it is impossible seriously to study the Old Testament without becoming aware that it reflects and contains the fruits of a centuries-long dialogue embracing the entire story of God's way with creation and humankind. Even in its much briefer time span the New Testament itself portrays a variety of theologies and modes of Christian discipleship, and frankly reveals (and, of course, deplores) the bitter acrimony with which the disputes were conducted. It is, in my view, the bitterness and inattention of the disputants which is scandalous to modern Anglicanism, as elsewhere. The disputes themselves are normal, and occur in every Christian church known to me.

S. W. Sykes, 'The Genius of Anglicanism', in G. Rowell (ed.), *The English Religious Tradition and the Genius of Anglicanism*, Ikon, 1992, page 236

The Elizabethan Articles of Religion set out the powers and the limitations of the authority of the Church in relation to the authority of the Bible. These two Articles do a neat job in relating Tradition and Scripture, and keeping an eye on State control of Church councils.

Of the Authority of the Church

The church hath power to decree Rites or Ceremonies, and authority in Controversies of Faith. And yet it is not lawful for the Church to ordain any thing that is contrary to God's Word written, neither may it so expound one place of Scripture, that it be repugnant to another. Therefore, although the Church be a witness and a keeper of holy Writ, yet, as it ought not to decree any thing against the same, so besides the same ought it not to enforce any thing to be believed for necessity of Salvation.

Article 20

Of the Authority of General Councils

General Councils may not be gathered together without the commandment and will of Princes. And when they be gathered together (forasmuch as they be an assembly of men, whereof all be not governed with the Spirit and Word of God,) they may err, and sometimes have erred, even in things pertaining unto God. Wherefore things ordained by them as necessary to salvation have neither strength nor authority, unless it may be declared that they be taken out of holy Scripture.

Article 21

Robert Sanderson (1587–1663), Bishop of Lincoln and a leading member of the Savoy Conference, affirms this declared power of the Church of England to make rules and ordinances but denies that she has departed in any way from the received tradition of the universal Church.

Now I appeal to any man that hath not run on madly with the cry for company, but endeavoured with the spirit of charity and sobriety to satisfy his own understanding herein, if the Church of England, both in the Preface before the Book of Common-Prayer, and in the Articles of her Confession, and in sundry passages in the Homilies occasionally – and these Books are acknowledged her most authentic Writings, the two former especially, and the just standard whereby to measure her whole doctrine – if, I say, she have not in them all, and that in as plain and express terms as can be desired, disclaimed all human traditions that are imposed upon the consciences of God's people either in point of faith or manners, and declared to the world, that she challenged no power to herself to order any thing by her own authority but only in things indifferent, and such as are not repugnant to the word of God; and that her Constitutions are but for order, comeliness, and uniformity sake, and not for conscience sake towards God; and that therefore any of those her Orders and Constitutions may be retained, abolished, or altered from time to time, and at all times, as the Governors for the time being shall judge to serve best unto edification. What should I say more? If men list to be contentious, and will not be satisfied, who can help it?

Works of Robert Sanderson, Oxford University Press, 1854, vol. 2, page 158

The Anglican regard for Tradition did not please all its members, and there was a lasting tendency in some quarters to rest on sola scriptura *and distrust any additions as popish innovation. Philip Shuttleworth, Warden of New College, Oxford, took this view at a time when the Tractarians were making a strong appeal to Tradition and some of their followers were introducing more ceremonial into Church services. The Article to which he refers is Article 20, above.*

God, we are told, is the author of order, not of confusion. Did we possess no other sanction for the establishment of Church government with its attendant ceremonials, this one would be sufficient, as binding upon the conscience of every well-intentioned Christian. The authority of the spiritual is, at all events, as sacred as that of the secular magistrate, when exercised in discretion, and with reference to the will of Him from whom all power is derived. The language of the 20th Article of our Church appears to reach that precise point, short of which none but the self-willed and arrogant would wish to stop, and beyond which none but the advocate of spiritual despotism would desire to advance. Forms and ceremonials there must be. But they can, by any possibility, exist only in concurrence with a feeling of deference to those who bear legitimate authority, and a predisposition to conform to those usages which a wise antiquity, or the common consent of our enlightened Christian brethren, have consecrated. The moment, however, that this reasonable boundary is passed, that things indifferent are enjoined as integral points of doctrine, and that man steps in to exercise an authority for which he has received no commission, then, indeed, it becomes every follower of Christ to stand forth in defence of that liberty which his Redeemer has established. Nor should it be forgotten, that great as the sin of schism undoubtedly is, its guilt attaches not so much to these who, solely from a wish to preserve their mode of divine worship in its primitive purity, withdraw from a community whose usages they disapprove, as to those who encumber their articles of fellowship with conditions which Scripture gives them no warrant to demand. Where, indeed, we are to draw that exact line, where the right of legitimate dictation ceases, and superstitious usurpation begins, will always be difficult to determine, and will be variously judged of according to the different modes of human feeling.

P. N. Shuttleworth, *Not Tradition but Scripture*, Rivington, 1839, pages 217–18

The appeal to Reason in establishing the authority of the Church has been particularly strong in the Church of England. In this as in many other ways, Richard Hooker (p. 10) made some early pronouncements.

Whatsoever our hearts be to God and to his truth, believe we or be we as yet faithless, for our conversion or confirmation, the force of natural Reason is great. The force whereof unto those effects is nothing without grace. What then? to our purpose it is sufficient, that whosoever doth serve, honour, and obey God, whosoever believeth in him; that man would no more do this than innocents and infants do, but for the light of natural Reason that shineth in him, and maketh him apt to apprehend those things of God, which being by grace discovered, are effectual to persuade reasonable minds and none other, that honour, obedience, and credit, belong aright unto God. No man cometh unto God to offer him sacrifice, to pour out supplications and prayers before him, or to do him any service which doth not at first believe him both to be, and to be a rewarder of them who in such sort seek unto him. Let men be taught this either by revelation from heaven, or by instruction upon earth; by labour, study, and meditation, or by the only secret inspiration of the Holy Ghost; whatsoever the mean be they know it by, if the knowledge thereof were possible without discourse of natural Reason; why should none be found capable thereof but only men, nor men till such time as they come unto ripe and full ability to work by reasonable understanding? The whole drift of the Scripture of God, what is it, but only to teach theology? Theology, what is it, but the science of things divine? What science can be attained unto without the help of natural discourse and Reason? [. . .] In vain it were to speak any thing of God, but that by Reason men are sometimes able somewhat to judge of that they hear, and by discourse to discern how consonant it is to truth. Scripture indeed teacheth things above Nature, things which our Reason by itself could not reach unto. Yet those things also we believe, knowing by Reason, that the Scripture is the Word of God.

The Works of Richard Hooker, Clarendon Press, 1820, vol. 1, pages 385–6 (Book 3, 6)

John Cosin (1594–1672) was Bishop of Durham and one of the principal members of the Savoy Conference which met in 1661 and produced the revised Book of Common Prayer in the following year. He gives a view, generally accepted then and later, of faith and reason as close though unequal partners. The Pauline text he cites is Romans 1. 19f.

If we find our natural faculties rectified, so as that understanding and reason, which we have in moral and civil actions be bent likewise upon the practice and exaltation of Christian and religious actions, we may be sure this other greater light is about us. But if we be cold in them, in actuating, in exalting, in using our natural faculties and light to the end, we shall be in danger to be deprived of all light, we shall not see the invisible God in visible things, (which St. Paul makes so inexcusable, so unpardonable a sin) we shall not see the light of God that shined upon us this day, nor the mind of God that was declared to us in this Gospel; we shall not see the hand of God in all our worldly crosses, nor the seal of God in any spiritual blessing or promise whatsoever. But the light of faith bears me witness that I see all this.

To conclude: the light of nature, in the highest exaltation of it, is not the light of faith; but yet if there be that use made of it that there should be, it will make somewhat towards it. Faith and nature are subordinate, and the one rules the other. The light of faith bears me witness that I have Christ with all the benefit of His incarnation; and the light of natural reason exalted to religious uses, bears me witness that I have faith whereby I apprehend Him. Only that man whose conscience testifies to himself, and whose actions testify to the world, that he does what he can to follow the true light of this text, and all the rules of religion, and them only which that Light set forth and revealed and in His own words, that man can only believe himself, be believed by others, that he hath the true light of faith and religion in him.

John Cosin, *Works*, Parker, 1855, vol. 1, pages 289–90

Thomas Wilson (1663–1755) was Bishop of Sodor and Man. He used his episcopal authority to improve the spiritual and pastoral life of his see and also to impose a firm church discipline. The following passage is supposed to be a dialogue between a Missionary and an Indian – that is, a Native American. The imagined relationship may be unacceptable to the modern reader, but what is said here about the value and limitations of reason in faith is worth noting.

Indian   You have convinced me, Sir, that our reason alone is not sufficient to make known to us the things which you say are most surely believed among Christians; that *reason* cannot tell us, with what *worship* the GREAT GOD will be pleased, nor give us any certainty of the *happiness or misery* of the life to come; which, to be sure, makes men less concerned how they lead their lives here. You have told me, and I am convinced of it, that our reason alone cannot assure us *upon what terms* the GREAT GOD will pardon us, when we have offended Him, as all men are apt to do; and we all know and feel how hard it is even to follow what our reason tells us we ought to do. *Of what use then is reason to us?*

Missionary Of very great use, most certainly. It will keep you from being imposed upon, when any thing is proposed to your belief, as coming from God; you will be able to judge whether you have sufficient proof to receive it as such: and then, if you find you have, your reason will convince you that it must be necessary for your happiness, because a God of truth and goodness cannot deceive His creatures, or require any thing of them but what must necessarily be for their good.

Indian   It is on this very account, Sir, I am now come to you, not only to learn from you, by what other ways God has made His will known unto Christians; but to enquire, whether those ways be such as no man of common sense and reason ought to call in question.

Missionary I hope I shall give you all the satisfaction in those things, that unprejudiced reason can desire. You will remember then what I told YOU before, that the GREAT GOD, in compassion to His poor bewildered creatures, sent His own Son to let them know how far they were departed from the ways of reason and truth; and that they would be for ever miserable, if they did not return to the duty they owed their Maker, and, lastly, that *God was in Christ reconciling the world unto Himself,* and would pardon mankind upon condition of their faith in Him, their repentance and future *obedience.* I told you also, that He gave them such evidences that this message came from God, as could not be justly called in question by any man, and, among the rest, this very extraordinary one; He declared, and His enemies knew it, *They will put Me to death, and after three days I will rise again from the dead;* which also came exactly to pass.

The Works of Thomas Wilson, Parker, 1851, vol. 4, pages 175–6

H. L. Mansel (1820–71) was Regius Professor of Ecclesiastical History at Oxford and Dean of St Paul's. He defended the importance of Reason in religious belief but held that the human intellect is itself a divine gift.

The intellectual stumbling-blocks, which men find in the doctrines of Revelation, are not the consequence of any improbability or error peculiar to the things revealed; but are such as the thinker brings with him to the examination of the question; – such as meet him on every side, whether he thinks with or against the testimony of Scripture; being inherent in the constitution and laws of the Human Mind itself. But must we therefore acquiesce in the melancholy conclusion, that self-contradiction is the law of our intellectual being; that the light of Reason, which is God's gift, no less than Revelation, is a delusive light, which we follow to our own deception? Far from it. The examination of the Limits of Thought leads to a conclusion the very opposite of this. Reason does not deceive us, if we will only read her witness aright; and Reason herself gives us warning, when we are in danger of reading it wrong. The light that is within us is not darkness; only it cannot illuminate that which is beyond the sphere of its rays. The self-contradictions, into which we inevitably fall, when we attempt certain courses of speculation, are the beacons placed by the hand of God in the mind of man, to warn us that we are deviating from the track that He designs us to pursue; that we are striving to pass the barriers which He has planted around us. The flaming sword turns every way against those who strive, in the strength of their own reason, to force their passage to the tree of life. Within her own province, and among her own objects, let Reason go forth, con-quering and to conquer. The finite objects, which she can clearly and dis-tinctly conceive, are her lawful empire and her true glory. The countless phenomena of the visible world; the unseen things which lie in the depths of the human soul; these are given into her hand; and over them she may reign in unquestioned dominion. But when she strives to approach too near to the hidden mysteries of the Infinite; when, not content with beholding afar off the partial and relative manifestations of God's presence, she would 'turn aside and see this great sight,' and know why God hath revealed Himself thus; the voice of the Lord Himself is heard, as it were, speaking in warning from the midst: 'Draw not nigh hither: put off thy shoes from off thy feet; for the place whereon thou standest is holy ground.'

H. L. Mansel, *Limits of Religious Thought*, Bampton Lectures, John Murray, 1859, pages 129–30

Arthur Middleton was a parish priest for many years, Honorary Canon of Durham, Tutor and for a time Acting Principal of St Chad's College. He has

*written widely about the history and nature of Anglicanism. He explains
and justifies the Anglican view on sources of authority.*

The Fathers were held in esteem not only as witnesses to the content of
the primitive faith but as a guide to the right interpretation of Holy
Scripture. Throughout, in Reformer, Caroline and Tractarian, the same
fundamental principle is present, that while Scripture is the supreme
standard of faith, the Fathers represented the tradition of the Church by
which Scripture was rightly interpreted. While initially the Reformers
used the Fathers chiefly as a means of proving what was and what was
not primitive doctrine and practice, the Carolines built on this principle
and developed this use of the Fathers by making patristic thought and
piety a vehicle in which to structure their own theological vision. In
neither is there any transformation of the Fathers into a formal and
infallible authority, nor the degeneration of their theology into a patristic scholasticism. For their concern is not merely to return to texts,
abstract tradition, formulas and propositions, but to recover the true
spirit of the Fathers, the secret inspiration that made them true witnesses
of the Church. Their appeal to the Fathers is much more than a historical reference to the past: it is an appeal to the *mind of the Fathers*, and to
follow them means to acquire their mind. This is what saves their use of
the Fathers from a mere appeal to authority as such, rigid masters from
whom no appeal is possible, and issues in an approach that is critical and
reasonable. This saved them from becoming preoccupied with the controversies of their time in the doctrines of justification and predestination, as they set out to restore the grandeur of Christian truth by following the Nicene Fathers in making the Incarnation the central doctrine of
the faith. It placed them beyond their age and culture and empowered
them to transcend the limitations of nationalism as well as enabling
them to avoid the temptation of building a scientific theology on the
plan of Calvin. This patristic basis is what makes their theology something quite different from Tridentinism or Continental Protestantism.
Furthermore, it was an ideal of theology that was not divorced from
prayer and liturgy, for it provided a way of life and worship informed
and structured by theological vision.

Arthur Middleton, *Fathers and Anglicans*, Gracewing, 2001, page 308

4

Holy Orders

Fit persons to serve in the sacred Ministry of thy Church

The claim of the Church of England to remain within the Holy, Catholic and Apostolic Church required the assurance that the threefold ministry of bishop, priest and deacon had been maintained and that these orders had been validly conferred in the Apostolic Succession. This claim has been continually defended by her apologists and denied by the Roman Catholic Church. The controversy began with the assertion that Mathew Parker, the first Elizabethan Archbishop of Canterbury, was not properly consecrated in 1559, since the consecrating bishops, who had held their sees in the reign of Edward VI, had not themselves received proper episcopal consecration. The scurrilous 'Nag's Head Fable', was put out early in the seventeenth century and continued to be cited in controversy for over two hundred years. This slander is no longer an issue, but in historical interest the refutation by John Bramhall (p. 14) may be quoted:

> They say, that Archbishop Parker and the rest of the Protestant bishops in the beginning of Queen Elizabeth's reign, or at least sundry of them, were consecrated at the Nag's Head in Cheapside together, by Bishop Scory alone, or by him and Bishop Barlow jointly, without sermon, without sacrament, without any solemnity, in the year 1559 [. . .] We say, Archbishop Parker was consecrated alone, at Lambeth, in the Church by four bishops, authorised thereunto by commission under the Great Seal of England, with sermon, with sacrament, with all due solemnities, upon the 17th day of Dec anno 1559, before four of the most eminent public notaries in England.

Even if the succession had been broken with Parker, it would be restored in William Laud, some at least of whose consecrating bishops were in undisputed succession.

In 1894 Pope Leo XIII set up a commission to examine the validity of Anglican orders. Although some of its members believed them to be valid, the final issue was the encyclical *Apostolicae curae* in 1896, declaring them to be 'utterly invalid and altogether void'. The Archbishops of York and Canterbury wrote a long and detailed reply, also in Latin, with the title *Saepius Officio* but with an English translation the opening of which is given below. Throughout later, and on the whole more hopeful, discussions with the Roman Catholic Church, the Church of England and others in the Anglican Communion continue to assert the full validity of their orders. These orders are accepted by the Old Catholics and, more cautiously, by some of the Eastern Orthodox.

A different dispute developed in the reign of Elizabeth I with those who regarded Episcopacy as inessential or even contrary to the purity of the Church. The Church line was that Bishops were of the *esse*, the essential quality of the Church, and not merely of the *bene esse*, desirable but dispensable. The argument which began with attacks from Puritans has continued to be a barrier in ecumenical discussions, the Free Churches being reluctant to agree that their ministers must receive episcopal ordination if they were to be accepted to officiate in the Church of England. This problem, sharply divisive for centuries, has not gone away but has been quietly softened by all parties. Hooker admits possible exceptions.

The rule of the Church of England is that Bishops form a separate order with reserved functions of confirmation and ordination as well as their pastoral and controlling authority over their dioceses. The deacon has been treated as a temporary role, seldom lasting more than a year, in final preparation for priestly ordination, although there are suggestions of a permanent diaconate, and some clergy have not moved beyond this first order. There have been changes affecting the function and deployment of some clergy, but making no difference to the means and authority of ordination. Apart from school and college chaplains, most priests in the past were employed in parish ministry. There are now many specialist chaplaincies to hospitals, prisons, industry and the armed services. The number of non-stipendiary clergy, exercising all the clerical functions but supported by paid work outside the Church, is increasing. The widespread and important role of lay Readers, established in 1866, has added a new dimension to the official ministry.

The question of ordination is inextricably connected with the celebration of Holy Communion, claimed to be a valid catholic Eucharist. Yet preaching and officiating at non-eucharistic services has also been regarded as highly important. Is the priest primarily a preacher or a minister of the sacraments? The Ordinal declares authority for both functions and gives them equal weight: 'Take thou authority to preach the Word of God, and to minister the holy Sacraments.'

The Reformation opened the way to the marriage of ordained clergy, forbidden in the Roman Catholic Church. It was not readily approved by all who accepted the new settlement. Even after the break with Rome, Henry VIII ruled in the third of his conservative *Six Articles* (1539) that priests 'may not marry, by the law of God'. Ten years later, a statute of Edward VI grudgingly permitted, in a Pauline tone, the marriage of clergy as a second-best option.

> Although it were not only better for the estimation of priests, and other ministers in the Church of God, to live, chaste, sole, and separate from the company of women and the bond of marriage, but also thereby they might the better intend to the administration of the gospel, and be less intricated and troubled with the charge of household, being free and unburdened from the care and cost of finding wife and children, and that it were most to be wished that they would willingly and of their selves endeavour themselves to a perpetual chastity and abstinence from the use of women: Yet forasmuch as the contrary has rather been seen, and such uncleanness of living, and other great inconveniences, not meet to be rehearsed, have followed of compelled chastity, and of such laws as have prohibited those (such persons) the godly use of marriage; it were better and rather to be suffered in the commonwealth, that those which could not contain, should, after the counsel of Scripture, live in holy marriage,

A major change in the matter of holy orders was made in 1992 when the General Synod of the Church of England passed a measure to allow the ordination of women to the priesthood. The diaconate had already been open to them and there were women priests in other provinces of the Anglican Communion. This decision followed years of debate in which feeling on both sides had been strongly expressed. The first women were ordained in 1994. An Act of Synod provided alternative episcopal oversight for those who were unable to accept this decision, and compensation for stipendiary clergy who left the Church of England as a result. A 'period of reception' continues, while many women are now exercising this ministry. The question of women in the episcopate remains undecided at the time of writing.

The preface to the Ordinal in the Book of Common Prayer sets out the position of the Church of England as it stands to this day. It is perhaps too confident about the very early evidence for the threefold order, but it places Anglican orders firmly in the catholic tradition and affirms their continuity.

It is evident unto all men diligently reading holy Scripture and ancient Authors, that from the Apostles' time there have been these Orders of Ministers in Christ's Church; Bishops, Priests, and Deacons. Which offices were evermore had in such reverend estimation, that no man might presume to execute any of them, except he were first called, tried, examined, and known to have such qualities as are requisite for the same; and also by publick Prayer, with Imposition of Hands, were approved and admitted thereunto by lawful authority. And therefore, to the intent that these Orders may he continued, and reverently used and esteemed, in the Church of England; No man shall be accounted or taken to be a lawful Bishop, Priest, or Deacon in the Church of England, or suffered to execute any of the said functions, except he be called, tried, examined, and admitted thereunto, according to the Form hereafter following, or hath had formerly Episcopal Consecration or Ordination.

The Romanist denial of the validity of Anglican orders and the Puritan denial of their necessity produced a stern warning in the Canons formulated in 1604.

Whosoever shall hereafter affirm or teach, that the form and manner of making and consecrating bishops, priests, or deacons, containeth any thing in it that is repugnant to the word of God, or that they who are made bishops, priests, or deacons, in that form, are not lawfully made, nor ought to be accounted, either by themselves or by others, to be truly either bishops, priests, or deacons, until they have some other calling to those divine offices; let him be excommunicated *ipso facts,* not to be restored until he repent, and publicly revoke such his wicked errors.

Richard Hooker (p. 10) set out at greater length, and with specific citations of authority, the claims of the Ordinal. He takes the commonsense view that the Apostolic Succession is to be understood within the intention and practice of the whole Church and does not mean that there has never been valid ordination without the laying on of episcopal hands traceable back to the New Testament times.

Inasmuch as there are but two main things observed in every Ecclesiastical function, power to exercise the duty itself, and some charge of people whereon to exercise the same; the former of these is received at the hands of the whole visible Catholic Church. For it is not any one particular multitude that can give power, the force whereof may reach far and wide indefinitely, as the power of order doth, which whoso hath once received, there is no action which belongeth thereunto, but he may exercise effectually the same in any part of the world without iterated ordination. They whom the whole Church hath from the beginning used as her agents in conferring this power are not either one or more of the Laity, and therefore it hath not been heard of that ever any such were allowed to ordain ministers: only persons Ecclesiastical, and they, in place of calling, superiors both unto Deacons, and unto Presbyters; only such persons Ecclesiastical have been authorised to ordain both, and give them the power of order, in the name of the whole Church. Such were the Apostles, such was Timothy, such was Titus, such are Bishops. Not that there is between these no difference, but so that they all agree in preeminence of place above both Presbyters and Deacons, whom they otherwise might not ordain. Now whereas hereupon some do infer, that no ordination can stand but only such as is made by Bishops, which have had their ordination likewise by other Bishops before them, till we come to the very Apostles of Christ themselves [. . .] to this we answer, that there may be sometimes very just and sufficient reason to allow ordination made without a Bishop. The whole Church visible being the true original subject of all power, it hath not ordinarily allowed any other than Bishops alone to ordain: howbeit, as the ordinary course is ordinarily in all things to be observed, so it may be in some cases not unnecessary that we decline from the ordinary ways. Men may be extraordinarily, yet allowably, two ways admitted unto spiritual functions in the Church. One is, when God himself doth of himself raise up any, whose labour he useth without requiring that men should authorise them; but then he doth ratify their calling by manifest signs and tokens himself from heaven: and thus even such as believed not our Saviour's teaching, did yet acknowledge him a lawful teacher sent from God; *Thou art a teacher sent from God, otherwise none could do those things which thou dost* [. . .] Another extraordinary kind of vocation is, when the exigence of necessity doth constrain to leave the usual ways of the Church, which otherwise we would willingly keep: where the Church must needs have some ordained, and neither hath, nor can have possibly a Bishop to ordain; in case of such Necessity, the ordinary institution of God hath given oftentimes, and may give place. And therefore we are not, simply without exception, to urge a lineal descent of power from the Apostles by continued succession of Bishops in every effectual ordination. These cases of necessity excepted, none may ordain but only Bishops. By the imposition of their hands it is that the Church giveth power of order, both unto Presbyters and Deacons.

The Works of Richard Hooker, Clarendon Press, 1820, vol. 3, pages 194–6 (Book 7, 14)

He emphasises the distinction between clergy and laity, and asserts the indelibility of orders which have been validly conferred.

To whom Christ hath imparted power both over that mystical body which is the society of souls, and over that natural which is himself for the knitting of both in one; (a work which antiquity doth call the making of Christ's body): the same power is in such not amiss termed a kind of mark or character and acknowledged to be indelible. Ministerial power is a mark of separation, because it severeth them that have it from other men, and maketh them a special *order* consecrated unto the service of the Most High in things wherewith others may not meddle. Their difference therefore from other men is in that they are a distinct *order*. So Tertullian calleth them [. . .] They which have once received this power may not think to put it off and on like a cloak as the weather serveth, to take it reject and resume it as oft as themselves list, of which profane and impious contempt these later times have yielded as of all other kinds of iniquity and apostasy strange examples; but let them know which put their hands unto this plough, that once consecrated unto God they are made his peculiar inheritance for ever. Suspension may stop, and degradations utterly cut off the use or exercise of power before given: but voluntarily it is not in the power of man to separate and pull asunder what God by his authority coupleth. So that although there may be through misdesert degradation as there may be cause of just separation after matrimony, yet if (as sometime it doth) restitution to former dignity or reconciliation after breach doth happen, neither doth the one nor the other ever iterate the first knot.

The Works of Richard Hooker, Clarendon Press, 1820, vol. 2, pages 424–5 (Book 5, 77)

While the Roman Catholic Church regarded all Anglican orders as invalid, the Protestant opposition, Presbyterian and Independent, denied the apostolic authority for a separate order of bishops. William Laud (1573–1645), Archbishop of Canterbury, took a firm line which eventually led to his execution. He defended himself against a strong attack by the Puritan Lord Say. His argument is eloquent, but even the most conservative modern scholar would have to say that he takes some liberties with the New Testament evidence.

For my own part, if it be thought fit to reduce the Christian Church to her first beginnings, give us the same power, and use us with the same reverence for our works' sake, as then our predecessors were used, and reduce us, in God's name, when you will. But this Lord's zeal burns quite another way. He tells us, indeed, that 'the question is no more but whether Bishops should be reduced to what they were in their first advancement over the presbyters'; but he means nothing less than their reducement thither and this is manifest out of his own next words. For there he says, their first advancement was 'but a human device for avoiding of schism'. But a human device? Why, first, our Saviour Himself chose twelve Apostles out of the whole number of His disciples, and made them bishops, and advanced over the presbyters and all other believing Christians, and gave them the name of Bishops as well as of Apostles; as appears, since that name was given even to Judas also, as well as to the other Apostles, and to the other Apostles as well as to Judas, since Matthias was chosen by God Himself, both into the bishopric and apostleship of Judas, Acts i. 20, 24, 25. Now that Christ Himself did ordain the Apostles over the ordinary disciples, presbyters or others, is evident also in the very text; for He chose them out of His disciples, S. Luke vi. And to what end was this choosing out, if after this choice they remained no more than they were before? Nay, He chose them out with a special ordination to a higher function, as appears S. Mark iii, where 'tis said, 'He ordained twelve that they should be with Him'; that is, in a higher and nearer relation than the rest were. Nay, more than so, the word there used by S. Mark is *epoiesen* 'He made' them; He made them somewhat which before that making they were not, that is, Apostles and Bishops. Had they been such before, it could not have been said that ' He made' them then. And our last translation renders it very well, 'He ordained them,' so belike this making was a new ordination of them.

Works of William Laud, Parker, 1847, vol. 6, pages 172–3

William Chillingworth (1602–44) entered the Roman Catholic Church for a short time but returned to the Church of England and became a chaplain in the Royalist army during the Civil War. He is remembered for his dictum, 'the Bible only is the religion of Protestants'. He engaged in a long and vehement controversy with a Jesuit called Knott, in defence of the Church of England as a true Church, in which he claimed that the validity of her orders was not affected by a break from the Roman succession.

The sum of your discourse [. . .] must be this: 'Want of succession of bishops and pastors, holding always the same doctrine, and of the forms of ordaining bishops and priests which are in use in the Roman church, is a certain mark of heresy: but protestants want all these things; therefore they are heretics'. To which I answer, That nothing but want of truth, and holding error, can make or prove any man or church heretical. For if he be a true Aristotelian, or Platonist, or Pyrrhonian, or Epicurean, who holds the doctrine of Aristotle, or Plato, or Pyrrho, or Epicurus, although he cannot assign any that held it before him for many ages together; why should I not be made a true and orthodox Christian, by believing all the doctrine of Christ, though I cannot derive my descent from a perpetual succession that believed it before me? By this reason, you should say as well, that no man can be a good bishop, or pastor, or king, or magistrate, or father, that succeeds a bad one. For if I may conform my will and actions to the commandments of God, why may I not embrace his doctrine with my understanding, although my predecessors do not so? You have above, in this chapter, defined faith, 'a free, infallible, obscure, supernatural assent to Divine truths, because they are revealed by God, and sufficiently propounded'. This definition is very fantastical; but for the present I will let it pass, and desire you to give me some piece or shadow of reason, why I may not do all this without a perpetual succession of bishops and pastors that have done so before me. You may judge as uncharitably, and speak as maliciously of me as your blind zeal to your superstition shall direct you; but certainly I know, (and with all your sophistry you cannot make me doubt of what I know,) that I do believe the gospel of Christ (as it is delivered in the undoubted books of canonical scripture) as verify as that it is now day, that I see the light, that I am now writing; and I believe it upon this motive, because I conceive it sufficiently, abundantly, superabundantly proved to be Divine revelation; and yet in this I do not depend upon any succession of men, that have always believed it without any mixture of error; nay, I am fully persuaded there hath been no such succession, and yet do not find myself any way weakened in my faith by the want of it.

The Works of William Chillingworth, Oxford University Press, 1838, vol. 2, pages 375–6

William Beveridge (1637–1708), Bishop of St Asaph, sympathised with the Nonjurors but remained within the Established Church. He writes about the essential giving of the Holy Spirit in ordination, referring to the words of Christ to the Apostles, 'Receive ye the Holy Ghost' (John 20.22).

[The order of priesthood] being instituted for the due administration of the ordinary means of grace, it was necessary that they, who were admitted into this Order also, should have the Holy Ghost, the Fountain of all Grace, conferred on them, to influence their several administrations, without which it is impossible they should ever attain their end. And hence it is, that according to the practice of the Catholic and Apostolic Church, though not in that of Deacons, yet in the Ordination of Priests, as you will see presently, the Bishop, when he lays his hands severally upon every one that receives that Order, saith, 'Receive the Holy Ghost for the office and work of a Priest in the Church of God, now committed unto thee by the imposition of our hands; whose sins thou dost forgive, they are forgiven; and whose sins thou dost retain, they are retained'. Where we may observe, that although some other words are inserted to determine and distinguish the office committed to them, yet all the same words are repeated, which our Lord Himself used at the Ordination of His Apostles; which the Catholic Church always judged necessary, not only in imitation of our Blessed Saviour, but likewise, because that the persons who are ordained Priests in His Church are to preach the same word, administer the same Sacraments, and exercise the same power in the Censures of the Church, as the Apostles themselves did. And therefore it is necessary that they should be endued with the same Spirit, ordained after the same manner, and entrusted with the same power of the keys as the Apostles themselves were. By which means, the means of grace and salvation administered by Priests thus ordained, become as effectual to those that use them aright, as when they were administered by the Apostles themselves; the Spirit, which they receive by this imposition of hands, being always ready to assist at their several administrations, and to bless and sanctify them to those who are duly prepared and disposed for them.

William Beveridge, *Theological Works*, Parker, 1844, vol. 1, pages 40–1

Daniel Waterland (1673–1740) held several senior clerical posts, becoming Archdeacon of Middlesex in 1730. He was a strong defender of orthodoxy against Deists and Arians. Here he recognises the idea of priesthood of all believers but affirms the special position of the ordained ministry in the public celebration of the sacraments.

Christian sacrifices may be divided into private and public: which is a distinction somewhat like to, but not altogether the same with the former. For though internal sacrifice, as such, is always secret, yet it may be performed in company with others, as well as when we are alone: and though external sacrifice, as to the outward part, is open to view, may be seen or heard, yet it may be performed in private as well as in company.

Therefore both external and internal sacrifices may be subdivided into private and public, accordingly as they are respectively offered up to God, either from the private closet in retirement, or from among our brethren met together in the public assemblies for the same purpose. Private prayer is private sacrifice, and public prayer is public sacrifice. Good works likewise are sacrifices, if really and strictly good, if referred to God and his glory: therefore when they are done in private, they are private sacrifices; but if so done as to 'shine before men,' for an example to them, then they become public sacrifices.

Christian sacrifices maybe distinguished likewise into lay-sacrifice and clerical. In a large sense, all good. Christians are sacrificers, and, so far, priests unto God. St. Austin [*Augustine*], in few words, well sets forth both the agreement and the difference; observing that all Christians are priests, as they are members of Christ, members of one and the same High Priest; but that Bishops and Presbyters are in a more peculiar or emphatical manner entitled to the name of priests. So I interpret *proprie* not to exclude Christian laics from being, properly speaking, sacrificers, but so only as to exclude them from being emphatically and eminently such as the clergy are, for though they are all equally sacrificers, they are not equally administrators of sacrifice, in a public, and solemn, and authorised way.

The Protestant doctrine, commonly, has run, that clergy and laity are equally priests: not equally Bishops, Presbyters, or Deacons, but equally priests, (in the sense of *hiereis)* that is, equally sacrificers. For like as when a senate presents a petition, by their speaker, to the crown, every member of that senate is equally a petitioner, though there is but one authorised officer, one speaker commissioned to prefer the petition in the name of the whole senate; so in this other case, the whole body of Christian people are equally sacrificers, though the clergy only are commissioned to preside and officiate in a public character. The sacrifice is the common sacrifice of the whole body, and so the name of sacrificer is also common: but the leading part, the administration of the sacrifice, is appropriate to the commissioned officers; and so also are the names of Bishops, Presbyters, and Deacons. This is all that any sober Protestants have meant; though their expressions have been sometimes liable to misconstruction, by reason of the latent ambiguity of words and names. The word priest is equivocal, as denoting either a presbyter or a sacrificer: and the word sacrificer is still further equivocal, as meaning either one who barely sacrifices, or one that administers a sacrifice in a public capacity, as the head or mouth of an assembly.

Daniel Waterland, *The Doctrine of the Eucharist*, Clarendon Press, 1896, pages 650–2

Robert Nelson (1656–1715) was a layman who joined the Nonjurors but later returned to the Established Church. He shared their high view of Church practice and principles. Here he affirms the importance and details of ordination, as traceable back to the usage of the Old Covenant.

[Ordination is] a privilege peculiar to the Character of a *Bishop* who is a Governor in the Church of God; whereby he conveys Authority to some to preach the Gospel, and to administer the Sacraments who are called *Presbyters*, and from whence is derived our word *Priest*; and to others to be Assistants to himself, and the *Presbyters* in their spiritual Administrations, who are called *Deacons*; which is performed by *Prayer* and the *Imposition of Hands,* a solemn Ceremony of blessing and devoting Persons to the sacred Function. For as the laying the Hands upon the Head, was a Rite of Benediction used by *Jacob* in blessing *Joseph's* Children, and by *Moses* in blessing *Joshua*; so by the Sinners laying their Hands on the Heads of the Sacrifice, it appears that it was a Ceremony used in devoting things to God; upon which accounts this was appropriated to the Ordination of *Churchmen,* who are to be blessed and devoted to God, and was made use of to express that Right and Authority which Persons do receive together with it, for *the Exercise* and *Discharge* of their *Ministerial Function.* [. . .] Our *Blessed Saviour,* while here upon Earth, was himself the great *Shepherd* and *Bishop of Souls*; an *High Priest* called of God; who in his Lifetime established under himself two distinct Orders of Church Officers, the one superior to the other, namely the *Twelve Apostles* and the *Seventy Disciples*; who are so distinguished from one another, that it implies a distinction in their Office; they are mentioned apart by different Names, and sent forth at different times. In which Establishment our *Lord* kept as nigh to the Form in use among the *Jews* as was possible, who had their *High Priest,* the *Priests* and the *Levites.*

Robert Nelson, *Companion for the Festivals and Fasts of the Church of England,* 1704, pages 526–8

The Oxford Movement opened a new question about Anglican orders. Did those who asserted their validity recognise them as being truly sacerdotal and sacramental? In the first of the Tracts for the Times, *addressed* Ad clerum – *to the clergy – John Henry Newman (p. 16) challenged them to regard themselves as true catholic priests. The inferior clergy should help and support their bishops, who were under pressure from state interference but who might not have been enthusiastic about his pious wish for them.*

Black event as it would be for the country, yet, (as far as they are concerned,) we could not wish them a more blessed termination of their course, than the spoiling of their goods, and martyrdom.

He turns to the words used at the ordination of priests.

These, I say, were words spoken to us, and received by us, when we were brought nearer to God than at any other time of our lives. I know the grace of ordination is contained in the laying on of hands, not in any form of words: yet in our own case, (as has ever been usual in the Church,) words of blessing have accompanied the act. Thus we have confessed before God our belief, that through the Bishop who ordained us, we received the HOLY GHOST, the power to bind and to loose, to administer the Sacraments, and to preach. Now *how*, is he able to give these great gifts? *Whence* is his right? Are these words idle, (which would be taking God's name in vain,) or do they express merely a wish (which surely is very far below their meaning,) or do they not rather indicate that the Speaker is conveying a gift? Surely they can mean nothing short of this. But whence I ask, his right to do so? Has he any right, except as having received the power from those who consecrated him to be a Bishop? He could not give what he had never received. It is plain then that he but *transmits* and that the Christian Ministry is a *succession*. And if, we trace back the power of ordination from hand to hand, of course we shall come to the Apostles at last. We know we do, as a plain historical fact: and therefore all we, who have been ordained clergy, in the very form of our ordination acknowledged the doctrine of the APOSTOLICAL SUCCESSION.

J. H. Newman, Tracts for the Times, vol. 1, Parker, 1839, pages 2–3

As the tenets of the Oxford Movement became more widely accepted, the preservation of the Apostolic Succession and the historic episcopate by the Church of England was defended in Lux Mundi, *a volume of essays by liberal Anglo-Catholics, influential and controversial in its time edited by Charles Gore (p. 19). The author of this passage, Walter Lock (1846–1933), Warden of Keble College, Oxford, was one of several Oxford dons among its contributors.*

As soon as we find the Christian episcopate universally organised, we find it treated as an institution received from the Apostles and as carrying with it the principle of historic continuity. So it has remained ever since, side by side with the other safeguards of unity, the sacraments and the common faith. The Roman Church has added to it what seemed a further safeguard of unity, the test of communion with itself; but this was a later claim, a claim which was persistently resented, and which was urged with disastrous results. The Reformed Churches of the Continent, in their protest against that additional test, have rejected the whole principle of historic continuity; they have remained satisfied with the bond of a common faith and of common sacraments: but the result can scarcely be said to be as yet a securer unity. Even an Unitarian historian recognises heartily that the characteristic of the Church in England is this continuity. 'There is no point,' urges Mr Beard, 'at which it can be said, here the old Church ends, here the new begins . . . The retention of the Episcopate by the English Reformers at once helped to preserve this continuity and marked it in the distinctest way . . . It is an obvious historical fact that Parker was the successor of Augustine, just as clearly as Lanfranc and Becket.'

   This, then, is what the Church claims to be as the home of grace, the channel of spiritual life. It claims to be a body of living persons who have given themselves up to the call of Christ to carry on His work in the world; a body which was organised by Himself thus far that the Apostles were put in sole authority over it; a body which received the Spirit to dwell within it at Pentecost; a body which propagated itself by spiritual birth; a body in which the ministerial power was handed on by the Apostles to their successors, which has remained so organised till the present day, and has moved on through the world, sometimes allied with, sometimes in separation from the State, always independent of it;

a body which lays on each of its members the duty of holiness, and the obligation of love, and trains them in both.

The words by Beard are taken from the 1883 Hibbert Lectures.
W. Lock, 'The Church', in C. Gore (ed.), *Lux Mundi,* John Murray, 1904, pages 278–9

The reply of the Archbishops to Apostolicae Curae *begins thus in the English version.*

The duty indeed is a serious one; one which cannot be discharged without a certain deep and strong emotion, But since we firmly believe that we have been truly ordained by the Chief Shepherd to bear a part of His tremendous office in the Catholic Church, we are not at all disturbed by the opinion expressed in that letter. So we approach the task which is of necessity laid upon us 'in the spirit of meekness'; and we deem it of greater importance to make plain for all time our doctrine about holy orders and other matters pertaining to them, than to win a victory in controversy over a sister Church of Christ. Still it is necessary that our answer be cast in a controversial form lest it be said by anyone that we have shrunk from the force of the arguments put forward on the other side.

Anglican Orders, SPCK, 1957, pages 23–4

The validity and necessity of Anglican ordination was defended again by the Doctrine Commission set up in 1922. The quotation in the extract is from 'A Letter to all Christian People' (see p. 243).

Since it is a function of the Ministry thus to be a symbol and effective instrument of the unity of the Church, it is appropriate that it should be constituted by a rite of ordination having an agreed, universal, and traditional character. The ideal of the Church's Ministry requires that it be 'acknowledged by every part of the Church as possessing . . . the authority of the whole body'. Such considerations make it clear why the Church has in fact preserved and set store by the continuity of the Ministry as, along with the Scriptures, Creeds, and Sacraments, a guarantee of its continuous identity. They also make it clear why, in our judgement, the acceptance of any Order of Ministry cannot be based on considerations of evangelistic effectiveness alone, apart from any regard for continuity and unity. The life of the Church is continuous from generation to generation; continuity of ministerial commission embodies in the sphere of Order the principle of Apostolicity in the sense of continuous mission from Christ and the Father.

The development of non-stipendiary ministry means that many priests who are active in parish work are also engaged in other paid employment. This has brought a tacit understanding that there must be some modification of the Bishop's charge in the traditional Ordination Service to 'forsake and set aside (as much as you may) all worldly cares and studies . . . you will apply yourselves wholly to this one thing'. Local ordained ministry, in which a person is called to train for service in a particular parish, might seem to question the indelibility and universal validity of holy orders. This idea is clearly refuted by John Tiller, emeritus Archdeacon of Hereford and formerly chef secretary of the Church's board for selection of candidates for the ordained ministry. The Anglican principle of ordination remains firm while the circumstances of ministry change.

Attempts are made to justify the dependence of the local church on a stipendiary sacramental ministry on the ground that the congregation receives a priest as an extension of the bishop's ministry. The fact that the incumbent is not 'home-grown' emphasises the fact that the diocese is the true definition of the local church, within which the bishop and the college of presbyters exercise pastoral oversight. This is to invent a theology of structures to do duty for a theology of orders. [. . .]

A local president of the eucharistic community, duly ordained to the ministry, is not a congregationalist subversion of episcopal oversight. Ordination, whether to stipendiary or to non-stipendiary ministry, whether to serve as deacon or priest in one's home church or in a distant parish, must always by definition involve an association with the bishop's ministry. Orders lose their significance if they are not recognised as authorisation to minister in the whole 'church of God'. Within a divided Christendom, of course, no orders are so recognised in practice. But there can be no partial or local form of ordination. The act of ordination brings a new relationship, not only to the local church, but also to the church universal. The theological distinctiveness of a local ordained ministry does not therefore lie in the form of ordination.

John Tiller, 'Towards a theology of a local ordained ministry', in J. M. M. Francis and L. Francis (eds), *Tentmaking*, Gracewing, 1998, page 385

As for the question of clerical marriage, John Jewel (p. 9) defended it largely on the grounds that enforced clerical celibacy led to immorality.

We say, that marriage is honourable and holy in all degrees of men, in patriarchs, in prophets, in apostles, in holy martyrs, in the ministers of the church, and in the bishops, and that, as St Chrysostom saith 'It is both lawful and just that he should ascend the episcopal throne with it'; and we say, as Sozomen did of Spiridion, and Nazianzen did of his own father, that 'A pious and industrious bishop is nothing the worse for being married, but rather much the better, and more useful in his ministry'. And we say that the law which by force takes away this liberty from men, and ties them to a single life against their wills, is, as St. Paul styles it, The doctrine of devils, (1 Tim. iv. 1) and that from hence, as is confessed by the bishop of Augusta, Faber, the abbot of Palermo, Latomus, the tripartite work, which is joined to the second volume of the councils, and other defenders of the papal party, and which is apparent from the thing itself, also confessed by all histories, an incredible impurity of life and manners, and horrible debaucheries in the ministers of God, have sprung and arisen; so that Pius II, bishop of Rome, was not out when he said, He saw many causes why the clergy should be denied wives, but he saw more and greater causes to allow them wives again.

Works of Bishop Jewel, ed. J. Ayre, Parker Society, 1847, pages 306–7

It took some time for the idea of married clergy to meet approval in all quarters. Queen Elizabeth I took a poor view of it, as evidenced by her reported farewell to Archbishop Parker's wife: 'Madam I may not call you, and Mistress I am ashamed to call you, so as I know not what to call you, but yet I do thank you.' Unable to reverse the new freedom, she did her best to restrict it.

Of the Injunctions which Elizabeth published, for the guidance of her clergy and laity in religious matters, in the first year of her reign, the twenty-ninth runs thus: 'Item, although there be no prohibition by the word of God, nor any example of the Primitive Church, but that the Priests and Ministers of the Church may lawfully, for the avoiding of fornication, have an honest and sober wife, and that for the same purpose the same was by Act of Parliament in the time of our dear brother King Edward the Sixth made lawful: whereupon a great number of the clergy of this Realm were then married, and so continue, yet because there hath grown offence, and some slander to the Church by lack of discreet and sober behaviour in many ministers of the Church, both in choosing of their wives and indiscreet living with them, the remedy whereof is necessary to be sought, it is thought therefore very necessary, that no manner of priest or deacon shall hereafter take to his wife any manner of woman without the advice and allowance first had upon good examination by the bishop of the same diocese, and two justices of the peace of the same shire, dwelling next to the place where the same woman hath most made her abode before her marriage, nor without the good will of the parents of the said woman, if she have any living, or two of the next of her kinsfolks, or, for lack of knowledge of such, of her master or mistress where she serveth. And before she shall be contracted in any place, she shall make a good and certain proof thereof to the minister, or to the congregation assembled for that purpose, which shall be upon some holyday where divers may be present. And if any shall do otherwise, that then they shall not be permitted to minister either the word or the sacraments of the Church, nor shall be capable of any ecclesiastical benefice, and for the manner of marriages of any bishops, the same shall be allowed and approved by the metropolitan of the province, and also by such commissioners as the Queen's Majesty thereunto shall appoint.

J. C. Jeafferson, *A Book about the Clergy*, Hurst and Blackett, 1870, page 257

Edward King (1829–1910), Bishop of Lincoln, was known for his sanctity of life and his pastoral care for both clergy and laity. He advises a young priest who is wondering whether it is right to marry.

As to the important matter on which you ask my advice, I will say that I think St Paul puts before us the unmarried life as the higher state; but then, you must remember, he adds 'for those who are called to it'. If you had been living as you were, or, if you thought the higher life would help your ministry best, then I should advise you to try for it. I gather, however, from your letter that you think a married priest would do most good in the sphere to which you have been called. I think, then, you are quite free to marry. I need not add 'only in the Lord,' which, as you know, would mean someone who would understand your priestly life and help you in it. I am single myself, but simply because I never felt called to anything else. I have the highest view of married life; indeed, I believe our English parsonages for purity of life may well compare with the old monasteries and the modern clergy houses. I should make it a matter of prayer, and feel quite free.

Edward King, *Spiritual Letters*, Mowbray, 1910, page 109

The measure to ordain women to the priesthood was passed after strong opinions for and against had been expressed over a number of years. So much has been said and written that one example from each side must suffice. It may be added that a result of the change has been the phenomenon of the 'parson's husband', and in some parishes a team of a married couple.

   The House of Bishops gave a majority in support when the vote was taken in the General Synod. The second report on their own discussions published in 1990 showed some disagreement. This is the statement of those in favour.

[Some of the bishops] believe that the continuation of an exclusively male priestly ministry in twentieth-century England actually obscures the truth of the Gospel. They believe that the insights and the experiences of the society around us stand in judgement upon our continuing exclusive practice. The persistence of an all male priesthood threatens our mission and our unity. The symbol of an all male priesthood no longer makes evident to the world what we believe about the unity and communion of men and women in creation and in the kingdom. The symbol of an exclusive ministry, some of us believe, reinforces patterns of inequality and alienation which make it difficult for many women (real and particular women), and some men, to belong to the Church. Those of us who hold this believe that it makes it hard for the world to recognise the Church as a community of liberty and reconciliation. An inclusive ministry, they believe, would point beyond human divisions towards the equality and dignity of women and men created in God's image and point the world to the communion of the kingdom. Further, they believe that an inclusive ministry would proclaim more fully truths about God the Holy Trinity, the God who is neither male nor female, in whom those qualities we call masculine and feminine are encompassed and transcended in the wholeness of divine life and love. An inclusive ministry would witness in our fragmented world that the Church is the place where the kingdom is being born, where the Holy Spirit breaks down the barriers that divide, breathes new life, heals and restores. Moreover a fully inclusive ministry will bring a greater wholeness as both male and female experience is brought to the deliberations and decisions of those who exercise oversight as bishops, or delegated oversight as presbyters. Those of us who are convinced that the Church of England should proceed to ordain women to the priesthood acknowledge that this may slow down the movement into deeper fellowship with some Churches, notably the Roman Catholic Church and the Orthodox Churches, but they cannot put the concern for ecclesial unity above that unity which they believe the values of the Kingdom of God demand.

The following was written by one of the many women who were against the proposal.

This demand is one to which we should accord careful thought. It is also a demand which we need to approach with great care in order to ensure that we are not merely jumping onto the bandwagon of 'equality for women'. We must beware of being influenced by those outside the church whose sole aim is to see women given equal opportunities in all professions – an aim laudable in itself, but one which ignores the uniqueness of the priesthood.

What then of those within the church who tell us that there are no good reasons why women should not become priests, and many why they should? These people suggest that at the root of the church's refusal to ordain women to the priesthood lies prejudice. We are told that Christ's failure to ordain women – to have them among the twelve –

does not mean that he wanted them excluded for ever; that Paul's state-ment in 1 Corinthians on which the church's teaching has been based, was addressed only to the Corinthians and was not meant to be obeyed by the whole church; that in any case Paul was influenced against women having any part to play in worship by his Hebrew training. Finally it is suggested that the church held on to this teaching because of the belief of the scholastic theologians of the middle ages that males are supreme and females subject to them! Side by side with these criticisms are put such arguments as the great need at the present time for more people to enter the priesthood, and the existence throughout the first Christian centuries of an order of deaconesses.

What are we to think of these ideas? Are we to throw overboard two thousand years of tradition and start ordaining women to the priest-hood? Or are we right in holding to our beliefs? It would seem that those who want the church to relinquish these beliefs would need to produce a great deal more evidence than they have so far done, for none of their reasons seem persuasive enough to be a basis for the demand for the ordination of women.

[. . .] Much more evidence is needed than that put forward by those who wish to see women in the priesthood before the church abandons the tradition based on the above facts. Especially these people need to be reminded of the belief of the church that tradition does reflect the guid-ance of the Holy Spirit throughout the ages, and that it is not purely an invention of prejudiced males.

Sue Flockton, *Why Not Ordain Women?*, Church Literature Association, 1977,
pages 1–2, 4

Some believe that recent changes have diminished the role of the clergy and diverted attention from the importance of the Apostolic Succession, which was urged so strongly by earlier writers. John Bishop (1930–92) was a devoted parish priest, a theological college lecturer and an insightful scholar.

Given the ambiguities of authority in the Church, where does this leave the parish priest? What is he to teach or do when the congregation is divided or sections of the Church speak in contradictory ways? What would George Herbert make of the Church of England now? How would the parish react if he got up into the pulpit the Sunday after his induction and said, 'I am the deputy under Christ for reducing man to the obedience of God'? Here and there pockets of deference survive. 'Ah, Vicar, how nice of you to call! If you go round to the front door I will unbolt it and let you in properly.' There are even parishes where, if your hearing is acute, you may catch one very old lady saying to another very old lady, 'Father says we must do so-and-so.' And in those other parishes, where the vicar is Fred to everyone except his wife, as he downs the Red Barrel in the public bar and dashes on to the club for a gin, the collar may be gone, the profile may be so low as to be detectable only to a second year sociology student, but Fred will wonder what is up if he is kept waiting when he orders drinks. Yet this deference amounts to very little. Even in the Roman Church, where the pope can command crowds numbering millions, he cannot stop his own people voting for abortion, a grave sin. The vicar is often the one who is expected to pack up the chairs in the hall, put out the dustbin and lock the church. Ruefully he may reflect that he is the servant of all. And then the irony, I hope, strikes him: is not this the mode in which Jesus exercised His own royal lordship?

We, as bearers of ministerial priesthood, sent by those who have been sent by the risen Lord, apostolic ministers indeed, have learnt (if we did not know it already) that it is not for us to dictate from the altar steps or lay down the law from the pulpit. In our teaching we have to be as wily as serpents. We have to be ready to answer for the truth entrusted to us by our Lord Himself, never swerving or compromising, and never smoothing away what He has put into our hands; yet simply and patiently explaining. The apostolic priesthood has an intrinsic authority of office within the Church.

John Bishop, *The Ultimate Mystery*, John Bishop Charitable Trust, 1998, page 239

5

Holy Communion

The most comfortable Sacrament of the Body and Blood of Christ

The first Book of Common Prayer in 1549 printed a new English order for 'The Supper of the Lord and the Holy Communion, Commonly called the Mass'. The title in the second book in 1552 was 'The Order for the Administration of the Lord's Supper or Holy Communion', and this is the heading in the book of 1662 which is still authorised and used today. The words reflect one of the major changes and causes of controversy, for the Church of England and for all the Reformation churches. The Mass had been central to worship all through the Middle Ages. Attendance on Sundays and Holy Days was required, but lay communion was infrequent, often only once a year at Easter. The basic duty was to be present at the time of the consecration and elevation of the sacred elements. In the sixteenth century, disagreement about the nature of the sacrament, the change in the elements and the frequency of communion made for continual debate not only with other churches but within the Church of England itself. It is a mistake to suppose that the Reformers, Lutheran, Calvinist or Zwinglian, took a low view of the Eucharist because of their insistence on Bible study and preaching. The passionate and sometimes bitter discussions sprang from the desire rightly to interpret the meaning of the Lord's instruction, 'Do this in remembrance of me'.

The Church of England has never made a definitive statement equivalent to the Tridentine affirming of Transubstantiation. That particular doctrine was denied in Article 28 and in the 'Black Rubric' which was printed at the end of the Communion service in 1552, omitted in 1559 and restored in a modified form in 1662. However, belief in the Real Presence of Christ in consecrated bread and wine, without dogmatic definition of the change of substance, has been, and continues to be, held by many

Anglicans. Others believe that communicants receive the grace of Christ when they come in faith, although the bread and wine have no objective difference after consecration. The history of the words of administration shows how the makers of the official liturgy were prepared and able to accommodate both opinions. The 1549 Book of Common Prayer orders that the bread shall be given with the words, 'The Body of our Lord Jesus Christ which was given for thee preserve thy body and soul unto everlasting life.' The more Protestant revision of 1552 substituted 'Take and eat this in remembrance that Christ died for thee, and feed on him in thy heart by faith with thanksgiving,' taking the service as a memorial of Christ's Passion by each communicant. The two sentences were combined in the Elizabethan compromise in 1559 and so remain, with similar words for the administration of the wine. More recent liturgies prefer the simple, 'the Body of Christ', 'the Blood of Christ'.

Those who might hold different views on this matter agreed that the Eucharist was a common meal for all believers who came together to share the sacrament. In opposition to the practice of mere presence at the Mass as a sufficient lay duty, non-communicating attendance was discouraged. It was a matter of controversy after the Oxford Movement, when the sung Eucharist where most of the congregation would not receive communion became the main Sunday service in some churches. Whereas attendance at Mass had been required at least on Sundays and Holy Days, and its celebration had been a daily obligation for the priest, Holy Communion in the Church of England was less frequent. The service until the Creed might be said after Matins and Litany, but consecration and communion did not follow in many parish churches. The minimum declared requirement for confirmed members of the Church was communion three times a year, of which Easter was to be one. The minimum did not satisfy everyone, as can be seen in the words of Allestree, quoted below. The members of the 'Holy Club' which John and Charles Wesley founded at Oxford in 1729 received communion frequently. By contrast, Anthony Trollope's Mr Harding, a worthy and holy man, celebrated the sacrament once every three months at his little church in Barchester (*The Warden*, 1855).

Despite variations in practice, many Anglican writers took a high view of the sacrament, and urged solemn preparation as well as more frequent reception. The Tractarians brought eucharistic worship back to the centre, although it was many years before it became the Sunday norm in parishes, and believed in the Real Presence rather than the simple memorialism. They were not themselves strong ritualists but their followers introduced ceremonial and practices which led to bitter opposition from the mainstream of the Church, with riots, persecution and even imprisonment of some priests who refused to follow the official line. Nearly all the practices once declared illegal – such as wafer bread, altar candles and the mixed chalice – are now to be found in the majority of churches.

The Tractarians taught the centrality of the Eucharist in parish worship as an act of obedience and adoration. Many of the founding Anglican writers and their successors taught the importance of regarding it as a common meal shared by Christians in remembrance of the Last Supper. Both ideas came together and changed the face of worship in the Church of England with the 'Parish and People' movement. It now seemed right to restore the Eucharist to the centre of parish worship, to give the laity greater participation in the service, and to order the church so that the celebrant faced the people in a way which symbolised a shared meal rather than a priestly sacrifice. The movement was strongly influenced by the work of A. G. Hebert: *Liturgy and Society* (1935) and his edited volume *The Parish Communion* (1937). Changes in the liturgy itself were partly, though not solely, a result of this new, or perhaps restored, emphasis and are considered later under *Public Worship*. There was an ecumenical dimension to this movement. More lay participation, and a sense of sharing rather than passively following the whole service, developed in most of the other churches. There is now a greater outward similarity in eucharistic services across the churches, though shared communion is still in the future. Within the Church of England, the Parish Communion has helped to heal some of the suspicion between sections which held different ideas about the nature of the sacrament.

Although such differences have in the past sometimes led to confrontation and unworthy accusations from both extremes, the attitude of Anglican writers towards the Holy Communion has been reverent and has urged similar reverence in preparation and reception. It has been seen a privilege given by grace alone, not dependent on the personal worthiness of the communicant, yet demanding true repentance and the resolve to amend and grow spiritually. In the words of the Book of Common Prayer, to 'intend to lead a new life, following the commands of God and walking from henceforth in his holy ways'. These things have sometimes been best expressed not by writers on eucharistic theology but by poets and mystics. Reverence which springs from joy and confidence, mingled with a sense of total need and dependence, has inspired some of the writings quoted below, telling of how the earthly feast of familiar bread and wine raises the faithful to a vision of the heavenly feast of the whole Church Triumphant.

Myles Coverdale (1488–1568) produced the first complete English Bible, became Bishop of Exeter under Edward VI, went into exile under Mary I and returned to be a leader of the Puritan party in the Church under Elizabeth I. He writes here as one if the early proponents of regular actual communion as a duty laid on all confirmed members of the Church of England.

In all congregations well ordered ought to be such custom, that the supper be celebrate so oft as may be, and so much as the people shall be able to receive. And every private person ought, so much as in him lieth, to be ready to receive it so often, as it shall be celebrate in a common assembly, unless he be by very urgent causes constrained to abstain. For albeit that the time is not assigned, nor the day expressed by any precept or commandment; yet ought this thing to suffice, that we know it to be the Lord's will we should use this sacrament oftentimes. Otherwise we know not the profit that cometh unto us thereby. The excuses that some men lay are void and vain. Some say, they are not worthy, and by that pretext they abstain all the year. Others do not only consider how unworthy they be; but they do also lay for them, that they cannot communicate with such as they see come thither unprepared. Also, other suppose, that the oft use of it is superfluous; neither do they think that it ought to be so often iterated and repeated, after that we have once received Christ.

I ask of those first, which lay for themselves their own unworthiness, how their conscience can sustain so great misery more than an year, and dare not call upon the Lord accordingly For they will grant it to be a point of rashness to call upon God as a Father, unless we be the members of Christ; which thing cannot be done, unless the substance and verity of the supper be fulfilled in us: and if we have the verity itself, we are, with much better reason, meet to receive the same. Whereby we perceive, that

they which would exempt themselves from the supper as unworthy, do
rob themselves of that great commodity of invocating and praying to
God. But I would not compel them, whose consciences be troubled and
feared by any religion, to the intent they should intermingle themselves
rashly. But rather I counsel them to tarry for a season, until the Lord
shall vouchsafe to deliver them from that anxiety. In like manner, if
there be any other cause, I do not deny but it is lawful to defer. I do only
purpose to declare, that no man ought to continue long in this thing,
that he may abstain for his unworthiness. For so is the congregation
robbed of the communication, wherein all our health consisteth. Let
him rather endeavour to fight against all the impediments which the
devil casteth against him, lest he be excluded from so great a good thing,
and consequently robbed of all the benefits together.

Writings and Translations of Myles Coverdale, ed. G. Pearson, Parker Society, 1844,
pages 448–9

*The same encouragement is given in the Prayer Book Exhortation which the
priest is to read 'in case he shall see the people negligent to come to the Holy
Communion'. It is a little less patient than Coverdale about good reasons
for temporarily abstaining.*

I bid you all that are here present, and beseech you, for the Lord Jesus
Christ's sake, that ye will not refuse to come thereto, being so lovingly
called and bidden by God himself. Ye know how grievous and unkind a
thing it is, when a man hath prepared a rich feast, decked his table with
all kind of provision, so that there lacketh nothing but the guests to sit
down; and yet they who are called (without any cause) most unthank-
fully refuse to come. Which of you in such a case would not be moved?
Who would not think a great injury and wrong done unto him?
Wherefore, most dearly beloved in Christ, take ye good heed, lest ye,
withdrawing yourselves from this holy Supper, provoke God's indigna-
tion against you. It is an easy matter for a man to say, I will not communicate, because I am otherwise hindered with worldly business. But such
excuses are not so easily accepted and allowed before God. If any man
'say, I am a grievous sinner, and therefore am afraid to come': wherefore
then do ye not repent and amend? When God calleth you, are ye not

ashamed to say ye will not come? When ye should return to God, will ye excuse yourselves, and say ye are not ready? Consider earnestly with yourselves how little such feigned excuses will avail before God. They that refused the feast in the Gospel, because they had bought a farm, or would try their yokes of oxen, or because they were married, were not so excused, but counted unworthy of the heavenly feast.

In 1657, towards the end of the Commonwealth, The Whole Duty of Man *was published; it was a popular book of devotion for many years. It appeared anonymously but is usually ascribed to Richard Allestree (1619–81), Regius Professor of Divinity at Oxford and Provost of Eton. He firmly advocates frequent communion.*

Though the obligation of every single vow reach to the utmost days of our lives, yet are we often to renew it, that is, we are often to receive the Holy Sacrament, for that being the means of conveying to us so great and invaluable benefits, and it being also a command of Christ, that we should do this in remembrance of Him, we are in respect both of reason and duty to omit no fit opportunity of partaking of that holy table.

Richard Allestree, *The Whole Duty of Man* (1657), 1700, pages 89–90

John Jewel (p. 9) took the more Reformed position about the nature of the sacrament.

When we speak of the mystery of Christ, and of eating his body, we must shut up and abandon all our bodily senses. And, as we cannot say that we see him with our bodily eyes, or hear him with our bodily ears, or touch him with bodily feeling; so likewise can we not, and therefore may we not, say we taste him or eat him with our bodily mouth. In this work we must open all the inner and spiritual senses of our soul: so shall we not only see his body, but hear him, and feel him, and taste him, and eat him. This is the mouth and the feeling of faith. By the hand of faith we reach unto him, and by the mouth of faith we receive his body.

Touching the eating of Christ's body St Augustine taught the people on this wise: *Crede, et manducasti. Credere in Christum, hoc est, manducare panem vivum*: 'Believe in Christ, and thou hast eaten Christ.' 'For believing in Christ is the eating of the bread of life.' Believe that he is that 'Lamb of God that taketh away the sins of the world.' Believe that there is no other name given unto men wherein we shall be saved, but the name of Jesus Christ. Believe that he hath paid the ransom for the sins of the whole world. Believe that he hath made peace between God and man. Believe that he hath reconciled all things by his blood. Here is nothing to be done by the mouth of the body. Whosoever thus believeth, he eateth, he drinketh him.

Works of Bishop Jewel, ed. J. Ayre, Parker Society, 1847, pages 118–19

According to words ascribed to her in an early record, Queen Elizabeth I had a pious but diplomatic view when asked about her opinion on the Real Presence.

'Twas God the word that spake it,
He took the Bread and brake it;
And what the word did make it,
That I believe and take it.

Thomas Pestell (?1584–?1659) was a Royal Chaplain to Charles I. He left many sermons and some poems which deserve to be better known, of which his meditation on coming to Holy Communion is one.

Lord to thy flesh and blood when I repair,
When dreadful joys and pleading tremblings are,
The most I relish, most it does me good,
When my soul faints and pines and dies for food;
Did my sins murder thee? To make that plain
Thy pierced dead-living body lives again.
Flow sweet sad drops; what differing things you do
Reveal my sins; and seal my pardon too.

The Poems of Thomas Pestell, Oxford University Press,
1940, page 6

George Herbert (1593–1633), leaving a career which was moving towards courtly advancement, was ordained and passed his last years as rector of Bemerton, near Salisbury. He is one of the greatest of Anglican devotional poets, well known through his hymns 'Teach me, my God and King' and 'Let all the world in every corner sing'. His poem on Holy Communion is ecstatic and deeply reverent, less easy on first reading than some of his work, but is worth taking slowly as a source for meditation. 'Impanation' was a word dear to some of the Reformers, as asserting the Real Presence without Transubstantiation.

O gracious Lord, how shall I know
Whether in these gifts Thou be so
As Thou art everywhere?
Or rather so, as Thou alone
First I am sure, whether bread stay,
Or whether bread doth fly away,
Concerneth bread, not me;
Tak'st all the lodging, leaving none
For thy poor creature there.

But that both Thou and all Thy train
Be there, to Thy truth and my gain
Concerneth me and Thee

And if in coming to Thy foes,
Thou dost come first to them, that shows,
The haste of Thy good will;
Or if that Thou two stations makest,
In Bread and me, the way Thou takest
Is more, but for me still.
Then of this also I am sure,
That Thou didst all those pains endure
To abolish Sin, not wheat;
Creatures are good and have their place
Sin only well did all deface
Thou drivest from his seat.
I could believe an Impanation
At the rate of an Incarnation

If Thou hadst died for Bread;
But that which made my soul to die,
My flesh and fleshly villainy,
That also made Thee dead
That flesh is there mine eyes deny
And what should flesh but flesh descry,
The noblest sense of five?
If glorious bodies pass the sight,
Shall they be food and strength and might,
Even there where they deceive?
Into my soul this cannot pass;
Flesh (though exalted) keeps his grass,
And cannot turn to soul.
Bodies and minds are different spheres
Nor can they change their bounds and meres [*limits*],
But keep a constant pole.

This gift of all gifts is the best,
Thy flesh the least that I request;
Thou took'st that pledge from me,
Give me not that I had before,
Or give me that so I have more;
My God, give me all Thee.

George Herbert, 'The Holy Communion', F. E. Hutchinson (ed.),
     The Works of George Herbert, Oxford University Press, 1941

*Daniel Waterland (p. 59) addressed the question of communicants who
thought that receiving the Sacrament was an act of virtue which made personal morality less important. After some typically Anglican weighing of
arguments, he warns against this error.*

It may be further pleaded . . . that the action of the Sacraments, as means
of grace (supposing it erroneous) is apt to lead men to rely upon the
Sacraments more than upon their own serious endeavours for the leading a good life, or to rest in the Sacraments as sufficient without keeping
God's commandments. But this is a suggestion built upon no certain
grounds. For suppose we were deceived (as we certainly are not) in our

high conceptions of the use and efficacy of this Sacrament; all that follows is, that we may be thereby led to frequent the Sacrament so much the oftener; to come to it with the greater reverence, and to repeat our solemn vows for the leading a good life by the assistance of Divine grace, with the more serious and devout affections. No divines amongst us, that I know of, ever teach that the use of the outward Sacrament is of any avail without inward faith and repentance, or entire obedience. Our Church at least, and, I think, all Protestant churches, have abundantly guarded against any one's resting in the bare outward work. The danger therefore on this side is very slight in comparison. For what if a man should erroneously suppose that upon his worthy receiving he obtains pardon for past sins, and grace to prevent future, will not this be an encouragement to true repentance, without which he can be no worthy receiver, and to watchfulness also for the time to come, without which the Divine grace can never have its perfect work? Not that I would plead for any pious mistake, (were it really a mistake) but I am answering an objection; and shewing, that there is no comparative force in it. Were the persuasion I am pleading for really an error, reason good that it should be discarded, religion wants not the assistance of pious frauds, neither can it be served by them. But as we are now supposing it doubtful on which side the error lies, and are arguing only upon that supposition, it appears to be a very clear case, that religion would suffer abundantly more by an error on the left hand, than by an error on the right; and that of the two extremes, profaneness, rather than superstition, is the dangerous extreme.

Daniel Waterland, *The Doctrine of the Eucharist*, Clarendon Press, 1896, pages 11–12

John Wesley (1703–91), the founder of Methodism, was a priest in the Church of England who never wished to begin a denomination outside that church but was driven by hostility from the church authorities to organise lay pastors to do the work of evangelism, and to ordain men as priests in North America. A tireless traveller and preacher, he practised and promulgated the duty of receiving Holy Communion frequently, as an act of obedience and as a source of grace.

I am to show that it is the duty of every Christian to receive the Lord's Supper as often as he can.

The first reason why it is the duty of every Christian so to do is because it is a plain command of Christ. That this is his command appears from the words of the text – 'Do this in remembrance of me' – by which, as the apostles were obliged to bless, break, and give the bread to all that joined with them in these holy things, so were all Christians obliged to receive those signs of Christ's body and blood. Here, therefore, the bread and wine are commanded to be received in remembrance of his death, to the end of the world. Observe, too, that this command was given by our Lord when he was just laying down his life for our sakes. They are, therefore, as it were, his dying words to all his followers.

A second reason why every Christian should do this as often as he can is because the benefits of doing it are so great to all that do it in obedience to him – namely, the forgiveness of our past sins, the present strengthening and refreshing of our souls. In this world we are never free from temptations. Whatever way of life we are in, whatever our condition be, whether we are sick or well, in trouble or at ease, the enemies of our souls are watching to lead us into sin. And too often they prevail over us. Now, when we are convinced of having sinned against God, what surer way have we of procuring pardon from him than the 'showing forth the Lord's death' – 1 Cor 11 26 – and beseeching him, for the sake of his Son's sufferings, to blot out all our sins?

The Works of the Rev John Wesley, Wesleyan Methodist Book Room, no date,
vol. 7, pages 147–8

Alexander Knox (1757–1831) was a descendant of John Knox of Scotland and a friend of John Wesley. He partly anticipated the Oxford Movement with his high view of the Church of England as a reformed part of the Catholic Church. He defended her maintenance of the Apostolic Succession and here asserts the Real Presence.

According to the Apostle, and that universal belief to which he appeals, the commemorative celebration of the Eucharist, as a devotional act, is not that which makes it peculiarly beneficial and venerable; but it is so, because in this ordinance, the aliments which Christ has appointed, become, through his designation and blessing, the direct vehicles of his own divine influences to capable receivers. Nothing short of this notion would accord with the ascribing of spiritual virtue, specially to each visible sign; and, what is still more, to each, not as becoming efficacious through *the act of receiving*, but as endued with efficacy through *the act of consecration.*

For, we must observe, it is not 'the cup of blessing which we *drink*,' nor 'the bread which we *eat*,' that are declared to be the communion of the blood, and the communion of the body of Christ; but it is said, 'the cup of blessing which we *bless*, and the bread which we *break*,' clearly indicating, that the eucharistic elements, when once solemnly sanctified according to our Lord's appointment, are to be regarded as being, in an inexplicable, but deeply awful manner the receptacles of that heavenly virtue, which his divine power qualifies them to convey. On such a subject it would be presumptuous to indulge in any hypothetic speculation. But it would be still more blameable, and at least as prejudicial, not to allow to the Apostle's words all their due import; especially as those very words contain the only direct definition of the Eucharist in the sacred writings.

The Remains of Alexander Knox, 1836, vol. 2, pages 45–6

Christina Rossetti (1830–94) led the apparently uneventful life of a Victorian spinster, but wrote poetry which was deeply emotional and insightful. Some was gently erotic, some playful, but much of it expressing the devotion of her Anglo-Catholic Christian faith, as in this sonnet.

Why should I call Thee Lord, Who art my God?
Why should I call Thee Friend, Who art my Love?
Or King, Who art my very Spouse above?
Or call Thy sceptre on my heart Thy rod?
Lo now Thy banner over me is love,
All heaven flies open to me at Thy nod:
For Thou hast lit Thy flame in me a clod,
Made me a nest for dwelling of Thy Dove.
What wilt Thou call me in our home above,
Who now hast called me friend? how will it be
When Thou for good wine settest forth the best ?
Now Thou dost bid me come and sup with Thee,

Now Thou dost make me lean upon Thy breast:
How will it be with me in time of love?

Christina Rossetti, 'After Communion', *Poems*,
Macmillan, 1904

E. B. Pusey, (1800–82) Regius Professor of Hebrew at Oxford, became the leader of the Oxford Movement after Newman left the Church of England in 1845. He asserted the Real Presence in the Eucharist as sound Anglican doctrine, though stopping short of Transubstantiation.

The outward and visible sign is (our Catechism teaches us) 'a means whereby we receive the inward'. As through the Baptism of water in the name of the Trinity we receive the inward part of Baptism, 'the death unto sin and the new birth unto righteousness', so, through the outward elements of the Lord's Supper, 'the bread and Wine', received as Christ has commanded, we receive the 'inward part', 'the Body and Blood of Christ'. But in order that we may receive them; they must be there, for us to receive them.

This, as it is the first teaching of our childish years, training us to look on, and to long for, what we are to receive thereafter, comes naturally, as the first, immediate instruction, preparatory to the first Communion. We had repeated from our early childhood, that 'the Body and Blood of Christ are verily and indeed taken and received by the faithful in the Lord's Supper'. And now, at the first Communion comes the great reality itself. 'Verily and indeed'; in deed and in truth; really and truly, are 'the Body and Blood of Christ taken and received in the Lord's Supper by the faithful', and so by each one of us, if we are faithful. 'If this be not the Real Presence', I heard in my youth from an old clergyman, 'I know not how it could be expressed'.

The gift, then, in the Sacrament of the Lord's Supper, according to our Catechism, is not only grace, nor even any spiritual union with our Lord wrought by God the Holy Ghost; it is no mere lifting up our souls to Him at the Right Hand of God; but it is His Body and Blood in deed and in truth, received by us, if faithful. And, at present, we are concerned with what it is to the faithful, not what it becomes to the unfaithful.

E. B. Pusey, *The Real Presence of the Body and Blood of our Lord Jesus Christ the Doctrine of the English Church*, Parker, 1869, pages 165–6

This view of the nature of the Eucharist, together with the growing practice of a Choral Eucharist as the chief Sunday morning service at which lay communion was not encouraged, led to disputes about the propriety of non-communicating attendance. Some maintained that it was mistaken and even sinful to come with the intention of not receiving the sacrament. The opposite view was held by Darwell Stone (1859–1941), Principal of Pusey House, Oxford, and a defender of the strong Anglo-Catholic position against the more liberal catholicism of writers like Charles Gore.

I do not think that one can say that communicants are not able to share in the offering if at any particular Celebration they do not communicate. By reason of their Communions their life is a Eucharistic life which goes on continuously from Communion to Communion. In the case of persons who have communicated at an early service and are present later in the day without communicating, I do not think between their power to join in the offering at the early service and their power to do so at the later service. And I should say that very much the same is true about persons who have communicated (say) on a Sunday and are present without communicating on the following weekdays; and that in a lessening degree this holds good about those who communicate rarely [...]

I think that in the present condition of the Western Church we really come nearest to the early Church if we allow baptised children and some other baptised persons to be present throughout the Eucharistic Service without communicating. Baptism, it seems to me, gives such union with our Lord as allows of a share in the Eucharistic offering.

One can hardly doubt that the custom of going out of church at an early point in the Celebration which the Prayer Books of 1552 and 1559 made prevalent has been a great failure as regards any right relation to the Eucharist; and I should say that a practice of non-communicating attendance – with a due emphasis on the importance of Communion comes much nearer the method of the early Church than what came to be the ordinary custom in England. Perhaps in view of (a) the Western refusal of communion to infants and young children, (b) the present lack of discipline as to who may come to church and the place which they are to fill, and (c) the rarity of Communion on the part of many, it gives effect to the principles of the early Church better than any other plan now possible on a wide scale.

From the point of view of the early Church it is, of course, abnormal that there should be any who have not communicated admitted thus far; but from that point of view it is abnormal also that children should have been baptised and not admitted.

F. L. Cross, *Darwell Stone*, Dacre Press, 1943, pages 267–8

Stewart Headlam (1847–1924) was a controversial figure who aroused much hostility by his championing of unpopular causes. As a parish priest in Bethnal Green, East London, he campaigned on behalf of the poor and exploited. He was the prototype of Morell in Bernard Shaw's Candida. *He worked to overcome the suspicion which still existed between the Church and the theatre. He was also, as this passage shows, a devout sacramentalist.*

'Why was the sacrament of the Lord's Supper ordained?' Such is the commonplace abrupt way in which the Child is brought face to face with his lesson on this great subject. But if his Godparents have done their duty by him, he must often already have seen the priest before the altar, and seen that his elders were taking their share in the most solemn, most unique, act of their weekly life. And now he is told in a few plain homely words, what it all means. There before the altar the priest is making 'a continual remembrance of the sacrifice of the death of Christ and of the benefit which we receive thereby.' Here in a few words and a few acts you got at the very centre of our worship, and of our life. At present few English Churchmen realise this; for priests and people all have allowed their pretty musical Matins to interfere in time or in dignity with this continual Remembrance. We verily believe that much of the infidelity and the degraded misery of England are the result of English Church-men having forgotten, that it was for a Continual Remembrance that the Lord's Supper was ordained. Restore the Mass, the Holy Communion, the Lord's Supper, the Holy Eucharist, call it what you will, the act is the same, to its true position, as the one common, necessary Service, and you preach a gospel which infidelity and plutocracy must give way to.

For see how simple God's own service is compared with the double chants, difficult passages of scripture, and perhaps the Athanasian Creed, of the Matins you substitute for it. The outward part or sign is simply Bread and Wine, which the Lord hath commanded to be received; the simple human elements, of strength and joy, these are taken by the Priest, offered and consecrated; and then the inward part or thing signified is the Body and Blood of Christ, which are verily and indeed taken and received by the faithful in the Lord's Supper; that is to say Jesus then and there gives Himself to us to strengthen and refresh us, as our bodies are strengthened and refreshed by bread and wine.

Stewart Headlam, *The Laws of Eternal Life*, Verinder, 1888, pages 58–9

A. G. Hebert, a member of the Society of the Sacred Mission at Kelham, was one of the strongest influences on the Parish and People Movement. His words about the centrality of the Eucharist and the importance of a general communion express its fundamental aims.

The Holy Eucharist is not one service among many, but the centre of all. The Church of God assembles to celebrate the One Sacrifice upon which the whole life of salvation depends: pays to God the adoration which the whole creation owes to Him as its Lord; gives thanks to Him for all His mighty works from the foundation of the world to the second Advent, and for all spiritual and bodily blessings which each member has received; offers up to God the offering of the whole creation symbolised in the oblation of bread and wine, which includes the will of each member who shares in it to offer up his own life to God. takes the bread and wine, and repeats with them the sacrificial rite, which Christ instituted at the Last Supper, as the sacrificial Memorial of His Death and Resurrection; and in the Communion is herself offered up, through union with Him, to be a reasonable, holy and living sacrifice, and to live a sacrificial life in the world. For the individual, this act is the summing-up of all that his Christian faith means: his reconciliation with God and with his brethren, when with the other members of the family he kneels at the Table of the Lord: self-dedication: dependence on God, from whom he receives the sustenance of his life: justification by faith: forgiveness of sins; the Divine peace [. . .]

The inclusion of the communion of the people at the Parish Eucharist is really a matter of importance. It is not merely that the late Sung

Eucharist does, in fact, lead many who should be weekly communicants to substitute attendance at Mass for communion: it is that when the service is the general communion its atmosphere and spirit becomes quite different. It becomes the worship of the Body: the eucharistic sacrifice is seen in its full glory when it is not only the Memorial of the sacrifice of Christ but also the offering-up of the members of the Body in union with the Head.

A. G. Hebert, Liturgy and Society, Faber, 1935, pages 207–8, 213

William Temple (1881–1944), Archbishop of Canterbury, was much concerned with the social and economic implications of the Christian faith, and the Ecumenical Movement. He was also a philosophical and spiritual writer, who influenced Anglican thought. In this extract he claims the universality of Christ as a presence in the world but follows the traditional Anglican line, as stated by Coverdale, above, of expecting actual communion by those who are present at the Eucharist.

It is in the whole repetition of Christ's act that the spiritual value or reality lies. The consecrated elements are the permanent witness of that repetition, and it is as such that they become the means or occasion of the special accessibility or presence of Christ. This is only beneficial, of course, to those who approach in faith. This value, like all values, is only fully actual when it is appreciated or appropriated. For this reason those were right who said that the Presence was in the faithful receiver. But they were wrong if they held that it was there exclusively; the receiver finds, and does not make, this Presence. By means of the elements Christ is present, that is, accessible; but the accessibility is spiritual, not material or local, and Christ is only actually present to the soul of those who make right use of the means of access afforded.

No doubt Christ is always and everywhere accessible; and He is always the same. Therefore it is possible to make a 'spiritual communion' which is in every way as real as a sacramental communion. But it is far harder. Our minds are greatly affected by our bodies. When with our very bodies we repeat the sacrificial act by which the Lord interpreted His death, we find ourselves empowered to intend with fuller resolve our union with

Him in His obedience to God. The consecrated elements are quite truly and certainly a vehicle of Christ's Presence to our souls.

That Presence is given under a form which at once indicates that it is given to be received. Any other use of it seems to me both unauthorised and dangerous. It is dangerous because it suggests that the value of the Sacrament is intended to reside in itself. But this is not so. The Presence is given to be received; when received it incorporates us into the Body of Christ, so that in the power of His eternal sacrifice we may take our allotted share therein, 'filling up what is lacking of the sufferings of Christ for His Body's sake, which is the Church'. The proof that we have received the Presence is the increase of love in our daily lives.

William Temple, Christus Veritas (1924), Macmillan, 1949, pages 240–1

J. A. T. Robinson, Bishop of Woolwich, caused much controversy with his book Honest to God *in 1963, which some readers took to be a denial of a transcendent and personal God. It is less often cited in the Church today, but some of its observations are still relevant. Here he explains and defends the rationale of the Parish Communion.*

The Holy Communion is the proclamation to the Church and to the world that the presence of Christ with his people is tied to a right receiving of the common, to a right relationship with one's neighbour. For it is given only in and through these things, both in church and out of it. What the action in church does is to set forth this truth in symbol and in power. And therefore the pattern of this action is formative for the whole of Christian living. It must be made to represent the truth that 'the beyond' is to be found 'at the centre of life', 'between man and man'. That is why the Prayer Book indicates that the bread to be used for Communion shall be 'such as is usual to be eaten'; that is why the deepest insights into the meaning of 'God's board' have come for many in our generation not in the 'glass case' of the sanctuary but at their own hearth; that is why the liturgical revival has expressed itself in the recovery of the central altar with the celebration by the whole people gathered *round* the table.

Indeed, the very difference of position at the Communion table, so trivial a thing and apparently so ritualistic and removed from life, is in itself symbolic of much of what we have been trying to say. The so-called 'eastward position', in which the priest stands with his back to the people, has the psychological effect of focusing attention upon a point somewhere in the middle distance beyond the sanctuary. It symbolises the whole way of thinking in which God is seen as a projection 'out there' to whom we turn from the world. By contrast the 'westward position', in which the president surrounded by his assistants faces the people across the table, focuses attention upon a point in the middle, as the Christ stands among his own as the breaker of bread. There is equally here – or should be – the element of 'the beyond', the transcendent, as they lift their hearts to him as their ascended and triumphant Lord. But the beyond is seen not as that which takes one out and away from the earth-ly and the common, but as the vertical of the unconditioned cutting into and across the limitations of the merely human fellowship, claiming it for and transforming it into the Body of the living Christ. Moreover, the whole tendency connected with this transition of thought and expres-sion is to strip away the associations of churchiness and religiosity and everything that sets apart the sanctuary from society, and to let the décor, the music and the architecture speak the language of the world it is meant to be transforming.

J. A. T. Robinson, *Honest to God*, SCM Press, 1963, pages 88–9

The Church of England has produced some fine eucharistic hymns, as well as borrowing such hymns from other churches. One of the best is by William Bright (1824–1901), Professor of Ecclesiastical History at Oxford. He was a great admirer of the Fathers of the Church and produced a collection of early Church prayers.

And now, O Father, mindful of the love
That bought us, once for all, on Calvary's tree,
And having with us him that pleads above,
We here present, we here spread forth to thee
That only offering perfect in thine eyes,
The one true, pure, immortal sacrifice.

Look Father look, on his anointed face
And only look on us as found in him;
Look not on our misusings of thy grace,
Our prayer so languid, and our faith so dim;
For lo, between our sins and their reward
We set the passion of thy Son our Lord.

And then for those our dearest and our best,
By this prevailing presence we appeal;
O fold them closer to thy mercy's breast,
O do thine utmost for their souls' true weal;
From tainting mischief keep them white and clear
And crown thy gifts with grace to persevere.

And so we come: O draw us to thy feet
Most patient Saviour, who canst love us still;
And by this food, so aweful and so sweet,
Deliver us from every touch of ill.
In thine own service make us glad and free,
And grant us nevermore to part from thee.

The New English Hymnal, Canterbury Press, 1986, no. 273

6

Baptism and Confirmation

Born anew of water and of the Holy Ghost

Baptism with water in the name of the Holy Trinity has been and still is accepted by most Christian denominations as the act of obedience to the command of Christ which brings the individual into membership of his Church. Yet it has been a source of controversy almost equal to disputes about the other Gospel sacrament, the Eucharist. Uncertainly about the details of practice in the Church of the New Testament has given material for arguments from all sides. Was baptism seen as a complete initiation into the Church, or was it necessary to have a further rite to receive the gift of the Holy Spirit? Was baptism given only to adult believers who could make an informed profession of faith? Was baptism always by total immersion? Scholars continue to offer different views on these questions. It is certain that infants were baptised early in the history of the Church and that confirmation as a separate service was practised by the early second century AD and was general by the fourth century.

The sixteenth-century Reformers held firmly to the importance and necessity of baptism and made their practice of it part of their claim to remain in the catholic Church. The Church of England continued the familiar usage, baptising infants very soon after birth, and requiring godparents who would make the necessary promises and affirmations. Threefold dipping was required in the 1549 Book of Common Prayer, but in 1552 sprinkling was permitted if the child was declared to be weak – a provision which came to be generally adopted without requiring any certification. The medieval practices of the white robe or 'chrisom' and the anointing with oil were at first continued, but were abandoned in 1552. The sign of the cross on the child's forehead was retained although it was a cause of objection by Puritans down to the Savoy Conference which produced the 1662 Prayer Book. The creedal affirmation of 'one baptism for the remission of sins' was invoked to defend the catholicity of the Anglican rite equally with all others, and also to oppose the Anabaptists who denied the validity of infant baptism.

The font remained in its prominent position near the door, a symbol of the liminal act of admission to the full privileges of the Church. Some of the old fonts were damaged or destroyed in later waves of iconoclasm. A prayer for the blessing of the water in 1549 was replaced in 1552 by a prayer for those about to be baptised in it. Provision was made for private baptism at home in case of emergency – and such cases were frequent then and for centuries after – with public reception in the church if the child survived. One of the services introduced in the 1662 Book of Common Prayer was an office for adult baptism. It was explained as being made necessary 'by the growth of Anabaptism through the licentiousness of the later time crept in among us . . . may always be useful for the baptizing of Natives in our Plantations, and others converted to the Faith'.

Catechising as a preparation for admission to communion was given prominence in all the major Reformed churches. In the Church of England children were to be instructed and examined in the Catechism, and when they could answer satisfactorily would be brought to the Bishop for Confirmation. Communion could be given only to those who were confirmed or 'ready and desirous to be confirmed'. As dioceses were large and travel difficult, it was not always easy to get confirmed as soon as one was ready and and desirous. Bishops varied in their commitment, but in many places confirmations were infrequent and often unedifying in the scramble of a large crowd eager to reach the bishop's hands, and the service might become very long. The Tractarians insisted on the importance and solemnity of the rite, and the situation rapidly improved during the nineteenth century.

What was to be done could be decided by authority, but what it meant when it was done might be harder to determine. From the sixteenth century onwards there was disagreement within the Church about the effect of the sacrament. Put simply, the Prayer Book declares the traditional doctrine that baptism cleanses from original sin and unconditionally regenerates those who receive it even as infants. The demands and obligations of Christian are still to be fulfilled, but there has been a real change in the spiritual condition. Many on the more evangelical side of the Church regarded this as denying the need for conversion and commitment as an informed choice in years of discretion. The act of baptism was a sign rather than a sacrament efficacious in itself. This disagreement brought about a celebrated case in 1848 when Henry Phillpotts, Bishop of Exeter, refused to license a priest called Charles Gorham on the grounds that he was unsound about baptismal regeneration. The case went eventually to the Judicial Committee of the Privy Council, which ruled in favour of Gorham, a judgement which dismayed Tractarian sympathisers and helped to push some of them towards the Roman Catholic Church. They were troubled by the judgement of a secular court on a question of doctrine as much as by the theological issue itself.

There were a few minor changes in the 1928 Prayer Book, with the restoration of a blessing over the water. More recent liturgies, including the Church of England *Common Worship*, prefer to group together baptism, confirmation and the first communion of the new members of the Church as 'Rites of Initiation'. This is held to follow the practice of the early Church when catechumens were received into full fellowship by the Bishop on Easter Eve. Many additional ceremonies have been restored, such as anointing, the giving of candles and welcoming by the whole congregation. It makes a long service if all the possibilities are used, but there is usually some judicious selection, leading the initiatory rites into the Eucharist. It is particularly effective with the growing number of adult baptisms, and it means that children who are old enough to be confirmed do not have to wait a week or more for their first communion as was once frequently the case. Infant baptism is still usually administered during one of the regular Sunday services. The common pattern of these services across the churches is seen, at least by Anglicans, as an ecumenical measure and an affirmation that baptism is admission into the universal catholic Church. Some still believe that the new services lack the force and clear declarations of the shorter rites of baptism and confirmation in the Book of Common Prayer. The admission of children to Holy Communion before confirmation raises questions about the nature of confirmation itself and the communicant status of baptised but unconfirmed adults. In short, controversy still surrounds these services, as it has done since the sixteenth century, but the Church continues faithfully to receive those who seek reception.

Baptismal regeneration and infant baptism are affirmed in number 27 of the 39 Articles, although as sign rather than sacrament.

Baptism is not only a sign of profession, and mark of difference, whereby Christian men are discerned from others that be not christened, but it is also a sign of Regeneration or new Birth, whereby, as by an instrument, they that receive Baptism rightly are grafted into the Church; the promises of forgiveness of sin, and of our adoption to be the sons of God by the Holy Ghost, are visibly signed and sealed; Faith is confirmed, and Grace increased by virtue of prayer unto God. The Baptism of young Children is in any wise to be retained in the Church, as most agreeable with the institution of Christ.

The service in the Book of Common Prayer is more affirmative of actual regeneration. After baptism the priest says:

Seeing now, dearly beloved brethren, that this Child is regenerate, and grafted into the body of Christ's Church, let us give thanks to Almighty God for these benefits; and with one accord make our prayers unto him that this child may lead the rest of his life according to this beginning.

And so is the Catechism:

Question. Who gave you this name?
Answer. My Godfathers and Godmothers in my Baptism; wherein I was made a member of Christ, the child of God, and an inheritor of the kingdom of heaven.

Richard Hooker (p. 10) explains the Anglican view of the universality of valid baptism, the effects of the sacrament, and the error of second baptisms.

They which have not at the first their right Baptism must of necessity be re-baptized, because the law of Christ tieth all men to receive Baptism. Iteration of Baptism once given hath been always thought a manifest contempt of that ancient Apostolic aphorism, *One Lord, one Faith, one Baptism*: Baptism not only one, inasmuch as it hath every where the same substance, and offereth unto all men the same grace; but one also, for that it ought not to be received by any one man above once. We serve that Lord which is but one, because no other can be joined with him: we embrace that Faith which is but one, because it admitteth no innovation, that Baptism we receive which is but one, because it cannot be received often. For how should we practise iteration of Baptism, and yet teach, that we are by Baptism born anew, that by Baptism we are admitted unto the heavenly society of Saints, that those things be really and effectually done by Baptism, which are no more possible to be often done than a man can naturally be often born, or civilly be often adopted into any one stock and family? This also is the cause, why they that present us unto Baptism are entitled for ever after our parents in God, and the reason why there we receive new names, in token, that by Baptism we are made new creatures. As Christ hath therefore died and risen from the dead but once, so that Sacrament which both extinguisheth in him our former sin, and beginneth in us a new condition of life, is by one only actual administration for ever available; according to that in the Nicene Creed, *I believe one Baptism for the remission of sins.* And because second Baptism was ever abhorred in the Church of God as a kind of incestuous birth, they that iterate Baptism are driven under some pretence or other to make the former Baptism void.

The Works of Richard Hooker, Clarendon Press, 1820, vol. 2, pages 263–4 (Book 5, 62)

Even the most convinced defenders of infant baptism are sometimes anxious about its later effect on those who have received it but can have no memory of it. Richard Allestree (p. 77) insists that every believer should reflect on its meaning throughout life.

Let this therefore be your first business; try whether you rightly understood what that covenant is which you entered into at your baptism, what be the mercies promised on God's part, and the duties on yours. And because the covenant made with each of us in baptism is only the applying to our particulars the covenant made by God in Christ with all mankind in general, you are to consider whether you understand that; if you do not, you must immediately seek for instruction in it. And till we have means of gaining better, look over briefly what is said in the entrance to this treatise concerning the second covenant, which is the foundation of that covenant which God makes with us in our baptism. And because you will there find that obedience to all God's commands is the condition required of us, and is also that which we expressly vow in our baptism, it is necessary you should likewise know what those commands of God are. Therefore if you find you are ignorant of them, never be at rest till you have got yourself instructed in them, and have gained such a measure of knowledge as may direct you to do that whole duty of man which God requires.

Richard Allestree, *The Whole Duty of Man* (1657), 1700, page 63

Simon Patrick (1627–1707) began as a Presbyterian minister, was ordained in the Church of England and became successively Bishop of Chichester and Ely. He makes a succinct and classic statement of the doctrine of baptism: that it takes away the taint of original sin and opens the way to repentance and pardon for actual sins committed later.

God receives us into a state of pardon and forgiveness. He assures us that Adam's sin shall not undo us, and that every sin of our own shall not exclude us out of heaven; but that we shall have the benefit of repentance, and an allowance to retract our follies; yea, and grace so to do if we will make use of it. He admits us into that covenant of grace, which accepts of repentance instead of innocence, and of amendment instead of an unerring obedience. This is one of the special favours of the gospel which by baptism is consigned unto us, that former iniquities shall not be remembered; and that every breach of our covenant, if there be a real change wrought in us, shall not void it, and make it null and ineffectual unto us. So in Mark i. 4, John is said to *preach the baptism of repentance for remission of sin.* And Ananias saith, *Arise, and be baptized, and wash away thy sins.* And the Greek church after baptism sings those words three times, 'Blessed is he whose iniquity is forgiven.' As those who came to the baptism of John did thereby receive a distinguishing mark and character, that they should not be destroyed in the ruin of the nation; insomuch that he saith to the Pharisees that desired baptism, *Who hath warned you to flee from the wrath to come?* so they that are baptized into Christ do thereby receive a pledge, that no sin which they stand guilty of shall bring the anger of God upon their heads if they will keep his covenant; but all shall be crossed out which they are charged with, and be like words writ in the water, that are obliterated and vanished, nowhere more to be found.

The Works of Simon Patrick, ed. A. Taylor, Oxford University Press, 1858, vol. 1, page 25

William Wordsworth (1770–1850), Poet Laureate and in his later years a stout defender of the Church of England, found poetic inspiration in the service of infant baptism.

Dear be the Church that, watching o'er the needs
Of infancy, provides a kindly shower
Whose virtue changes to a Christian Flower
A Growth from sinful Nature's bed of weeds! –
Fitliest beneath the sacred roof proceeds
The ministration; while parental Love
Looks on, and Grace descendeth from above
As the high service pledges now, now pleads.
There, should vain thoughts outspread their wings and fly
To meet the coming hours of festal mirth,
The tombs – which hear and answer that brief cry,
The Infant's notice of his second birth –
Recall the wandering Soul to sympathy
With what man hopes from Heaven, yet fears from earth.

William Wordsworth, 'Baptism', *Ecclesiastical Sonnets* XX,
Poetical Works, Oxford University Press, 1942

Wordsworth's contemporary and friend Samuel Taylor Coleridge (1772–1834) recorded more personally his thoughts on his own baptism.

God's child in Christ adopted – Christ my all –
What that earth boasts were not lost cheaply, rather
Than forfeit that blest name, by which I call
The Holy One, the Almighty God, my Father? –

Father! in Christ we live, and Christ in Thee –
Eternal Thou, and everlasting we.
The heir of heaven, henceforth I fear not death
In Christ I live! In Christ I draw the breath
Of the true life! – Let, then, earth and sea and sky
Make war against me! On my front I show
Their mighty Master's seal. In vain they try
To end my life, that can but end its woe. –
Is that a deathbed where a Christian lies? –
Yes! but not his – 'tis Death itself that dies.

S. T. Coleridge, 'My Baptismal Birthday', *Collected Poems*,
Oxford University Press, 1912

At the time of the Gorham controversy, W. F. Hook (p. 18) stoutly defended the doctrine of baptismal regeneration, taking his stand on the prayer for regeneration in the baptismal service and the subsequent thanksgiving 'that it hath pleased thee to regenerate this infant with thy Holy Spirit'.

The prayer and thanksgiving to which I have called your special attention are used also in the Office for the Private Baptism of Children in Houses. With the exception of the Lord's Prayer, this is the only prayer especially enjoined. We are to use as many of the others 'as the time and present exigence will suffer'; but this thanksgiving prayer we must invariably use – no option, no latitude is permitted. For every child that is baptized we must give hearty thanks to our most merciful Father that it hath pleased Him to regenerate this child with His Holy Spirit. It seems that the Church was providentially guided to insist upon this, lest any doubt should exist as to the fact, that every infant, whether baptized in the church or in a house, in public or in private, is in his Baptism regenerated by the Holy Spirit.

This great doctrine, indeed, lies at the very foundation of Christianity; the amount of evil resulting from the fact, that some who profess and call themselves Christians are unbelievers in this eternal truth, is incalculable. How unequivocally it is asserted in our Baptismal Offices you have heard: and every clergyman, when, according to the technical term, he 'reads in', declares his 'unfeigned assent and consent to all and every thing contained and prescribed in and by the book entitled the Book of

Common Prayer, and Administration of the Sacraments and other Rites and Ceremonies of the Church, according to the Use of the Church of England, together with the Psalter, or Psalms of David, pointed as they are to be sung or said in Churches; and the Form or manner of making, ordaining, and consecrating Bishops, Priests, and Deacons.'

Therefore it would appear, that any one who denies the regeneration of all infants in holy Baptism, if he ministers in the Church of England, ventures publicly to declare his unfeigned assent and consent to that which in his heart he denies.

W. F. Hook, *The Church and its Ordinances*, Bentley, 1876, pages 325–6

J. F. Bethune-Baker, a leader of the Modern Churchmen's Union (now the Modern Churchpeople's Union) attacked one of the changes made in the baptismal service in the 1928 Prayer Book. He and his supporters were hoping to work towards more radical changes in this and other matters and objected to doctrinal points being, as it seemed to them, introduced through verbal changes in the liturgy. This matter of liturgy as reflecting doctrine has been the cause of controversy between many groups over more recent new services.

But more instructive still for our purpose is an instance to which special attention is due, for it exhibits definitely doctrinal reformulation – the new Order for the Baptism of Infants. There are changes which nearly everyone will welcome. But, but! The old Order contains a highly technical term which has been the subject of much controversy: 'seeing now . . . that this child is regenerate'. Various interpretations of this term have been given and allowed in the Church of England as expressing the effects of baptism. It has become, as it were, a blank cheque on which you can write values in your own coinage. It is replaced by the good plain English 'born again'. True, 'born again' stands in the Authorized Version of the Nicodemus episode in the Fourth Gospel. But it was corrected to 'anew', or 'from above', in the Revised Version, and even in our Order of 1662 it stands as 'born anew'. It was only Nicodemus who thought it must mean being born a second time, and we ourselves only use the phrase 'twice-born' of adults who have had some conscious experience, which is impossible in infants. To assert it as the result of the baptism of an infant, to say in plain English that this is what Baptism does, is to take back from us the freedom of interpretation of a technical term that had been won in the process of moralising our traditional doctrine of sacraments. And it is extraordinarily hard to devise an ethical *rationale* of the sacrament of Baptism in the case of infants. This is the only instance of outspoken reformulation that has caught my eye, and in it Modernism loses heavily by the change as I imagine its opponents must have realised with some amusement, if membership of such learned assemblies does not atrophy the sense of humour.

So I am led, by this evidence of the results of the laborious and prayerful work of good and learned men today, to the conclusion that the Church of England as a whole is not ready for reformulation of doctrine. Let us have no attempts at present at formal replacements by anything like official authority of the technical terms of traditional Christianity. It is not in that way that the refashioning we want can be done.

J. F. Bethune-Baker, *The Way of Modernism*, Cambridge University Press, 1927,
pages 144–5

The introduction to Holy Baptism in Common Worship *is more cautious. The word 'sign' is used with a declaration of 'new birth' and an implication rather than a direct reference about original sin. Like the rest of the new book it tries not to be partisan, satisfies many and disturbs some.*

Our Lord Jesus Christ has told us
that to enter the kingdom of heaven
we must be born again of water and the Spirit,
and has given us baptism as the sign and seal of this new birth.
Here we are washed by the Holy Spirit and made clean.
Here we are clothed with Christ,
dying to sin that we may live his risen life.
As children of God, we have a new dignity
and God calls us to fullness of life.

Amid all the arguments about baptism, the Church of England held firmly to the need for Confirmation and in the Canons of 1604 tried to ensure that it should be conferred regularly. This rule was not always obeyed.

Forasmuch as it hath been a solemn, ancient and laudable custom in the Church of God, continued from the Apostles' times, that all Bishops should lay their hands upon children baptized and instructed in the Catechism of Christian Religion, praying over them, and blessing them, which we commonly call *Confirmation*; and that this holy action hath been accustomed in the Church in former ages, to be performed in the Bishop's visitation every third year; we will and appoint, That every Bishop or his Suffragan, in his accustomed visitation, do in his own person carefully observe the said custom. And if in that year, by reason of some infirmity, he be not able personally to visit, then he shall not omit the execution of that duty of Confirmation the next year after, as he may conveniently.

Canon LX

Hooker had already defended Confirmation as a primitive practice which was not to be neglected.

Because it might be objected, that if the gift of the Holy Ghost do always join itself with true Baptism, the Church, which thinketh the Bishop's Confirmation after other men's Baptism needful for the obtaining of the Holy Ghost, should hold an error; St Jerome hereunto maketh answer, that the cause of this observation is not any absolute impossibility of receiving the Holy Ghost by the Sacrament of Baptism, unless a Bishop add after it the imposition of hands, but rather a certain congruity and fitness to honour prelacy with such pre-eminences, because the safety of the Church dependeth upon the dignity of her chief superiors, to whom if some eminent offices of power above others should not be given, there would be in the Church as many schisms as priests. By which answer it appeareth his opinion was, that the Holy Ghost is received in Baptism; that Confirmation is only a sacramental complement; that the reason why Bishops alone did ordinarily confirm, was not because the benefit, grace, and dignity thereof is greater than of Baptism; but rather, for that by the Sacrament of Baptism men being admitted into God's Church, it was both reasonable and convenient that if he baptize them not unto whom the chiefest authority and charge of their souls belongeth, yet for honour's sake, and in token of his spiritual superiority over them, because to bless is an act of authority, the performance of this annexed ceremony should be sought for at his hands. Now what effect their imposition of hands hath, either after Baptism administered by heretics or otherwise, St Jerome in that place hath made no mention, because all men understood that in converts it tendeth to the fruits of repentance, and craveth in behalf of the penitent such grace as David after his fall desired at the hands of God; in others, the fruit and benefit thereof is that which hath been before shewed. Finally, sometime the cause of severing Confirmation from Baptism was in the parties that received Baptism being infants, at which age they might be very well admitted to live in the family; but because to fight in the army of God, to discharge the duties of a Christian man, to bring forth the fruits, and to do the works of the Holy Ghost, their time of ability was not yet come, (so that Baptism was not deferred) there could, by stay of their Confirmation, no harm ensue, but rather good.

The Works of Richard Hooker, Clarendon Press, 1820, vol. 2, pages 321–2

Thomas Ken (1637–1711), Bishop of Bath and Wells, became one of the Nonjurors who refused to take the oath of allegiance to William III. He was himself a saintly man, a writer of devotional works, poems and hymns. He firmly exhorted those who were bringing up children to see that their charges learned their Catechism and came to be confirmed, explaining the purpose and benefits of that rite.

As for you who have families, I beseech you to instil into your children and servants their duty, both by your teaching, and your example. In good earnest it is less cruel and unnatural to deny them bread for their mortal bodies, than saving knowledge for their immortal souls.

Ye that are fathers or mothers, I exhort you to tread in the steps of Abraham, the father of the faithful, and the friend of God, and like him, to command your children and households to keep the way of the Lord.

Ye that are mothers or mistresses, I exhort you to imitate that un-feigned faith which dwelt in young Timothy's grandmother Lois, and his mother Eunice, who taught him from a child to know the Holy Scriptures, which were able to make him wise to salvation; and like them, to bring up your children and servants in the nurture and admonition of the Lord.

I passionately exhort and beseech you all of either sex, never to cease your conscientious zeal for their instruction, till ye bring them to confirmation; to renew their baptismal vow; to make open profession of their Christianity; to discharge their godfathers and godmothers, to receive the solemn benediction of the bishop; to share in the public intercessions of the Church, and to partake of all the graces of God's Holy Spirit, implored on their behalf; that God, who has begun a good work in them, may perfect it till the day of Christ; and that I myself at that dreadful day, may render an account of you with joy.

The Prose Works of Thomas Ken, Rivington, 1838, page 114

Thomas Wilson (p. 46) addressed the clergy of his diocese with equal seriousness on the matter of Confirmation. His insistence on the importance of previous instruction through the Catechism, with other members of the parish there to hear what is being taught, may have some resonance for our present discussions about admission to communion and knowledge of the Christian faith.

There is no question to be made of it but that most of that ignorance, impiety, profaneness, want of charity, of union and order, which we complain of, is owing to the neglect or abuse of this one ordinance; which being appointed by the Apostles, and practised even when baptism was administered to people of full age, it is no wonder that God punishes the contempt of it, by withholding His Holy Spirit and those graces which are necessary and would certainly accompany the religious use of it.

If this were well considered, and pastors would resolve to discharge their duty in this particular faithfully, we should soon see another face of religion: Christians would be obliged to study their religion, and to think it something more than a work of the lips and of the memory, or the mere custom of the place where they live. And being made sensible of their danger (being liable to *sin,* to *death* and to *damnation*) this would make them *serious* and *thoughtful* and *inquisitive* after the manner of their redemption and the means of salvation; and their consciences being awakened and informed, sin would become more uneasy to them and virtue more acceptable. In short, by this means people would know their duty, the Sacraments would be kept from being profaned, and pastors would be respected – and obeyed, as being very truly the fathers of their flock.

And certainly no greater injury can be done to religion than to suffer young people to come to confirmation before they know the reason of this service, and have been well instructed in the principles and duties of Christianity. This being the very time of seasoning their minds with sound knowledge, of fortifying their wills with sober resolutions, and of engaging them to piety, before sin has got the possession of their affections; this being also the time of qualifying them to receive benefit by all our future labours, and of arming them against apostasy, heresy, schism, and all other vices to which we are subject in this state of trial.

In short, I do not know how, a clergyman could possibly spend one month better than by leading young people, as it were, by the hand, into the design of Christianity, by some such easy method as this following: which, if deliberately proposed to every single person in the bearing of all the rest (who should be obliged to be every day present) and familiarly explained, not the most ignorant (supposing he had learned, as he ought, the Church Catechism) but would be *able to give a reason of the hope that is in him*; and his faith being thus built upon a solid and sure foundation, would, by the grace of God now imparted to him in a greater measure, withstand all future trials and temptations.

The Works of Thomas Wilson, Parker, 1851, vol. 7, pages 8–9

William Nicholson (1591–1672), Bishop of Gloucester, in his Exposition of the Catechism *(1655) gave great importance to the rite of Confirmation for which the Catechism was to prepare candidates.*

The reasons are weighty. For, the child being grown up, before God, the Bishop, and the congregation, with his own mouth takes upon him that same obligation, which at his Baptism his sureties had undertaken for him: so that he frees them, and binds himself, renewing the old bond to perform the conditions, in believing, doing, and forsaking what is to be believed, done, or forsaken. Which double vow, made first by others solemnly for him, then again as solemnly renewed by him, sadly thought on, in all reason will have a powerful impression on the heart, for the present, and an effectual influence on whole life for the future. Which work, because it is difficult, and beyond the power of man, therefore the Bishop was to impose his hands upon him, to bless him, to pray for him, that God would strengthen him, and daily increase in him His manifold gifts of grace; that He would bestow upon him the spirit of wisdom and understanding, the spirit of counsel and ghostly strength, the spirit of knowledge and true godliness, and fill him with the spirit of His holy fear; with much more to the same purpose, as it is to be seen in those pious prayers appointed to be used at Confirmation. Which the Church held fit then to be administered when temptations, in respect of the child's proclivity to vice, might most strongly assault him. And that which moved our Church of England to retain this, was because the first reformers in it found that this rite was agreeable to the usage of the Church in times past. Which is very true. There be, that make it an Apostolical institution, having an eye to the sixth chapter of the Epistle to the Hebrews, verse 2. And Calvin, Beza, and Aretius seem (upon the place) to like well of it. Sure I am that the ancient Fathers and Councils are full and evident witnesses for it.

William Nicholson, *An Exposition of the Catechism* (1665), Parker, 1842, pages 5–6

Robert Nelson (p. 69) gives several reasons for the importance of Confirmation. The Nonjurors had a particular regard for this rite, anticipating the later demands of the Tractarians.

Since Confirmation is an Authentic Renewal of the Baptismal Vow, and capacitates those that receive it to be admitted Guests to the Table of the Lord, and is an act not to be repeated, the Candidates ought to be thoroughly instructed in the Nature of those Holy Promises they then renew, and of that Obligation they lie under to perform them. They ought to be acquainted with the meaning of this Holy Rite and whose

Office alone it is to administer it. They ought to have a competent degree of Knowledge in those Christian Duties that relate to God, their Neighbour and Themselves. And they must farther prepare themselves for this Ordinance by Prayer and Fasting, and a serious Resolution of living answerable to their Obligations. And in order to there Ends it is advisable that the Candidate should frequently read over the Confirmation Office. [...] It tends to preserve the Unity of the Church, by making Men sensible that their Obedience is due to such Ecclesiastical Governors, who are endued with all those Powers that were left by the Apostles to their Successors. It is a new Engagement to a Christian Life, and is a lasting Admonition and Check not to dishonour or desert our Christian Profession. It is a Testimony of God's Favour and Goodness to those that receive it, when his lawful Minister declares that God accepts their Proficiency, and advances them to a higher degree in the Church, by placing them among the Faithful; and thereby giving them a Title to approach the Holy Table of the Lord. It conveys Divine Grace to encounter our spiritual Enemies, and to enable us to perform what we undertake.

Robert Nelson, *Companion for the Festivals and Fasts of the Church of England*, 1704, pages 542–3.

At the end of the nineteenth century, when the service of Confirmation had become regular and frequent, its proper observance in the Church of England is commended by A. J. Mason, Fellow of Trinity College, Cambridge.

We have been preserved from any expression which would have robbed Confirmation of its glory by attributing to the initial part of Baptism that which Holy Scripture and the Fathers attribute to the second. No word in the baptismal offices can be taken to imply that the Holy Ghost is 'given' in that part of the sacrament. One phrase, which appears to approach to such a statement, is found on examination to guard most carefully against the error of the later Roman theology, and by its explicit terms is a witness for the older doctrine. 'Give Thy Holy Spirit to this infant', so the Church prays immediately before the christening of the child, but adds at once, 'that he may be born again, and be made an heir of everlasting salvation'. The nature and extent of the gift to be expected at the font is defined and restricted. It is such a gift or impartition as regenerates, not that which takes up its abode in the regenerate. By other expressions in the baptismal offices we are taught to expect that the baptized will be 'born anew of Water and of the Holy Ghost', 'baptized with Water and the Holy Ghost', 'washed and sanctified with the Holy' Ghost', 'receive the fullness of God's grace'; but never that he will receive that special 'promise' of the Holy Ghost for which S. Peter on the day of Pentecost said that repentance and Baptism would qualify his hearers, or that 'abundant outpouring' of which S. Paul spoke to Titus. These promises and outpourings are reserved for the moment when those whom God has already 'vouchsafed to regenerate by Water and the Holy Ghost'; come to the bishop to be, through his prayer and the laying on of his hands, 'strengthened' with the sevenfold Spirit.

A. J. Mason, *The Relation of Confirmation to Baptism*, Longmans Green, 1891,
pages 427–9

Those who were confirmed after proper instruction understood the solemnity of the occasion. Quiet Anglican devotion is well shown in two accounts, the first a diary record of the service in Worcester Cathedral in 1854 and the second from a novel published in the same year. Frances Havergal (1836–79) was a poet and hymnwriter. Charlotte M. Yonge (1823–1901) was a novelist, a pupil of Keble (p. 108) and a devotee of Tractarianism. Each of them emphasises the importance of the response 'I do' to the Bishop's question whether the candidates are prepared to renew the vows made for them at their baptism.

My heart beat very fast, and my breath almost seemed to stop, while the solemn question was being put by the Bishop. Never I think did I feel my own weakness and utter helplessness so much. I hardly dared answer; but 'the Lord is my strength' was graciously suggested to me, and then the words came quickly from (I trust) my very heart; 'Lord, I cannot without Thee, but oh, with Thy almighty help – I Do'.

I believe that the solemnity of what had just been uttered, with its exceeding comprehensiveness, were realised by me as far as my mind could grasp it. I thought a good deal of the words 'now unto Him that is able to keep you from Falling'; and that was my chief comfort. We were the first to go up, and I was the 4th or 5th on whom the bishop laid his hands. At first, the thought came as to who was kneeling next to me, but then the next moment I felt alone, unconscious of my fellow candidates, of the many eyes fixed upon us, and the many thoughts of and prayers for me, alone with God and His chief minister. My feelings when his hands were placed on my head (and there was solemnity and earnestness in the very touch and manner) I cannot describe, they were too confused; but when the words 'Defend, O Lord, this Thy child with Thy heavenly grace, that she may continue Thine for ever, and daily increase in Thy Holy Spirit more and more, until she come unto Thy everlasting Kingdom', were solemnly pronounced, if ever my heart followed a prayer it did then, if ever it thrilled with earnest longing not unmixed with joy, it did at the words 'Thine forever'. We returned to our seats, and for some time I wept, why I hardly know, it was not grief, nor anxiety, nor exactly joy. About an hour and a quarter elapsed before all the candidates had been up to the rails. Each time that the 'Amen' was chanted in a more distant part of the Cathedral, after the 'Defend' had been pronounced, it seemed as though a choir of angels had come down to witness, and pour out from their pure spirits a deep and felt 'Amen'.

M. V. G. Havergal, *Memorials of Frances Ridley Havergal*, Nisbet, 1880, 17 July 1854

And now the time is come. The demand is made, to be answered once and for ever, whether they renew the vows of their Baptism, and take on themselves the promise they never can unsay, engaging in their own persons to fulfil the *perfect* law.

'I do'.

Multitudes of clear young trembling voices make answer in one note. 'I do'. Wavering, unstable Emmeline, unreflecting, easily-led Katherine, how can you dare to bind yourselves to such an awful covenant with Him who is Justice itself

Hear the answer.

'Our help is in the name of the Lord:

Who hath made heaven and earth'.

And now their brother in his white robe stands at the entrance of the Chancel, and signs to them, and his face seems, in one look of love and earnest hope, to sum up all that he has striven so long to infuse into them.

They kneel on that Altar step where they never have before approached, and the Apostolic hand is on their heads; the blessing is spoken, that unspeakable Gift imparted, that, unless they fall away, will increase daily more and more, till they come to the everlasting kingdom.

Charlotte M. Yonge, *The Castle Builders*, Mozley, 1854, chapter 21

Edward King (p. 67) addresses the candidates he is about to confirm. He also emphasises the solemnity of the response 'I do'.

You have come with a special meaning to-night. You have come in a way in which you never came before, and never will come again, for it is only once in your life that you come to be confirmed; so that it is a special act on your part – you wish to do better. And that, in one way, is what is contained in those words, that you have 'come to years of discretion'. It says in the Prayer Book, you know, that you must not come to be confirmed until you have come to years of discretion. What does that mean? Well, it means, on the one hand, that you have learnt to know that sin is a much worse thing than once you thought it was. Of course, a little child, when its mother tells it not to do anything and it does it, knows that it has done wrong. Ay, but when we have come to years of discretion we mean that we have found out that sin is a hard thing to get rid of – a worse thing than we used to think it – something which we now see we must either conquer and drive away, or it will conquer us and lead us captive, miserable slaves, for the rest of our life here, and slaves through eternity! Take the case of lying, for example. A little child is sometimes afraid to speak the truth, and says it did not, when it did, and so on. When we come to years of discretion we see that a lie has something more in it, and that, generally speaking, when you tell one lie it will lead you to tell two or three others to try and get out of it. Yes, sin is a worse thing than we used to think it. Or you may have found it out in some other way – you have found out in some way or other that sin is a hard thing, a troublesome thing, a miserable thing, a thing which has given you more trouble and more misery than anything else in your life; and you have come to years of discretion, and you intend, in a minute, to say

'I do', and that means – 'I do renounce and put away what I have found out to be sinful and bad', on the one hand, and on the other it means 'I do believe all the articles of the Christian Faith'.

Edward King, *Sermons and Addresses*, Longman, 1911, pages 179–80

More recent liturgical opinion, while not seeking to do away with confirmation, has tended towards the sufficiency of baptism, at least in some cases, for full communicant membership of the Church. B 28 in the Canons, authorised in 1969, deals with reception into the Church of England from other communions.

1. Any person desiring to be received into the Church of England, who has not been baptized or the validity of whose baptism can be held in question, shall be instructed and baptized or conditionally baptized, and such baptism, or conditional baptism, shall constitute the said person's reception into the Church of England.

2. If any such person has been baptized but not episcopally confirmed and desires to be formally admitted into the Church of England he shall, after appropriate instruction, be received by the rite of confirmation, or, if he be not yet ready to be presented for confirmation, he shall be received by the parish priest with appropriate prayers.

3. If any such person has been episcopally confirmed with unction or with the laying of hands he shall be instructed, and with the permission of the bishop, received into the Church of England according to the Form and Reception approved by Convocation, or with other appropriate prayers, and if any such person be a priest he shall be received into the said Church only by the bishop of the diocese or by the commissary of such bishop.

7

Public worship

When we assemble and meet together

Michael Ramsey said that the Church of England 'does theology to the sound of church bells'. It is true that the parish church is still a prominent feature of most localities, whether it be a medieval edifice much restored, or an exercise in the latest architectural fashion. The sound of church bells may bring delight or annoyance according to proximity and temperament, but they continue to announce our services, both regular Sunday worship and the weddings and other occasional offices. The divines and scholars of the Church have seldom been purely speculative in their writings, but have envisaged doctrine being focused and experienced in public worship. For many centuries the Book of Common Prayer ensured a basic uniformity, in the diocesan cathedral as much as in the small chapel of ease.

The publication and enforcement of the first book in 1549 brought a new sense of congregational participation. The liturgy was now in the common tongue of the people. Matins and Evensong took the place of the Mass as the principal public services. Drawn largely from the Breviary and the monastic hours, they gave a new shape to the services and more opportunity for a congregation to join in and respond. From being the daily offices of the religious orders, they became the shared worship of all, laity and clergy alike. The service of Holy Communion, less often fully celebrated than in the past, also became more participatory. The intentions of the Reformers were made clear by rubrics and by exhortations in the words of the service. For example the people 'as many as are here present' were to join in the General Confession at Matins and Evensong, and for the Confession at Holy Communion to be 'meekly kneeling upon your knees'.

Acts of Uniformity between 1549 and 1662 ensured that there should be no significant deviations from what was set down. Uniformity across the country was in fact even greater than it had been. The preface to the new service book explained how 'hitherto there has been great diversity in saying and singing in Churches within this Realm . . . now from henceforth all the whole Realm shall but one Use'. The danger of losing spontaneity and true devotion in this canonical obedience was felt by some from the start and has always been something to be kept in mind and avoided. Discontent with a set form was one of the several reasons for the objections of the early Puritans and the subsequent emergence of free nonconformist churches. After the Parliamentary victory in the First Civil War, a Directory for the Public Worship of God was authorised for use in churches. As its name implies, it was a set of guidelines and directions rather than a book of services, a reaction against the doctrine of the Book of Common Prayer but even more against its regular order which was thought to result in 'vain repetitions'.

Despite such actual and potential problems, the Book of Common Prayer was the great strength of the evolving Church of England. It is a new comprehensive worship book for the regular services and for the occasional offices from Infant Baptism and the Churching of Women after childbirth to the Burial of the Dead. It is a source of doctrine, in the words of the services themselves and in the appended Articles. It is in fact the nearest thing to a foundation document for the Church of England. It is significant that the essence of that Church is to be found not in a single formal declaration or agreement but in its book of public worship. It is also its own instruction manual, leaving few doubts about the conduct of services to be resolved by either clergy or laity.

Those who attended these services daily would have heard the whole of the New Testament read through twice in the year and most of the Old Testament once. The early lectionary provided for long portions, working steadily through each book with only a few variations for special days. In addition, the services themselves were strongly based in Scripture, both by direct quotation and clear reference. There has probably never been a more Bible-based liturgy. With the publication of the Authorised or King James Version of the Bible in 1611 the Church of England had the resources which would determine the language register of worship in England for centuries to come.

Worship following the Book of Common Prayer gives a strong sense of sin, with the assurance of pardon following repentance. Some of its modern critics have accused it of too much emphasis on human sinfulness. Each individual reader can decide whether the present state of things suggests that sin is less apparent and less serious than it was in the sixteenth century. It combines proper awe and reverence with confidence in the near presence of God. As well as the main Sunday services, the occasional offices have become familiar to generations, undergirding and strengthening ordinary lives. These and other services have given idioms to the common language.

Musical settings of the Communion service were made in the sixteenth century and there have been many since. In parish churches singing was mainly confined to the metrical Psalter, versions of the Psalms appended to the book, first those by Sternhold and Hopkins and then from 1696 by Tate and Brady. Hymns were at first regarded with some suspicion as being more suited to unstructured nonconformist services, and their legality was even challenged in the courts, but a succession of Anglican hymnologists in the eighteenth century – Cowper, Newton, Toplady and others – eventually made them an essential part of principal Sunday services. *Hymns Ancient and Modern* (1861) and the *English Hymnal* (1906), with their revisions and successors, are as basic to the resources of a church as the service books themselves. If Anglicans do their theology to the sound of church bells they may be said to learn much of their theology from their hymnals. Choirs came to be no longer confined to cathedrals and college chapels; most parishes could produce a rehearsed choir at least for the principal Sunday service. The church orchestra in the gallery was gradually replaced by the organ, a transition recorded by Thomas Hardy in *Under the Greenwood Tree* (1872).

Attendance at public worship on Sunday was at first compulsory, with fines for 'recusancy' aimed mainly against Roman Catholics. In time it came to be socially rather than legally enforced. Attendance was compulsory in the Oxford and Cambridge colleges, the Public Schools and the Armed Forces. The danger of resentment and carelessness was not always recognised, or was considered less important than conformity. We may regret the growth of casual and irreverent behaviour in churches but conduct in the past was not always good, as witnessed by the extract below from *Verdant Green*. The established privilege of the Church of England also brought the niceties of social hierarchy into parish worship. The private pews and pew rents were accepted until the Tractarians and their successors began a campaign against them. The pew of the squire or local magnate might be like a small room of its own, shut off from the rest of the nave and sometimes even with its own fireplace. The congregation would give precedence to the family coming from these pews, and wait, standing, until they had left the church. The squire would keep an eye on attendance and censure misbehaviour in church. Sir Roger de Coverley would enquire after the health of anyone he did not see, 'which is understood as a secret reprimand to the person that is absent'. In fairness, it may be said that hierarchy and censure might sometimes be found in nonconformist churches as well.

The early Anglican apologists were eager to defend the authorised services. Roman Catholic critics found them doctrinally false and sacramentally inadequate. The growing voice of Protestant Dissent denounced them as sterile, formal and lacking in spontaneity. However, some of them, particularly the Methodists, made use of the Book of Common Prayer. Aware of these attacks, Anglican writers emphasised the need for personal devotion in services. It was recognised that the familiarity of the words, and perhaps even their literary beauty, could make their recital an end in itself without personal application.

Except for a few minor changes, the 1662 Book of Common Prayer provided the only authorised Church of England services until the twentieth century. The proposal for a revised version, keeping everything in 1662 but with substantial additions, was twice defeated in Parliament. Although it was never officially authorised the '1928 Book' was widely used and tacitly accepted. The Church of England was influenced by the liturgical movement which was touching many of the churches, and by the social changes following two world wars. Some experimental services were tried after the middle of the century, particularly directed towards the idea of the Parish Communion. The Worship and Doctrine Measure in 1975 gave the Church authority to create new services through a Liturgical Commission and the approval of the General Synod. The *Alternative Service Book* came out in 1980 and was superseded by *Common Worship* in 2000. The Preface to this most recent publication makes it clear that 'The Book of Common Prayer remains the permanently authorized provision in the Church of England, whereas the new liturgies are authorized until further resolution of the General Synod.'

The Preface to the First Prayer Book of 1549, printed since 1662 as 'Concerning the Service of the Church', declared what the reformed Church

*of England intended in the content of services and the concomitant liturgical
discipline, a question which would cause much dispute in the years ahead.
After recalling the inconveniences of the previous multiple service books, it
explains and commends the new order.*

Yet, because there is no remedy, but that of necessity there must be some
Rules; therefore certain Rules are here set forth; which, as they are few in
number, so they are plain and easy to be understood. So that here you
have an Order for Prayer, and for the reading of the holy Scripture,
much agreeable to the mind and purpose of the old Fathers, and a great
deal more profitable and commodious, than that which of late was used.
It is more profitable, because here are left out many things, whereof
some are untrue, some uncertain, some vain and superstitious; and
nothing is ordained to be read, but the very pure Word of God, the holy
Scriptures, or that which is agreeable to the same; and that in such a
Language and Order as is most easy and plain for the understanding
both of the Readers and Hearers. It is also more commodious, both for
the shortness thereof, and for the plainness of the Order, and for that the
Rules be few and easy.

And whereas heretofore there hath been great diversity in saying and
singing in Churches within this Realm; some following *Salisbury* Use,
some *Hereford* Use, and some the Use of *Bangor*, some of *York*, some of
Lincoln; now from henceforth all the whole Realm shall have but one Use.

And forasmuch as nothing can be so plainly set forth, but doubts may
arise in the use and practice of the same; to appease all such diversity (if
any arise) and for the resolution of all doubts, concerning the manner
how to understand, do, and execute, the things contained in this Book;
the parties that so doubt, or diversely take any thing, shall alway resort to
the Bishop of the Diocese, who by his discretion shall take order for the
quieting and appeasing of the same; so that the same order be not contrary to any thing contained in this Book. And if the Bishop of the
Diocese be in doubt, then he may send for the resolution thereof to the
Archbishop.

*Richard Hooker (p. 10) stoutly defended the use of set order in public wor-
ship, claiming it as the proper usage of the Church from the beginning and
censuring unstructured services and the use of unauthorised buildings.*

Of all helps for due performance of this service, the greatest is that very set and standing order itself, which, framed with common advice, hath both for matter and form prescribed whatsoever is herein publicly done. No doubt, from God it hath proceeded, and by us it must be acknowledged a work of singular care and providence, that the Church hath evermore held a prescript form of Common Prayer, although not in all things every where the same, yet for the most part retaining still the same analogy. So that if the Liturgies of all ancient Churches throughout the world be compared amongst themselves, it may be easily perceived they had all one original mould, and that the public Prayer of the people of God in Churches thoroughly settled, did never use to be voluntary dictates, proceeding from any men's extemporal wit. To him which considereth the grievous and scandalous inconveniences whereunto they make themselves daily subject, with whom any blind and secret corner is judged a fit house of common Prayer; the manifold confusions which they fall into, where every man's private spirit and gift (as they term it) is the only bishop that ordaineth him to his ministry; the irksome deformities whereby, through endless and senseless effusions of indigested prayers, they oftentimes disgrace in most insufferable manner the worthiest part of Christian duty towards God, who herein are subject to no certain order, but pray both what and how they list; to him, I say, which weigheth duly all these things, the reasons cannot be obscure why God doth in public Prayer so much respect the solemnity of places where the authority and calling of persons by whom, and the precise appointment even with what words or sentences, his name should be called on amongst his people.

The Works of Richard Hooker, Clarendon Press, 1820, vol. 2, pages 106–7 (Book 5, 25)

Lewis Bayly (?–1631), although a royal chaplain and Bishop of Bangor, was censured for his Puritan tendency. His book The Practice of Piety was popular with nonconformists, particularly John Bunyan. Somewhat outside the mainstream, he nevertheless represents a powerful influence in the seventeenth-century Church of England.

When prayers begin, lay aside thy own private meditations, and let thy heart join with the minister and the whole church, as being one body of

Christ (1 Cor. xii. 12) and because that God is the God of order, he will have all things to be done in the church with one heart and accord (Acts ii. 46) and the exercises of the church are common and public (chap. iv. 32). It is therefore an ignorant pride, for a man to think his own private prayers more effectual than the public prayers of the whole church. Solomon therefore advises a man not to be rash to utter a thing in the church before God. Pray, therefore, when the church prayeth, sing when they sing; and in the action of kneeling, standing, sitting, and such indifferent ceremonies (for the avoiding of scandal, the continuance of charity, and in testimony of thine obedience), conform thyself to the manner of the church wherein thou livest (Ezek. xlvi 10 Psal. cx. 3).

Whilst the preacher is expounding and applying the word of the Lord, look upon him; for it is a great help to stir up thine attention, and to keep thee from wandering thoughts: so the eyes of all that were in the synagogue are said to have been fastened on Christ whilst he preached, and that all the people hanged upon him when they heard him. Remember that thou art there as one of Christ's disciples, to learn the knowledge of salvation, by the remission of sins, through the tender mercy of God (Luke i. 77) [. . .]

When baptism is to be administered, stay and behold it with all reverent attention, that so thou mayest – First, shew thy reverence to God's ordinance. Secondly, that thou mayest the better consider thine own ingrafting into the body of Christ's church, and how thou performest the vows of thy new covenant; Thirdly, That thou mayest repay thy debts, in praying for the infant which is to be baptised (as other Christians did in the like case for thee), that God would give him the inward effects of baptism, by his blood and Spirit; Fourthly, That thou mayest assist the church in praising God for grafting another member into his mystical body; Fifthly, That thou mayest prove whether the effects of Christ's death killeth sin in thee, and whether thou be raised to newness of life by the virtue of his resurrection; and so to be humbled for thy wants, and to be thankful for his graces; Sixthly, To shew thyself to be a freeman of Christ's corporation, having a voice or consent in the admission of others into that holy society.

Lewis Bayly, *The Practice of Piety* (1611), London, 1820, pages 197–200

William Sherlock (1641–1707) was Dean of St Paul's, a firm supporter of monarchy and Divine Right. Here he warns even more strongly than Bayly against irreverence in church. The defiant habits of the Puritans in refusing formal postures of worship had slipped into the slackness and indifference of some Anglicans after the Restoration. Sherlock's regard of the early Church as a model for his own is typical of Anglican thought.

Another great miscarriage which many professed Christians are guilty of, is an irreverent performance of public worship; if that may be called religious worship, which is not attended with all the solemn expressions of reverence and devotion.

There are so many instances of this, that the very naming of them will be thought sharp and satirical. There are but few Christians who put on that true gravity and seriousness of looks and behaviour as becomes the presence of God and the solemnity of religious worship. You shall see some gazing about them with a roving and wandering eye, as if they came only, to see and to be seen, to observe every new face or new dress and garb, and therefore too often set themselves out with that fantastic gaiety which more becomes a play-house than a church. You shall see others talk, or whisper, or laugh, to the great offence and scandal of all serious and devout minds. Others, instead of worshipping God, sleep away the prayers or sermon, or both, as if they were not concerned in either. It is possible, indeed, for very devout men sometimes to be surprised with sleep; but it is a great indecency whenever it is so, and requires great care to prevent it in ourselves and others and is a great contempt of God and of his worship when it grows into a custom, and men as naturally dispose themselves to a sleeping posture, as if it were the design of their coming to church. You shall see others *sit* all the time of divine service; which would be thought a very great rudeness when we put up a petition to an earthly prince. This was unknown in the ancient Church, wherein for some ages they did not so much as sit either while the Scriptures were read or expounded: and Eusebius relates a famous story of Constantine the first Christian emperor, that when he made a speech to him in his own palace concerning the sepulchre of our Saviour, he heard it standing, though it were very long, and would not be persuaded to sit down, saying, that it was not fit to consult our ease while we hear any discourses concerning God; and that it was more agreeable to piety to hear religious discourses standing. And what would that religious emperor have thought to have seen Christians in public assemblies pray sitting? And, indeed, I have often thought, what should be the reason of that universal practice of sitting when we sing psalms; for psalms of praise and thanksgiving are as much the worship of God as prayer, and therefore equally require a posture of devotion.

William Sherlock, *A Practical Discourse of Religious Assemblies* (1681), Burns, 1840,
pages 177–8

Long afterwards, and coming from a different level of churchmanship, Evelyn Underhill (1875–1941) similarly stressed the essential symbiosis of personal piety and public worship. She was one of the most important Anglican devotional writers of her time, introducing many to the mystics and spiritual masters of the past.

Christian worship is never a solitary undertaking. Both on its visible and invisible sides, it has a thoroughly social and organic character. The worshipper, however lonely in appearance, comes before God as a member of a great family; part of the Communion of Saints, living and dead. His own small effort of adoration is offered 'in and for all'. The first words of the Lord's Prayer are always there to remind him of his corporate status and responsibility in its double aspect. On one hand, he shares the great life and action of the Church, the Divine Society; however he may define that difficult term, or wherever he conceives its frontiers to be drawn. He is immersed in that life, nourished by its traditions, taught, humbled and upheld by its saints. His personal life of worship, unable for long to maintain itself alone, has behind it two thousand years of spiritual culture, and around it the self-offering of all devoted souls. Further, his public worship and commonly his secret devotion too, are steeped in history and tradition; and apart from them cannot be understood. There are few things more remarkable in Christian history than the continuity through many vicissitudes and under many disguises of the dominant strands in Christian worship. On the other hand the whole value of this personal life of worship abides in the completeness with which it is purified from all taint of egotism, and the selflessness and simplicity with which it is added to the common store. Here the individual must lose his life to find it; the longing for personal expression, personal safety, joy, must more and more be swallowed up in Charity. For the goal alike of Christian sanctification and Christian worship is the ceaseless self-offering of the Church in and with Christ her Head, to the increase of the glory of God.

Evelyn Underhill, *An Anthology of the Love of God*, Mowbray, 1953
(*The School of Charity*), page 84

William Law (1686–1761) took an entirely different view from Bayly and Underhill. Law was a Fellow of Emmanuel College Cambridge who was deprived on refusing the Oath of Allegiance to George I and became a Nonjuror. He was for a time tutor to the father of the historian Edward Gibbon. His strong insistence on the need for regular and frequent private prayer (p. 179) made him suspicious of the contemporary conformist attitude to church attendance. However, the evidence of the Acts of the Apostles and many of the Epistles makes it clear that there was regular corporate if not 'public' worship in the New Testament churches.

It is very observable, that there is not one command in all the Gospel for *Public Worship*; and perhaps it is a duty that is least insisted upon in Scripture of any other. The frequent attendance at it is never so much as mentioned in all the New Testament. Whereas that *Religion or Devotion* which is to govern *the ordinary actions* of our life, is to be found in almost every verse of Scripture. Our blessed Saviour and his Apostles are wholly taken up in Doctrines that relate to *common life*. They call us to renounce the world, and differ in every *temper* and *way* of life, from the spirit and way of the world: to renounce all its goods, to fear none of its evils, to reject its joys, and have no value for its happiness: to be as new *born babes*, that are born into a new state of things; to live as *Pilgrims* in spiritual watching, in holy fear, and heavenly aspiring after another life: to take up our daily cross, to deny ourselves, to profess the blessedness of mourning, to seek the blessedness of poverty of spirit: to forsake the pride and vanity of Riches, to take no thought for the morrow, to live in the profoundest State of Humility, to rejoice in worldly sufferings: to reject the lust of the flesh, the lust of the eyes, and the pride of life; to bear injuries, to forgive and bless our enemies, and to love mankind as God loveth them: to give up our whole hearts and affections to God, and strive to enter through the strait gate into a life of eternal Glory.

This is the *common Devotion* which our Blessed Saviour taught, in order to make it the *common life* of all Christians. Is it not therefore exceeding strange, that People should place so much piety in the attendance upon public worship, concerning which there is not one precept of our Lord's to be found, and yet neglect these common duties of our *ordinary* life, which are commanded in every Page of the Gospel? I call these duties the devotion of our *common life,* because if they are to be practised, they must be made parts of our common life, they can have no place anywhere else.

William Law, *A Serious Call to a Devout and Holy Life* (1728), Epworth Press, 1961, page 7

George Borrow (1803–81), traveller, philologist and student of Romany life, worked as an agent of the British and Foreign Bible Society, In his partly fictionalised autobiography Lavengro *he remembers his early experience of worship at the church in East Dereham, Norfolk. It is probably a fair picture of parish services in the early nineteenth century.*

Twice every Sunday, I was regularly taken to the church, where, from a corner of the large spacious pew, lined with black leather, I would fix my eyes on the dignified high-church rector, and the dignified high-church clerk, and watch the movement of their lips, from which, as they read their respective portions of the venerable liturgy, would roll many a portentous word descriptive of the wondrous works of the Most High [. . .] Peace to your memories, dignified rector, and yet more dignified clerk. By this time ye are probably gone to your long homes, and your voices are no longer heard sounding down the aisles of the venerable church.

George Borrow, *Lavengro* (1851), John Murray, 1904, pages 20–1

A humorous novel about early Victorian life at Oxford shows the possibly negative effects of compulsory attendance. Verdant Green is a very innocent Freshman, on his first morning in the college chapel. William Sherlock, above, would certainly have disapproved

The lesson had just begun; and the man on Verdant's right appeared to be attentively following it. Our freshman, however, could not help seeing the book, and, much to his astonishment, he found it to be a Livy, out of which his neighbour was getting up his morning's lecture. He was still more astonished, when the lesson had come to an end, by being suddenly pulled back when he attempted to rise, and finding the streamers of his gown had been put to a use never intended for them, by being tied round the finial of the stall behind him – the silly work of a boyish gentleman, who, in his desire to play off a practical joke on a freshman, forgot the sacredness of the place where college rules compelled him to show himself on morning parade.

'Cuthbert Bede' (Edward Bradley), *The Adventures of Mr Verdant Green,
an Oxford Freshman* (1857), Nelson, no date, page 92

Herbert Thorndike (1598–1672) suffered ejection under the Commonwealth but after the Restoration was reinstated as a Fellow of Trinity College, Cambridge and later became a Prebendary of Westminster. His high view of the Eucharist endeared him to the Tractarians in the nineteenth century. Here he defends the use of ceremonial in worship, recognising the needs of worshippers as physical as well as spiritual beings.

God hath made Christians, though governed by the Spirit of His grace, as gross in their bodily senses and faculties of their minds, as other men of like education are: and it is a debt which the guides of the Church owe to the wise and unwise of God's people, to conduct them in the way of godliness by means proportionable to their faculties. The outward form of public service availeth much, even with them whose minds are best in tune, to corroborate their reverence and devotion at the service of God, by the exercise of it: but speaking of them whose minds are less withdrawn from their senses, how great impression shall the example of the world, practising the service of God in an orderly and reverent form, make in the minds of men that cannot receive it from their reason, but from their senses? This effect in things of slight consequence in particular, which nevertheless altogether amount to a considerable sum, is better seen by the gross in practice, than convinced by retail in dispute. Yet since the importunities of men have caused false reasons to prevail with weak people, it is requisite the true reasons be pleaded, lest it be thought there are none such, because not so fit to be pleaded.

The circumstances and ceremonies of public service are indeed a kind of discipline and pedagogy, whereby men subject to sense are guided in the exercise of godliness: it is, as it were, the apparel of religion at the heart; which some think, like the sun, most beautiful when it is most naked; and so it were indeed, did men consist of minds alone without bodies, but as long as our bodily senses are manageable to our soul's advantage, the heat within will starve without this apparel without.

Theological Works of Herbert Thorndike, Parker, 1844, vol. 1, pages 301–2

At the height of the ritualist controversy, the Judicial Committee of the Privy Council ruled that a number of ceremonial practices were illegal in the Church of England. The verdict was given against John Purchas (1823–72), vicar of St James's Church, Brighton, and reversed a previous judgement in his favour by an ecclesiastical court. The decision, which came to be known as the 'Purchas Judgement', was invoked in similar cases. Purchas robustly defends ritual practice as not only not being acceptable to the rules of the Book of Common Prayer but as restoring what had been neglected.

Every part of the Church must have a ritual, and as there is but one Catholic Church, so the ritual of every portion thereof will have a family likeness, and be one in spirit though diverse in details. Ritual and Ceremonial are the hieroglyphics of the Catholic religion, a language understood of the faithful, a kind of parable in action, for as of old when He walked the earth, our blessed Lord, still present in His divine and human nature in the Holy Eucharist on the altars of His Church, still spiritually present at the Common Prayers, does not speak unto us 'without a parable'. But as our Lord's 'visage was marred more than any man, and His form more than the sons of men', so has it fared, at least in His Church in this land, with the aspect of His worship on earth. For the last three hundred years, brief but brilliant periods excepted, our ritual has lost all unity of significance of expression. We have treated 'The Book of Common Prayer and Administration of the Sacraments, and other Rites and Ceremonies of the Church' much as if it were simply a collection of sundry Forms of Prayer, overlooking the fact that besides these there are acts to be done, and functions to be performed. And these have been done infrequently, not to say imperfectly.

The old Puritan idea of Divine Service is confession of sin, prayer to God and intercession for our wants, bodily and spiritual. Another theological school, more perhaps in vogue, looks upon praise as the great element of worship – praise, that is, apart from *Eucharistia*, itself, in one sense, a mighty Act of Praise. Hence one Priest with his form-of-prayer theory affects a bald, chilling, and apparently indevout worship, whilst another lavishes all the splendour of his ritual upon his forms of prayer which are said in choir; and both depress, by defective teaching and a maimed ritual, the distinctive service of Christianity. Matins and Evensong are performed with a severe simplicity by the one, in an ornate manner by the other.

J. Purchas, *The Directorium Anglicanum*, 1858, pages vii–viii

Evan Daniel's history of the Prayer Book is still a standard work on the subject. In his Preface he reflects on the evolution of Anglican worship. Daniel was the Principal of St John's College, Battersea, in London.

Looking back on the eventful history of the Prayer-book, we are stirred by much the same feelings as are evoked by the contemplation of some venerable cathedral, whose origin is hidden in a remote antiquity, whose various parts are known to have been designed and built in widely separated ages, and whose very stones, like those of St Mark's at Venice, show that they have been brought from many distant quarters. Here we see signs of work done and undone, it may be, many times; changes precipitately undertaken and, perhaps, as suddenly abandoned; here traces of some fierce outburst of iconoclastic zeal, reckless and indiscriminating in its work of destruction; here again the reparation made by some age of pious zeal and enlightened devotion; here some relic of the simplicity of primitive art, and here, side by side with it, some specimen of the highest development to which art ever attained; yet, through all these indications of divergent and sometimes conflicting influences, one central and dominant idea of a noble temple reared for the worship and service of God asserts itself; old and new, under the harmonising power of that idea, are happily blended together without incongruity, and essential unity is preserved under much external heterogeneousness.

Evan Daniel, *The Prayer Book its History, Language and Contents*, Gardner, 1901, page vi

Gregory Dix (1901–52) was an Anglican Benedictine monk at Nashdom Abbey, elected as its Prior in 1948. His book The Shape of the Liturgy *was one of the strongest influences on subsequent liturgical change in the Church of England. As appears in this extract, he took a poor view of the Book of Common Prayer, but acknowledged that Cranmer's Communion Service was 'the most effective attempt ever made to give liturgical expression to the doctrine of justification by faith alone'.*

The depth and breadth and allusiveness of the classical rites comes just from this, that their real author is always the worshipping church, not any individual however holy and gifted, any committee however representative, or any legislator however wise. The results in every tradition were codified from time to time by men with a gift or a taste for this sort of work. But all the time such men were working within a tradition, with materials supplied them by the immense eucharistic experience of the whole worshipping church of the past, of other churches as well as their own. [. . .] No one man is great enough or good enough to fix the act of the Body of Christ for ever according to his own mind and understanding of it. The good liturgies were not written; they grew.

About the beginning of the sixteenth century it did look as though something of this kind needed to begin again. The eucharistic practice of the church no longer fully expressed her contemporary mind and life and needs; but a fairly brief period of liturgical experiment might well have enabled it to do so. Instead, one man's personal and quite unrepresentative opinion, come to before ever the first changes were tried out in practice, was clamped upon the Church of England in a fixed form, which it was never afterwards free to alter. Now that stage is over, and the opportunity missed in the sixteenth century has come again. In spite of all the well-intentioned efforts of the bishops to prevent it, a good deal of the necessary 'liturgical experiment' has been carried out by the clergy in the last forty years. But it has had to be done with so little guidance from authority that most of the results have been uncoordinated and many have not been observed. We need a new 'custom', with the stability and self-enforcement that any satisfactory custom has in itself. Can we reproduce deliberately and consciously and in a reasonably short space of time – say five to ten years – that process by which *the church* produced the great liturgies naturally and instinctively in a period of centuries?

Gregory Dix, *The Shape of the Liturgy*, Dacre Press, 1945, pages 718–19

Roger Beckwith was, before retirement, Warden of Latimer House, Oxford. He is one of the leading Evangelical writers in the Church today and a defender of Prayer Book Worship.

All in all, Cranmer was a child of the Renaissance no less than of the Reformation. He was a scholar, learned in the ancients as well as the moderns, but chiefly concerned to follow the Holy Scriptures, as now known in the original tongues. His greatest gifts became apparent when he took a share in the task of reviving English vernacular literature, by creating an English liturgy. The Book of Common Prayer has an originality and power which are often lacking both in Reformation liturgies and in attempts to restore the worship of the primitive Church. His English liturgical style is not the least part of what he accomplished. Though owing something to its Latin antecedents, and sharing the redundancies and antitheses characteristic of existing religious English, it achieves the difficult art of being contemporary without being colloquial, of having dignity without sacrificing vigour, and of expressing fervour without lapsing into sentimentality.

Cranmer's general liturgical aims are clear from his Prayer Book itself, and especially from the two prefatory statements 'Concerning the Service of the Church' and 'Of Ceremonies'. He seeks to attain intelligibility, edification, and corporateness, by producing, for regular use, a single, simple liturgy in the vernacular, in which the Scriptures are read and expounded in an orderly way, biblical teaching is incorporated throughout, all that is misleading or meaningless is excluded, words are audible, actions are visible, and congregational participation in speaking, singing, and reception of the sacrament (in both kinds) is encouraged. In pursuing these aims, there were limits to what he achieved. Like other students

of the Bible, he had his blind spots. Being confronted with a largely illit-
erate Church, and long-standing habits of infrequent lay communion, he
was not able to implement his principle of congregational worship as
fully as he wished, and he had to carry simplicity to lengths which
restricted variety and freedom, and sacrificed some of the riches of the
pre-Reformation liturgy. He curbed music and ceremonial to an extent
which may have been necessary at the time, but was not permanently
desirable. He made rather too much use of exhortations. Yet, when all
necessary deductions have been made, his achievement remains extraordinary. When compared with the state of the liturgy at the beginning of
Henry's reign, Cranmer's Prayer Books show the following significant
changes: the language has been altered from Latin to English; a multi-
plicity of service books has been reduced to one; a number of regional
uses has been reduced to one national use; the rubrics have been pruned
(even to excess), simplified, and fully integrated with the liturgical texts;
the lectionary has been reformed; preaching has been revived; the congregation has been given a considerable part in the service; the cup has
been restored to the laity, and the rule of receiving the sacrament once a
year has been increased threefold; an impressive new structure has been
given to the Communion service; the eight daily offices have been combined into two; the biblical content of most services has been greatly
increased; and traditional doctrines and practices which Cranmer judged
to be in conflict with biblical theology (notably the sacrifice of the Mass,
transubstantiation, and the invocation of saints), have been reformed or
entirely removed. The fact that his second Prayer Book received only
minor revisions in 1559, 1604, and 1662, and in its 1662 form is still widely
used in England and other parts of the world, is a tribute to his achievement which is not easy to gainsay.

Roger Beckwith, *Thomas Cranmer after Five Hundred Years*, The Prayer Book Society,
1989, pages 15–16

*The official case for an alternative to the Book of Common Prayer was made
in 1980.*

It is a remarkable fact that for over three hundred years and despite all
attempts at revision, the Book of Common Prayer has remained the

acknowledged norm for public worship in the Church of England, as well as a model and inspiration for worship throughout most of the Anglican Communion.

Rapid social and intellectual changes, however, together with a world-wide reawakening of interest in liturgy, have made it desirable that new understandings of worship should find expression in new forms and styles. Christians have become readier to accept that, even within a single church, unity need no longer be seen to entail strict uniformity of practice. The provision of alternative services is to be welcomed as an enrichment of the Church's life rather than as a threat to its integrity. As long ago as 1906 a Royal Commission reported that 'the law of public worship in the Church of England is too narrow for the religious life of the present generation'. Three-quarters of a century later it can be said with even greater certainty that the gospel of the living Christ is too rich in content, and the spiritual needs of his people are too diverse, for a single form of worship to suffice.

Preface to *The Alternative Service Book, 1980*

Dr Peter Mullen, Rector of St Michael's, Cornhill in the City of London, is one of the most vigorous of many defenders of the Book of Common Prayer against new liturgies.

We have to hold fast to that which is good. The Prayer Book, along with what is broadly called literature, lets into our modern life so much sense of a kind we don't otherwise know. It can and does give to life a weight in the age of Nietzsche's 'weightlessness'. It offers still, as it did in Cranmer's time, the Christian way for this nation. (The Prayer Book is much more likely to be superseded by political change – a French-style secular republic, or European federation – than by linguistic change.) Christians are walkers in a way. But we now, as always, need repentance, the Greek of which means literally a change of mind.

'You can't put the clock back' (though we do that once a year in this country) and 'you want the Church to be stuck in a time-warp'. Not exactly, though the noble example of the Eastern churches should be kept in mind; their survival of centuries of subordination to kings and emperors and then in some cases seventy years of savage atheistic persecution owes much to their reliable unchangingness. But as a matter of fact the Byzantine way does not seem an option for the West. For all the sameness and fixity of modern life, and *pace* Spengler, it is still true that 'Sensibility changes in us all from age to age, whether we will or no'. The fixity belongs to those who want to saddle us with the mechanism and thickness of the age, to stick us in the 1960s.

Peter Mullen (ed.), The Real Common Worship, Edgeways, 2000, page 194

Another prominent Prayer Book advocate is Dr Peter Toon, who was a parish priest in the United States and then the incumbent of two parishes in the English Diocese of Lichfield. He is particularly strong on the traditional language of worship which has become familiar over the centuries.

There are many examples of *style* in English – e.g., that used for debates in the British House of Commons, for addressing judge and jury in courts of law, for the composing of pop songs, for the working of computers, for describing American football, and so on. The form of language in each of these examples is clearly recognisable as belonging to a specific context and serves little or no purpose outside of that context.

Is there a *style* for public worship in English that is recognisable? Yes there is and it is that found in *The Book of Common Prayer*, the King James Version of the Bible and in classic English hymnody (Watts, Wesley, Keble etc.). Certainly this *style* was much better known in 1960 than it is today but it is still known and recognised today. People who are not regular churchgoers recognise this *style* immediately when, for example, the traditional forms of the Ten Commandments or the Lord's Prayer or the Apostles' Creed or 'Thus saith the Lord' are quoted. If people hear, 'And with thy spirit', most recognise religious language but this is hardly the case if they hear its modern replacement 'And also with you'. This point also applies in the use of phrases ('world without end'), clauses ('hallowed be thy Name') and sentences (e.g., 'those whom God has joined together let no man put asunder'.

Peter Toon and Louis R. Tarsitano, Neither Archaic nor Obsolete, Edgeways Books,
2003, page 68

Michael Perham, now Bishop of Gloucester, was the Vice-Chairman of the Liturgical Commission which produced Common Worship. *He makes a judicious and reasoned case for holding tradition and innovation together.*

Why a new round of liturgical change after only twenty years? Obviously that is a complex question with a variety of answers. But it needs to be remembered that the Church of England embarked in the 1960s on the most far-reaching liturgical changes since the sixteenth century. It is not surprising that, while some of the reforms introduced then have won general approval and established themselves securely in only a generation, others have not stood the test even of a short time. In the sixteenth century there was a period during which there were successive changes. The twentieth century is different. We have not lived through the kind of political and religious changes of direction that marked the reigns of Henry VIII, Edward VI, Mary and Elizabeth, and which were partly responsible for the changes to the liturgy, but we have lived through enormous cultural changes and it is possible to discern that the liturgical revisions of the 1960s and 1970s reflect a cultural fashion that has dated quickly. One only has to look at the world of architecture and buildings to see what one generation regards as innovative, exciting and catching the spirit of the age can, only a few years later, seem transitory and tired.

As we move into a new century, there is a greater willingness to reverence the past and to value the heritage, than there was a generation ago.

There is also in the Church, some evidence of a greater desire to relate to the wider community, to be in dialogue with 'folk religion', and to build bridges, compared to twenty-five years ago. There is also a clearer vision of the need for a Church that gives evangelism priority and that provides worship that serves that priority. In brief, it is a strangely different world from the one in which our new services were devised only a generation ago. That is in itself a warning against imagining that every age can make all things new in liturgy in a way that can last, and, unless we want to live with constant change, that argues for a liturgy that evolves slowly rather than one that changes rapidly. But it does not remove from the present generation the responsibility to create the best liturgy it can for the years ahead.

Michael Perham, *Celebrate the Christian Story*, SPCK, 1997, pages 2–3

Baroness Phyllis James, better known to many as the novelist P. D. James, was with Michael Perham a member of the Liturgical Commission. She recalls the value of the Book of Common Prayer in a more respected and confident Church of England.

The Church of England in my childhood was the national church in a very special sense, the visible symbol of the country's moral and religious aspirations, a country which despite great differences of class, wealth and privilege, was unified by generally accepted values and by a common tradition, history and culture, just as the church was unified by Cranmer's magnificent liturgy. There were, of course, varieties of practice and little superficial resemblance between the multi-candled ceremonial, the incense and Stations of the Cross found in the extreme High Church and the simplicities of an evangelical church which could have been mistaken for a Nonconformist chapel. But it was possible to attend different churches – on holiday, for example – and feel immediately at home, finding in the pew, not a service sheet with a series number, but the familiar and unifying Book of Common Prayer. The importance of the Church of England as the national church was perhaps most clearly shown on Armistice Day when whole communities gathered in their parish church, united in sorrowful remembrance. To be born in 1920, two years after the end of the slaughter of a generation, was to be aware from one's earliest years of a universal grieving which was almost part of the air one breathed. Today I frequently hear people and families referred to as being Christian as if they were members of a minority and slightly eccentric sect. In my childhood the great majority of the population, whether or not they regularly attended a place of worship, thought of themselves as Christians, and most described themselves as C. of E. The English have always respected and felt a devotion to their church, provided they are not expected regularly to attend its services.

P. D. James, in M. Furlong (ed.), *Our Childhood's Pattern*, Mowbray, 1995, pages 50–1

Geoffrey Rowell, Bishop of Gibraltar in the Diocese of Europe, sums up loss and gain in the round of recent liturgical change.

The revisions of the later part of the twentieth century, the *Alternative Service Book 1980* in England and parallel revisions elsewhere, have led to an increasing use of contemporary language, and the disappearance of a single, unifying liturgical text used by all Anglicans. *Common Worship* (2000) is a further English revision, no longer published in a single book and with a much wider range of options. As the change from manuscript to printing standardised liturgy, so the information technology revolution has created liturgy shaped in a broad common pattern but no longer a common prayer whose words can be engraved on the worshipper's heart. If there is gain in being able to compile special services for special occasions, and in an ever-increasing ecumenical exchange, there is loss undoubtedly in the weakening of the memory of common prayer. The days when the Sunday collect was learned by heart have gone for ever. The 1998 Lambeth Conference witnessed to an energy of liturgical revision around the Communion, and also to a variety of cultural styles of presentation, yet the shape of the eucharistic liturgy was recognisably the same and it would be too drastic a judgement to say that common prayer as a unifying constituent of Anglicanism, and the essential foundation of growth in holiness, has evaporated.

Geoffrey Rowell, *Love's Redeeming Work*, Oxford University Press, 2001, page 371

Hymns may sometimes be the best way to express the feelings of worshippers, as Arthur Middleton (p. 48) reminds us.

Nicholas Lossky, the Russian Orthodox theologian, advised his fellow orthodox to search in the *English Hymnal* as one way of discovering Anglican doctrine and devotion. [. . .] It is impossible to overrate the value of good hymns for personal as well as public use. Next to the Bible itself, hymns have done more to influence our views, and mould our theology. There is a power in them that never dies. Easily learned in the days of childhood and of youth, often repeated, seldom, if ever, forgotten; they live with us, a most precious heritage through all the changes of our earthly life. They form a fitting and most welcome expression for every kind of deep religious feeling and speak to us of faith and hope in hours of trial and sorrow. They can stimulate our Christian efforts, remaining in us as the rich consolation of heart and mind, and as one common bond of fellowship between the living members of Christ's mystical Body.

There in the hymnal you will learn about God the Father, God the Son, God the Holy Spirit, God the Holy and Blessed Trinity, the life of grace. Hymns celebrating Our Lady, saints, martyrs, and confessors remind us that the Church embraces the communion of saints in which we live with our forbears in the faith. Herbert's hymns and those for morning and evening can provide nourishment for our personal prayer as Keble and Ken demonstrate. There you will find pure doctrine in poetically evocative language, a compendium of theology to stimulate devotion and duty, the discipline of Christian living.

Arthur Middleton, *Loving Learning and Desiring God*, Address to the
Prayer Book Society, 2004, pages 21–2

This hymn by William Bullock and H. W. Baker well expresses the mingled fervour and moderation which mark the best Anglican services.

We love the place, O God,
Wherein thine honour dwells;
The joy of thine abode
All earthly joy excels.

We love the house of prayer,
Wherein thy servants meet;
And thou, O Lord, art there
Thy chosen flock to greet.

We love the sacred font
For there the holy Dove
To pour is ever wont
His blessing from above.

We love thine altar, Lord
O, what on earth so dear!
For there, in faith adored,
We find thy presence near.

We love the word of life,
The word that tells of peace,
Of comfort in the strife,
And joys that never cease.

We love to sing below
For mercies freely given;
But O, we long to know
The triumph-song of heaven!

Lord Jesus, give us grace
On earth to love thee more,
In heaven to see thy face,
And with thy saints adore.

The New English Hymnal,
Canterbury Press, 1986, no. 471

8

Preaching

Take thou authority to preach the Word of God

In the Church of England the sermon has not held the central place which has been given to it in some of the Protestant Free Churches, where the 'call' of a new minister may depend largely on a trial performance in the pulpit. Anglicans seldom have the opportunity of hearing their new incumbent preach before he or she is licensed, unless some of them pay a covert visit to the parish of a likely candidate. Yet the popular view of the church service, as held by those who seldom attend one, is that people have to listen to a sermon. The 'vicar' as presented in fiction or the media is quite likely to be engaged in 'Writing my sermon for Sunday'. It is also assumed that this will be largely about sin, and that the preacher will be against it. The first use of the verb 'to preach' as meaning to give censorious and unsought advice, is given by the Oxford English Dictionary as 1523, so the clergy of the Church of England cannot be blamed for having debased a good ecclesiastical word.

It is not easy to characterise the typical Anglican sermon. In delivery it has tended towards the restrained style which can come to be regarded as 'dry'. In content it has ranged widely over social and political as well as doctrinal topics, but with a central regard for the exposition of Scripture. The norm today is to preach on one of the lessons read during the service, though the announcement of a specific text at the beginning, once normal practice, is now less common. Although everyone, including the clergy, makes jokes about the sermon as the tedious part of the service, congregations expect to hear something from the pulpit, especially at the great festivals and the other focal times like Harvest Thanksgiving and Remembrance Sunday. In many cathedrals and some churches there are endowed sermons or sermon series to which distinguished speakers are invited. In the parish church a visiting preacher may interest the regular congregation, and give some relief to the incumbent, who needs to find something to say on most Sundays in the year.

Like so many things in people's experience of public worship, preaching was not an innovation in the sixteenth century. Homilies in Anglo-Saxon were preached before the Norman Conquest, and vernacular sermons instructed and exhorted congregations during the medieval period. The orders of Friars were particularly popular preachers. The Counter-Reformation preachers brought renewed emphasis on the sermon in the Roman Catholic Church.

Yet the Reformers did give new importance to preaching. Hostility to the idea of the sacrificial Mass as the centre of all church worship made the Ministry of the Word of equal importance with the sacramental life. The Bible in English, and in other vernacular languages, made it possible for all to hear, and to read if they were literate, the whole of the Scriptures in their own tongue. The Bible was not only a court of appeal for authority in the new ecclesiastical jurisdictions but a means of instruction in doctrine which was claimed to be reformed and purged of error. The emphasis of preaching in the reformed churches was on the exposition of the Bible. Although the sermon was not so dominant in Anglican services as in the new free and independent churches, it was regarded as important, so much so that some could fear that it might marginalise the Eucharist (see Thorndike below).

For many years the sermon in the Church of England was commonly at Matins and Evensong, after the appointed office had been said. The Book of Common Prayer, however, makes no mention of a sermon except after the Creed at Holy Communion. When notices have been given:

> Then shall follow the Sermon, or one of the Homilies already set forth, or hereafter to be set forth, by authority.

The order envisaged, was for Matins, Litany and Antecommunion, with the full eucharistic rite only on certain Sundays. But sermons were not confined to the statutory services in the parish church. Public sermons in the open air attracted crowds at such locations as St Paul's Cross, in front of St Paul's Cathedral in London. A permanent stone pulpit, roofed to protect the preacher from rain and to aid the projection of his voice, was erected in such places. In the churches, the new emphasis on the sermon caused internal re-ordering so that the pulpit rather than the altar was the dominant feature. New church buildings featured a large pulpit and a small sanctuary.

Whether in a church or outside, sermons were formidably long by present-day expectations; an hour was not considered too much of a strain on congregations in the sixteenth century, but after the Restoration, as the passage by Gilbert Burnet suggests, shorter discourses were beginning to seem desirable. Although the exposition of Scripture was the Reformation ideal for a sermon, national and local controversies, and divisions within the Church, were often matter for the pulpit. In the early years, Puritans who disliked the preaching of the parish incumbent might endow a Lectureship to preach more acceptable doctrine. When Richard Hooker became Master of the Temple Church in London, the Calvinist Walter Travers was already established there as Lecturer. It was said that 'Canterbury was preached in the morning, Geneva in the afternoon'.

Not all was controversial; the sermon had a vital part in giving people the teaching of the reformed church and explaining basic Christian doctrine to the majority who could not read and received little or no other education. The Elizabethan Puritans were insistent that there should be a preacher in every parish. But not all the clergy could be trusted in the pulpit without guidance. There were many who were themselves not well educated, and others who it was feared might knowingly preach heresy or sedition. Shakespeare's well-named Oliver Martext in *As You Like It* is an example of the first type. The danger was controlled by the issue of Books of Homilies in 1547 and 1571, with model discourses to be read by clergy who were not licensed to preach in their own words. Although the Homilies gradually fell into disuse, the practice of reading a sermon remained, whether composed by the preacher or another, as Addison and Borrow recall. Sermons written by others are seldom if ever read from the pulpit today, but there seems to be a steady sale for sermon notes and outlines. The disputatious sermon gave way in some cases, though not all, to the anodyne described by Alexander Pope:

> To rest the cushion and soft Dean invite,
> Who never mentions Hell to ears polite.

Epigram 3 (1733)

The Oxford Movement brought back controversial sermons, as supporters and opponents of the revival laid into each other from the pulpit. The Movement is generally taken to begin with John Keble's Assize Sermon at Oxford in 1833 against State interference in Church affairs. But while the Tractarians and their followers could preach strongly in defence of their beliefs, they also showed a typically Anglican restraint when it came to basic doctrine, especially about the central dogma of the Atonement. They invoked the principle of Reserve, of unfolding the mysteries of faith carefully and with regard to the capacity and state of mind of the hearers (see below, pp. 148–50). Their enemies accused them of Jesuitical subterfuge but they were a necessary corrective to the ranting style of some preachers who offered free pardon for sin without also stressing repentance and amendment.

Today the sermon is commonly a ten-minute period at the Parish Communion, with signs of congregational impatience beginning if it goes beyond fifteen. It is an age of literacy and texts rather than orality, and the span of listening attention has diminished. But people will tolerate a longer sermon on special occasions, and a visiting preacher can still be an attraction. On church noticeboards, it is usually the preacher rather than the officiant or celebrant whose name is announced.

The importance which the Reformers attached to preaching is shown in a sermon preached in 1548 by Hugh Latimer (c. 1485–1555), Bishop of Worcester, who became one of the first martyrs of the Church of England in the reign of Mary I. His comparison between the preacher and the ploughman is an example of the desire to bring the developing Church close to the daily life of its people, a path which later clergy have tried to follow.

Well may the preacher and the ploughman be likened together: first, for their labour of all seasons of the year; for there is no time of the year in which the ploughman hath not some special work to do: as in my country in Leicestershire, the ploughman hath a time to set forth, and to assay his plough, and other times for other necessary works to be done. And then they also may be likened together for the diversity of works and variety of offices that they have to do. For as the ploughman first sets forth his plough, and then tills his land, and breaks it in furrows, and sometime ridges it up again; and at another time harrows it and clots it, and sometime dungs it and hedges it, digs it and weeds it, purges and makes it clean: so the prelate, the preacher, hath many diverse offices to do. He hath first a busy work to bring his parishioners to a right faith, as Paul calleth it, and not a swerving faith; but to a faith that embraces Christ, and trusts to his merits; a lively faith, a justifying faith; a faith that makes a man righteous, without respect of works: as ye have it very well declared and set forth in the Homily. He hath then a busy work, I say, to bring his flock to a right faith, and then to confirm them in the same faith: now casting them down with the law, and with threatenings of God for sin; now ridging them up again with the gospel, and with the prom- ises of God's favour: now weeding them, by telling them their faults, and making them forsake sin; now clotting them, by breaking their stony hearts, and by making them supplehearted, and making them to have hearts of flesh; that is, soft hearts, and apt for doctrine to enter in: now teaching to know God rightly, and to know their duty to God and their neighbours: now exhorting them, when they know their duty, that they do it, and be diligent in it; so that they have a continual work to do.

Sermons by Hugh Latimer, Dent, 1906, page 56

The purpose of the Books of Homilies referred to above was clearly set out early in the reign of Elizabeth I.

Considering how necessary it is, that the word of God, which is the only food of the soul, and that most excellent light that we must walk by, in this our most dangerous pilgrimage, should at all convenient times be preached unto the people, that thereby they may both learn their duty towards God, their Prince, and their neighbours, according to the mind of the Holy Ghost, expressed in the Scriptures; and also to avoid the manifold enormities, which heretofore by false doctrine have crept into the Church of God; and how that all they, which are appointed Ministers, have not the gift of preaching sufficiently to instruct the people, which is committed unto them, whereof great inconveniences might rise, and ignorance still be maintained, if some honest remedy be not speedily found and provided: the Queen's most excellent Majesty, tendering the souls' health of her loving subjects, and the quieting of their consciences in the chief and principal points of Christian religion;

and willing also, by the true setting forth and pure declaring of God's word – which is the principal guide and leader unto all godliness and virtue – to expel and drive away as well all corrupt, vicious, and ungodly living, as also erroneous and poisoned doctrines, tending to superstition and idolatry; hath, by the advice of her most honourable Counsellors, for her discharge in this behalf, caused a Book of Homilies, which heretofore was set forth by her most loving brother, a Prince of most worthy memory, Edward the Sixth, to be printed anew; wherein are contained certain wholesome and godly exhortations, to move the people to honour and worship Almighty God and diligently to serve him, every one according to their degree, state, and vocation.

Preface to the *Second Book of Homilies, Sermons and Homilies Appointed to be read in Churches* (1562), Prayer Book and Homily Society, 1840

Lancelot Andrewes (1555–1626), Bishop of Winchester, was one of the greatest churchmen of his time. Preacher, writer of prayers and scholar, he was a leading member of the Hampton Court Conference in 1604, from which came the Authorised Version of the Bible. Andrewes was the principal translator of the Pentateuch and the historical books. He was admired by T. S. Eliot, who dedicated a book of essays to his memory and took the beginning of one of his sermons for the first lines of 'The Journey of the Magi'. Here Andrewes gives wise, and perhaps typically Anglican, advice to the preacher.

Let the preacher labour to be heard intelligently, willingly, obediently. And let him not doubt that he will accomplish this rather by the piety of his prayers than by the eloquence of his speech. By praying for himself, and those whom he is to address, let him be their beadsman before he becomes their teacher, and approaching God with devotion let him first raise to Him a thirsting heart before he speaks of Him with his tongue; that he may speak what he hath been taught and pour out what hath been poured in.

I cease not therefore to ask from our Lord and Master, that He may, either by the utterances of His Scriptures or the conversations of my brethren, or the internal and sweeter doctrine of His own inspiration, deign to teach me things so to be set forth and asserted, that in what is set forth and asserted I may ever hold me fast to the Truth; from this very Truth I desire to be taught the many things I know not, by Him from whom I have received the few I know.

Lancelot Andrewes, *Sermons*, ed. J. P. Wilson Parker, 1841–3, page 105

George Herbert (p. 79) gives equally moderate but firm advice to the ordinary parish priest.

The Country Parson preacheth constantly, the pulpit is his joy and his throne. If he at any time intermit, it is either for want of health, or against some great Festival, that he may the better celebrate it, or for the variety of the hearers, that he may be heard at his return more attentively. When he intermits, he is ever very well supplied by some able man who treads in his steps, and will not throw down what he hath built; whom also he intreats to press some point, that he himself hath often urged with no great success, that so in the mouth of two or three witnesses the truth may be more established. When he preacheth, he procures attention by all possible art, both by earnestness of speech, it being natural to men to think, that where is much earnestness, there is somewhat worth hearing; and by a diligent, and busy cast of his eye on his auditors, with letting them know, that he observes who marks, and who not; and with particularising of his speech now to the younger sort, then to the elder, now to the poor, and now to the rich. This is for you, and This is for you; for particulars ever touch, and awake more than generals. Herein also he serves himself of the judgements of God, as of those of ancient times, so especially of the late ones; and of those most, which are nearest to his Parish; for people are very attentive at such discourses, and think it behoves them to be so, when God is so near them, and even over their heads. Sometimes he tells them stories, and sayings of others, according as his text invites him; for them also men heed, and remember better then exhortations; which though earnest, yet often die with the Sermon, especially with Country people; which are thick, and heavy, and hard to raise to a point of Zeal, and fervency, and need a mountain of fire to kindle them; but stories and sayings they will well remember. He often tells them, that Sermons are dangerous things, that none goes out of Church as he came in, but either better, or worse; that none is careless before his judge, and that the word of God shall judge us. By these and other means the Parson procures attention; but the character of his Sermon is Holiness; he is not witty, or learned, or eloquent, but Holy.

George Herbert, *The Country Parson*, chapter 7, F. E. Hutchinson (ed.), *The Works of George Herbert*, Oxford University Press, 1941

Gilbert Burnet (1643–1715) was Professor of Divinity at Glasgow and later Bishop of Salisbury. He was an opponent of James II and accompanied William III when he landed in England to claim the throne. Despite his formidable details of application in a sermon, he suggests that the preacher could profitably manage it in half the regular time.

When the explanatory Part of the Sermon is over, the Application comes next. And here great Judgement must be used, to make it fall the heaviest, and lie the longest, upon such Particulars as may be within the Compass of the Auditory. Directions concerning a high Devotion, to a stupid, ignorant Company, or of Generosity and Bounty, to very poor People, against Pride and Ambition, to such as are dull and low-minded, are ill suited, and so must have little Effect upon them. Therefore Care must he taken that the Application be useful and proper; that it make the Hearers apprehend some of their Sins and Defects, and see how to perform their Duty, that it awaken them to it, and direct them in it: And therefore the most common Sins, such as Men's neglecting their Duty to God, in the several Branches of it, their setting their Hearts inordinately upon the World, their Lying in Discourse, but chiefly in Bargainings, their Evil-speaking, and their Hatred and Malice, ought to be very often brought in. Some one or other of these, ought to be in every Application that is made, by which they may see, that the whole Design of Religion lies against them. Such particular Sins, Swearing, Drunkenness, or Lewdness, as abound in any Place, must likewise be frequently brought in here. The Application must be clear and short, very weighty, and free of every Thing that looks like the Affectations of Wit and Eloquence; here the Preacher must be all Heart and Soul, designing the Good of his People. The whole Sermon is directed to this. Therefore, as it is fit that the chief Point which a Sermon drives at, should come often over and over, that so the Hearers may never lose sight of it, but keep it still in View, so, in the Application, the Text must be shewed to speak it; all the Parts of the Explanation must come in to enforce it: The Application must be opened in the several Views that it may have, but those must be chiefly insisted on, that are most suitable both to the Capacities and the Circumstances of the People: And in Conclusion, all ought to be summed up in a weighty Period or two; and some other signal Passages of the Scriptures relating to it may be sought for, that so the Matter may be left upon the Auditory in the solemnest Manner possible.

Thus I have led a Preacher, through the Composition of his Sermon; I will next lay before him some Particulars relating to it. The shorter Sermons are, they are generally both better heard, and better remembered. The Custom of an Hour's Length forces many Preachers to trifle away much of the Time, and to spin out their Matter, so as to hold out. So great a Length does also flat the Hearers, and tempt them to sleep; especially when, as is usual, the first Part of the Sermon is languid and heavy. In half an Hour, a Man may lay open his Matter in its full Extent, and cut off those Superfluities which come in only to lengthen the Discourse. And he may hope to keep up the Attention of his People all the while.

Gilbert Burnet, *A Discourse of the Pastoral Care* (1692), London, 1766, pages 196–8

Herbert Thorndike (p. 123) commended sermons but, influenced by some of the excesses during the Commonwealth, hoped the balance of word and sacrament would not be lost.

It is to be wished, indeed, that continual preaching be maintained in all churches, as it is to be wished that all God's people were prophets; and it is to be commended that the abuse of private masses is taken away. But if order be not taken that those which are set up to preach, may preach no more than they have learned out of the Scriptures, it will be easy to drive a worse trade of preaching than ever priests did of private masses, the one tending only to feed themselves, the other to turn the good order of the world, which is the harbour of the Church, into public confusion, to feed themselves; the profaning of God's ordinance being common to both.

And if the taking away of private masses must be by turning the Eucharist out of doors, saving twice or thrice a year, for fashion's sake, it is but Lycurgus's reformation, to stock up the vines, for fear men be drunk with the wine. [Lycurgus was a legendary king of Nemea in Greece.]

Theological Works of Herbert Thorndike, Parker, 1844, vol. 1, part 2, page 841

Sir Roger de Coverley explains how he made sure of a good sermon from his domestic chaplain, preferring established quality to originality.

At his first settling with me, I made him a present of all the good sermons which have been printed in English, and only begged of him that every Sunday he would pronounce one of them in the pulpit. Accordingly, he has digested them into such a series, that they follow one another naturally, and make a continued system of practical divinity.

As Sir Roger was going on in his story, the gentleman we were talking of came up to us; and upon the Knight's asking him who preached to-morrow (for it was Saturday night) told us, the Bishop of St. Asaph in the morning, and Dr. South in the afternoon. He then shewed us his list of preachers for the whole year, where I saw with a great deal of pleasure Archbishop Tillotson, Bishop Saunderson, Dr. Barrow, Dr. Calamy, with several living authors who have published discourses of practical divinity. I no sooner saw this venerable man in the pulpit, but I very much approved of my friend's insisting upon the qualifications of a good aspect and a clear voice; for I was so charmed with the gracefulness of his figure and delivery, as well as with the discourses he pronounced, that I think I never passed any time more to my satisfaction. A sermon repeated after this manner, is like the composition of a poet in the mouth of a graceful actor.

I could heartily wish that more of our country-clergy would follow this example; and, instead of wasting their spirits in laborious composi-tions of their own, would endeavour after a handsome elocution, and all those other talents that are proper to enforce what has been penned by greater masters. This would not only be more easy to themselves, but more edifying to the people.

Joseph Addison, *The Spectator*, 1711, no. 106

When two eighteenth-century clergymen meet at an inn, they compare notes about the market for printed sermons, which seems to have been overstocked.

Barnabas greatly discouraged poor Adams; he said, 'The age was so wicked, that nobody read sermons: would you think it, Mr. Adams?' said he, 'I once intended to print a volume of sermons myself, and they had the approbation of two or three bishops; but what do you think a bookseller offered me?' 'Twelve guineas perhaps,' cried Adams. 'Not twelve pence, I assure you,' answered Barnabas: 'nay, the dog refused me a Concordance in exchange. At last I offered to give him the printing them, for the sake of dedicating them to that very gentleman who just now drove his own coach into the inn; and, I assure you, he had the impudence to refuse my offer; by which means I lost a good living, that was afterwards given away in exchange for a pointer, to one who – but I will not say anything against the cloth. So you may guess, Mr. Adams, what you are to expect; for if sermons would have gone down, I believe – I will not be vain; but to be concise with you, three bishops said they were the best that ever were writ: but indeed there are a pretty moderate number printed already, and not all sold yet.'

'Pray, sir,' said Adams, 'to what do you think the numbers may amount?'– 'Sir,' answered Barnabas, 'a bookseller told me, he believed five thousand volumes at least.' 'Five thousand?' quoth the surgeon: 'What can they be writ upon? I remember when I was a boy, I used to read one Tillotson's sermons, and, I am sure, if a man practised half so much as is in one of those sermons he will go to heaven.' – 'Doctor,' cries Barnabas, 'you have a profane way of talking, for which I must reprove you. A man can never have his duty too freely inculcated into him. And as for Tillotson, to be sure he was a good writer, and said things very well; but comparisons are odious; another man may write as well as he – I believe there are some of my sermons,' – and then he applied the candle to his pipe. – 'And I believe there are some of my discourses,' cries Adams, 'which the bishop would not think totally unworthy of being printed; and I have been informed I might procure a very large sum (indeed an immense one) on them.' 'I doubt that,' answered Barnabas: 'however, if you desire to make some money of them, perhaps you may sell them by advertising the manuscript sermons of a clergyman lately deceased, all warranted originals, and never printed. And now I think of it, I should be obliged to you, if there be ever a funeral one among them, to lend it to me; for I am this very day to preach a funeral sermon, for which I have not penned a line, though I am to have a double price.' – Adams answered, 'He had but one, which he feared would not serve his purpose, being sacred to the memory of a magistrate, who had exerted himself very singularly in the preservation of the morality of his neighbours, insomuch that he had neither alehouse nor lewd woman in the parish where he lived.' 'No,' replied Barnabas, 'that will not do quite so well, for the deceased upon whose virtues I am to harangue, was a little too much addicted to liquor, and publicly kept a mistress. I believe I must take a common sermon, and trust to my memory to introduce something handsome on him.'

Henry Fielding, *The Adventures of Joseph Andrews*, 1742, book 1, chapter 16

George Borrow (p. 122) thought that sermons in the Church of England should be read rather than extempore. He was regularly combative in his views on most things, but perhaps some of his fellow-churchmen would have agreed on this one.

[T]he clergyman preached long and well: he did not read his sermon, but spoke it extempore; his doing so rather surprised and offended me at first; I was not used to such a style of preaching in a church devoted to the religion of my country. I compared it within my mind with the style of preaching used by the high-church rector in the old church of pretty D<ereham>, and I thought to myself it was very different, and being very different I did not like it, and I thought to myself how scandalised the people of D<ereham> would have been had they heard it, and I figured to myself how indignant the high-church clerk would have been had any clergyman got up in the church of D<ereham> and preached in such a manner. Did it not savour strongly of dissent, Methodism, and similar low stuff? [. . .]. However, long before the sermon was over, I forgot the offence which I had taken, and listened to the sermon with much admiration, for the eloquence and powerful reasoning with which it abounded.

George Borrow, *The Romany Rye* (1857), John Murray, 1903, page 51

Henry Thornton (1760–1815), banker and politician and a lay member of the Evangelical Clapham Sect, wrote a book of Family Prayers which was widely used throughout the nineteenth century. In a prayer for Sunday morning he shows the deep concern of devout laypeople for those charged with preaching the gospel at home and abroad.

We beseech Thee, O Lord, to bless the preaching of Thy Gospel on this day to all who shall be the hearers of it. Send forth Thy light and Thy truth to every part of our benighted world; and shower down, especially on these nations, the abundance of Thy grace, through the diligent and faithful ministry of Thy word among us. Purify every part of Thy professing Church. Unite us in the bonds of a common faith; and teach us all to love one another. Give success to every endeavour to enlighten the ignorant; to relieve the poor; to comfort the afflicted; to deliver the oppressed from him who spoileth him; and to promote peace and good-will among men. Pour into the hearts of all who know Thy truth a spirit of enlarged benevolence; and raise up many who shall go forth in Thy strength, both to multiply their deeds of charity, and to carry Thy Gospel into all lands.

Henry Thornton, *Family Prayers* (1834), Hatchards, 1869, pages 214–15

John Keble (1792–1866), Fellow of Oriel College, Oxford, Professor of Poetry at Oxford and later Vicar of Hursley near Winchester, was one of the leaders of the Oxford Movement. His volume of devotional poems The Christian Year *was first published in 1827 and went through many editions before the end of the nineteenth century. This recommendation of reserve and reverence is taken from his poem for the Fourth Sunday in Lent.*

E'en human love will shrink from sight
Here in the coarse rude earth
How then should rash intruding glance
Break in upon her sacred trance
Who boasts a heavenly birth?

So still and secret is her growth,
Ever the truest heart,

Where deepest strikes her kindly root
For hope or joy, for flower or fruit,
Least knows its happy part.

God only, and good angels look,
Behind the blissful screen –
As when, triumphant o'er His woes,
The Son of God by moonlight rose,
By all but Heaven unseen.

John Keble, *The Christian Year* (1827),
Oxford University Press, 1914, page 69

Charlotte M. Yonge (p. 108), in a commentary on Keble's poems, gives a summary account of why Reserve in preaching and evangelism was important to the Tractarians.

Reserve, reverent reserve, was ever a characteristic of the teaching of the school of divines of which the 'Christian Year' was the first utterance. Those who had gone before them, in their burning zeal to proclaim the central truth of the Gospel, had obtruded it with little regard to the season of speaking or the frame of mind of the hearer; and moreover, there was a habit of testing the sincerity of personal religion by requiring that its growth should be constantly proclaimed and discussed with great fullness of detail.

Charlotte M. Yonge, *Musings over the Christian Year*, London, 1871, page 90

Isaac Williams (1802–65) was one of the poets of the Oxford Movement as well as a prolific theological writer. He gave the fullest exposition of the doctrine of Reserve in numbers 80 and 87 of the Tracts for the Times, *'On Reserve in Communicating Religious Knowledge'. He claimed warrant for it in the Bible and in the works of the Fathers, and was highly critical of the emotional and unguarded preaching which he found in some of his contemporaries. He expresses something of the tension between personal preaching and Church discipline which has been part of the Anglican story since the sixteenth century. One thing which may seem remote today is his easy appeal to classical authorities as support.*

If people in general were now asked what was the most powerful means of advancing the cause of religion in the world, we should be told that it was eloquence of speech or preaching: and the excellency of speech we know consists in delivery; that is the first, the second, and the third requisite. Whereas, if we were to judge from Holy Scripture, of what were the best means of promoting Christianity in the world, we should say obedience; and if we were to be asked the second, we should say obedience; and if we were to he asked the third, we should say obedience. And it is evident, that if the spirit of obedience exists, simple and calm statement of truth will go far. Not that we would be thought entirely to depreciate preaching as a mode of doing good: it may he necessary in a weak and languishing state; but it is the characteristic of this system as opposed to that of the Church, and we fear the undue exaltation of an instrument which Scripture, to say the least, has never much recommended. And, indeed, if from Revelation we turn to the great teachers of morals which have been in the world, we shall be surprised to find how little they esteemed it useful for their purpose. The exceeding jealous apprehension of rhetoric which Socrates evinces is remarkable, as shown throughout the Gorgias. Nor does it ever seem to have occurred to the sages of old, as a means of promoting morality; and yet some of them, as Pythagoras and Socrates, made this purpose, viz., that of improving the principles of men, the object of their lives: and the former was remarkable for his mysterious discipline, and the silence he imposed; the latter for a mode of questioning, which may be considered as entirely an instance of this kind of reserve in teaching.

Tracts for the Times, vol. 4, Rivington, 1840, pages 74–5

Benjamin Jowett (1817–93), classical scholar and Master of Balliol College, Oxford, was a contributor to the volume Essays and Reviews *(1860). This collection by seven liberal churchmen caused great controversy and accusations of heresy against its contributors. Jowett's essay 'On the Interpretation of Scripture' was one of the main targets for attack. In it he takes the Reformation approach to preaching firmly based on the Bible, but his ideas are somewhat removed from those of the sixteenth century.*

Another use of Scripture is that in sermons, which seems to be among the tritest, and yet is far from being exhausted. If we could only be natural and speak of things as they truly are with a real interest and not merely a conventional one! The words of Scripture come readily to hand, and the repetition of them requires no effort of thought in the writer or speaker. But, neither does it produce any effect on the hearer, which will always be in proportion to the degree of feeling or consciousness in ourselves. It may be said that originality is the gift of few; no Church can expect to have, not a hundred, but ten such preachers as Robertson or Newman. But, without originality, it seems possible to make use of Scripture in sermons in a much more living way than at present. Let the preacher make it a sort of religion, and proof of his reverence for Scripture, that he never uses its words without a distinct meaning; let him avoid the form of argument from Scripture, and catch the feeling and spirit. Scripture is itself a kind of poetry, when not overlaid with rhetoric. The scene and country has a freshness which may always be renewed; there is the interest of antiquity and the interest of home or common life as well. The facts and characters of Scripture might receive a new reading by being described simply as they are. The truths of Scripture again would have greater reality if divested of the scholastic form in which theology has cast them. The universal and spiritual aspects of Scripture might be more brought forward to the exclusion of questions of the Jewish law, or controversies about the sacraments, or exaggerated statements of doctrines which seem to be at variance with morality. The life of Christ, regarded quite naturally as of one 'who was in all points tempted like as we are, yet without sin', is also the life and centre of Christian teaching. There is no higher aim which the preacher can propose to himself than to awaken what may be termed the feeling of the presence of God and the mind of Christ in Scripture; not to collect evidences about dates and books, or to familiarise metaphysical distinctions; but to make the heart and conscience of his hearers bear him witness that the lessons which are contained in Scripture – lessons of justice and truth – lessons of mercy and peace – of the need of man and the goodness of God to him, are indeed not human but divine.

Benjamin Jowett, 'On the Interpretation of Scripture' in *Essays and Reviews*, Parker, 1860, pages 429–30

Lay Readers, now simply called Readers, were at first restricted in their permission to preach but now exercise a valuable ministry of preaching in many services. Edward King (p. 67) gave them encouragement and advice in 1908.

In delivering a gospel message, if it is to be a life-giving message, there must be in the preacher a sense of message, and a desire to deliver it. A sense of message. This is included in what is technically called 'Mission'; it belongs to the Church doctrine of 'apostolic succession', both of which are included in the gift of Ordination.

This has always been a great support and strength to those who have been ordained. It is a safeguard against the feeling of personal weakness; at the same time it has, I fear, been a temptation and a ground for complaint against the Church. It has given an occasion to adversaries to say that we trust to our official position, and not to the real inward gift of the Holy Spirit.

I speak of this to you, dear friends, this afternoon, because, though you have not received the full gift of Holy Orders, yet you have come to receive a special licence or commission from the Church to enable you to take a share in her ministration, more especially in the ministry of the Word, in the reading and expounding the Holy Scriptures.

I wanted, therefore, to say to you that, while this licence or commission which you have received should rightly give you a sense of authority and power, and lead you to trust to God's sustaining Presence with you, yet I earnestly hope and trust that this sense of mission will be in each and all not merely an official sense of mission, but what I venture to call a personal sense of message, a feeling of having something you want to say.

Edward King, *Sermons and Addresses*, Longman, 1911, pages 134–5

David Edwards, formerly Dean of Norwich and Provost of Southwark, describes the current position of preaching in the Church of England and sees encouraging signs for the future.

There remains to be considered the greatest Protestant means of grace – the sermon. The traditional Anglican view is that the preacher ought to be the parish priest, and that he ought to be familiar alike with Scripture, with the theological thought of his time, and with the needs of his people as a result of constant visiting. In the midst of many distractions the priest is expected to prepare for the pulpit with great humility, and then when he preaches be humble enough not to 'steal the show' from the Prayer Book worship. This conception of preaching obviously makes great demands of the clergy, and it must be confessed that the actual performance in many pulpits is far short of the ideal. Nevertheless, Anglicanism has proved itself to be not so hostile to true preaching as the Puritans feared. There are to-day significant movements – the super-vision of junior clergy by senior priests in the diocese largely for the sake of their preaching, for example; some use of the laity in the pulpit; a return to the great Biblical themes, getting away from moral exhorta-tions and topical commentaries; greater attention to speaking tech-niques, in an age accustomed to the skills of broadcasters and television personalities; the popularity of Sunday Evensong as a 'preaching ser-vice', perhaps with a sermon of up to half an hour in length, leading into prayer; more frequent preaching at celebrations of the Holy Commu-nion, even if the sermon is only a paragraph long. 'Sir', ran the text affixed to the pulpit of Charles Simeon, 'we would see Jesus'. The Church of England has still far to go before it offers the treasure of Jesus from its pulpits as faithfully as, say, the Church of Scotland, but its laity have never ceased to appreciate faithful preaching, and its priests to-day are increasingly ashamed of unfaithfulness here.

D. L. Edwards, *Not Angels but Anglicans*, SCM Press, 1958, pages 84–5

Those who are often called upon to preach know that it is advisable to have a few adaptable sermons in reserve, following the practice of Canon Chasuble.

My sermon on the meaning of the manna in the Wilderness can be adapted to almost any occasion, joyful, or, as in the present case, dis-tressing. I have preached it at Harvest celebrations, christenings, confir-mations, on days of humiliation and festal days. The last time I delivered it was in the Cathedral, as a charity sermon on behalf of the Society for the Prevention of Discontent Among the Upper Classes.

Oscar Wilde, *The Importance of Being Earnest* (1895)

A more serious thought will close this chapter. Since there have sometimes been disputes about the comparative importance of the Ministry of the Sacrament and the Ministry of the Word, the wise words of Lancelot Andrewes (p. 141), preaching on Easter Day 1620, may effect a sound balance.

It were a folly to fall to comparisons, to set them at odds together these two ways, as the fond fashion now-a-days is, whether is better, Prayer or Preaching; the Word or the Sacraments. What needs this? Seeing we have both, both are ready for us; the one now, the other by-and-by; we may end this question soon. And this is the best and surest way to end it; to esteem of them both, to thank Him for both, to make use of both; having now done with one, to make trial of the other. It may be, who knows? if the one will not work, the other may. And if by the one or by the other, by either if it be wrought, what harm have we? In case it be not, yet have we offered to God our service in both, and committed the success of both to Him. He will see they shall have success, and in His good time, as shall be expedient for us, vouchsafe every one of us as He did Mary Magdalene in the text, 'to know Him and the virtue of His resurrection'; and make us partakers of both, by both the means before remembered, by His blessed word, by His holy mysteries; the means to raise our souls here, the pledges of the raising up of our bodies hereafter. Of both which He make us partakers, Who is the Author of both, Jesus Christ the Righteous.

Lancelot Andrewes, *Sermons*, ed. J. P. Wilson Parker, 1841–3, vol. 3, page 22

9

Pastoral care

Search for the sick, poor, and impotent people of the Parish

The 'Parson' of the parish has been a familiar figure ever since the parochial system was developed in England, as early as the seventh century. In the villages, and also in the towns when urban communities were smaller and more stable, he would be seen weekly in the church and, if he was a conscientious incumbent, almost daily about his rounds. In some parishes he would stay for many years or even for a lifetime. Sometimes a son would succeed his father as curate and then as the incumbent. Living among his people, he might know them through two or three generations, receiving the same persons in baptism, marriage and burial. He would know who was confirmed, who was regular in church attendance, whose way of life seemed to need his rebuke. In the more remote places he might be the only learned man in the parish. Where there was no local doctor, teacher or lawyer, people would turn to him for advice in more than spiritual matters. After the clergy were allowed to marry, the parson's family often played a large part in parish life, helping with visits, providing poor relief when public assistance was doubtful and grudging, and trying to organise some kind of school. Visiting, either for specific care or general inquiry, was easier than it is now. He or his family could walk or ride around the parish at leisure, and be reasonably sure of finding at least the woman of the house at home during the day.

The clergy did not come into existence as a new species. They inherited a position which was generally taken over smoothly despite changes in liturgy and the patronage system. Chaucer's Poor Parson in the *Canterbury Tales* is perhaps an idealised portrait, but he shows what many of the best clergy did in practice, and which their post-Reformation successors continued. He anticipates the pattern given by Herbert and Ken, below.

He was benign, extremely diligent,
Patient in every bad predicament –
Adversity was often on him laid.
He did not like to curse for tithes unpaid,
But rather would have given, without doubt,
To poor folk in his parish round about,
Both from church offerings and his private store,
For little wealth gave him enough, and more.
His parish wide, with houses far asunder –
But he'd not fail in either rain or thunder,
In sickness or distress, to visit duly
The farthest in his parish, high or lowly,
Going on foot, and in his hand a stave.
This fine example to his sheep he gave
That first he acted, afterwards he taught
In words which from the Gospel he had caught.

Geoffrey Chaucer, *The Canterbury Tales: General Prologue*,
lines 477–99 (Editor's translation)

This fourteenth-century priest would recognise a brother nearly four hundred years later, as described by Oliver Goldsmith:

His pity gave ere charity began.
Thus to relieve the wretched was his pride,
And e'en his failings leaned to Virtue's side;
But in his duty prompt at every call,
He watched and wept, he prayed and felt, for all.
And, as a bird each fond endearment tries
To tempt its new-fledged offspring to the skies,
He tried each art, reproved each dull delay,
Allured to brighter worlds, and led the way.
Beside the bed where parting life was laid,
And sorrow, guilt, and pain by turns dismayed,
The reverend champion stood. At his control
Despair and anguish fled the struggling soul;
Comfort came down the trembling wretch to raise,
And his last faltering accents whispered praise.

The Deserted Village (1770), *Goldsmith's Complete Poetical
Works*, Oxford University Press, 1906, pages 27–8

This was the good side, a vocation which was often at least partly fulfilled. It was not a consistent picture, for clergy than and now are seldom either earthly saints or depraved characters. There were great inequalities of income for incumbents until well into the nineteenth century, while assistant curates were always poor and, without patronage, might never rise to have their own parish. The records of good priests, and there were many even at times when religious fervour seemed to be generally lacking, have to be taken together with stories of neglect, indifference and incompetence. On the bad side there was pluralism: a priest, holding more than one benefice, sometimes together with a cathedral prebend or even a bishopric, leaving parish duties to an underpaid and sometimes ignorant curate. The holder of even a single benefice, if it was a rich one, might also be absent for much of the year and leave all to his hired assistant. One such was satirised in fiction by Anthony Trollope.

> Among the greatest of the diocesan sinners in this respect was Dr. Vesey Stanhope. Years had now passed since he had done a day's duty; and yet there was no reason against his doing duty except a want of inclination on his own part. He held a prebendal stall in the diocese; one of the best residences in the close; and the two large rectories of Crabtree Canonicorum, and Stogpingum. Indeed, he had the cure of three parishes, for that of Eiderdown was joined to Stogpingum. He had resided in Italy for twelve years. His first going there had been attributed to a sore throat; and that sore throat, though never repeated in any violent manner, had stood him in such stead, that it had enabled him to live in easy idleness ever since.

Barchester Towers (1857), Oxford University Press, 1998, chapter 9

While the parson's more secular advice might be beneficent in matters of law and learning, there were ways in which his position in the parish might be less admired. With the force of Establishment behind him, he could be seen as the representative of privilege and class hierarchy, even in places where his income might not be much above that of some of his poorest parishioners. Many parsons were Justices of the Peace who sat to determine and punish minor offences, or to remit more serious charge to a trial by jury. If the benefice was in the gift of the Lord of the Manor or the major landowner, it would be a bold priest who would make adverse comment on his doings. There were places where the incumbent was also a powerful landlord: the 'Squarson' was seldom popular. There was also the burden of the tithes, which Chaucer's Poor Parson was unwilling to exact by threat of excommunication. This complicated system of levy on agricultural produce was usually commuted to a fixed, but still unwelcome, money payment. The obligation was not completely abolished until the twentieth century. The fact that in many parishes the incumbent received only the 'small tithes' did not lessen resentment against him. Church Rates for parochial repairs and maintenance were levied on occupiers of land in the parish until 1868.

Despite their special status, the clergy were not of a different breed from other men, or totally remote from the society of their times. In schools and universities they were educated with those who would follow many other callings, keeping company with a range of social classes from nobleman to the 'servitors' and 'sizars' who made their way to a degree by doing menial work for the more privileged. In their parishes they read the same newspapers and heard the same facts and rumours as other people. They held opinions on the political and social questions of the time and were affected by economic changes. The idea that the clergy know little of the 'real' world and are not subject to the prejudices and passions of laypople still persists to this day.

Since history tends to record the extreme cases, both in fact and in fiction, it is well to remember that most parsons fulfilled most of their duties most of the time. Books to guide pastoral work, and bishops' charges to their diocesan clergy may aim high, but there is no reason to suppose that they were impossibly idealistic. The liminal moments of life, the rites of passage, the unheralded misfortunes, were provided for in the Book of Common Prayer. Babies were baptised soon after birth, their mothers churched a few weeks later. When the child was capable of learning, he or she would be taught the Catechism and presented to the bishop for confirmation. Marriage followed for most, beginning again the cycle of birth and growth. Illness was frequent, usually sudden, and often fatal. The office for the Visitation of the Sick is intimidating to modern ears and looks more towards death than recovery. When death came, the rite of burial – there was no cremation until late in the nineteenth century – was provided.

It is often the little things rather than the great events which give a true picture of the past. Consider the rubric in the Prayer Book order for the Communion of the Sick. After an initial instruction that 'three, or two at the least' shall communicate with the sick person, there is a further provision:

> In the time of the Plague, Sweat, or other like contagious times of sickness or disease, when none of the Parish or neighbours can be gotten to communicate with the sick in their houses, for fear of the infection, upon special request of the diseased the Minister may only communicate with him.

We cannot know how many acts of courage and sacrifice those words imply.

Today the 'Vicar', as clergy of the Church of England are generally known irrespective of proper title, is a less prominent figure in the wide community, and no longer exclusively male. But everyone in the land, churchgoer or not, is a member of a parish and entitled to pastoral care. When it is needed, it is often sought and happily received.

The Ordinal appended to the Book of Common Prayer explains what is expected of the parish clergy, both in pastoral care and sound teaching.

It is his Office, where provision is so made, to search for the sick, poor and impotent people of the Parish, to intimate their states, names, and places where they dwell, unto the Curate, that by his exhortation they may be relieved with the help of the Parishioners, or others.

The Ordering of Deacons 1662

Will you be ready, with all faithful diligence, to banish and drive away all erroneous and strange doctrines contrary to God's word; and to use both publick and private monitions and exhortations, as well to the sick as to the whole, within your Cures, as need shall require, and occasion shall be given?

The Ordering of Priests 1662

George Herbert (p. 79) was a devoted and conscientious priest during his short incumbency at Bemerton. What he wrote has been a model for parish clergy through the centuries.

The Country Parson upon the afternoons in the weekdays, takes occasion sometimes to visit in person, now one quarter of his Parish, now another. For there he shall find his flock most naturally as they are, wallowing in the midst of their affairs, whereas on Sundays it is easy for them to compose themselves to order, which they put on as their holyday clothes, and come to Church in frame, but commonly the next day put off both. When he comes to any house, first he blesseth it, and then as he finds the persons of the house employed, so he forms his discourse. Those that he finds religiously employed, he both commends them much, and furthers them when he is gone, in their employment; as if he finds them reading, he furnisheth them with good books; if curing poor people, he supplies them with Receipts, and instructs them further in that skill, showing them how acceptable such works are to God, and wishing them ever to do the Cures with their own hands, and not to put them over to servants. Those that he finds busy in the works of their calling, he commendeth them also, for it is a good and just thing for every one to do their own business. But then he admonisheth them of two things; first, that they dive not too deep into worldly affairs, plunging themselves over head and ears into carking, and caring; but that they so labour, as neither to labour anxiously, nor distrustfully, nor profanely. Then they labour anxiously, when they overdo it, to the loss of their quiet, and health: then distrustfully, when they doubt God's providence, thinking that their own labour is the cause of their thriving, as if it were in their own hands to thrive, or not to thrive.

George Herbert, *The Country Parson*, ch. 14, F. E. Hutchinson (ed.), *The Works of George Herbert*, Oxford University Press, 1941

This is one of several stories related by his seventeenth-century biographer Izaac Walton which show that Herbert lived up to his own precepts.

There came to him a poor old woman, with an intent to acquaint him with her necessitous condition, as also with some troubles of her mind:

but after she had spoke some few words to him, she was surprised with a fear, and that begot a shortness of breath, so that her spirits and speech failed her; which he perceiving, did so compassionate her, and was so humble, that he took her by the hand, and said, 'Speak, good mother; be not afraid to speak to me; for I am a man that will hear you with patience; and will relieve your necessities too, if I be able: and this I will do willingly; and therefore, mother, be not afraid to acquaint me with what you desire'. After which comfortable speech, he again took her by the hand, made her sit down by him, and understanding she was of his parish, he told her, 'He would be acquainted with her, and take her into his care'. And having with patience heard and understood her wants – and it is some relief for a poor body to be but heard with patience – he, like a Christian clergyman, comforted her by his meek behaviour and counsel; but because that cost him nothing, he relieved her with money too, and so sent her home with a cheerful heart, praising God, and praying for him. Thus worthy, and – like David's blessed man – thus lowly, was Mr. George Herbert in his own eyes, and thus lovely in the eyes of others.

Izaak Walton, *The Life of Mr George Herbert* (1670), Methuen, 1905, pages 72–3

George Herbert might qualify to be nominated as the ideal priest described by Thomas Ken (p. 103).

Give me the priest these graces shall possess –
Of an ambassador the just address.
A father's tenderness, a shepherd's care,
A leader's courage, which the cross can bear;
A ruler's awe, a watchman's wakeful eye,
A pilot's skill, the helm in storms to ply;
A fisher's patience, and a labourer's toil,
A guide's dexterity to disembroil,
A prophet's inspiration from above,
A teacher's knowledge, and a Saviour's love.

Give me the priest, a light upon a hill,
Whose rays his whole circumference can fill;

In God's own word and sacred learning versed,
Deep in the study of the heart immersed;
Who in sick souls can the disease descry,
And wisely for restoratives apply;
To beatific pastures leads his sheep,
Watchful from hellish wolves his fold to keep;
Who seeks not a convenience but a cure,
Would rather souls than his own gain ensure.
Instructive in his visits and converse,
Strives everywhere salvation to disperse;
Of a mild, humble, and obliging heart,
Who with his all will to the needy part;
Distrustful of himself, in God confides,
Daily himself among his flock divides;
Of virtue uniform, and cheerful air,
Fixed meditation, and incessant prayer,
Affections mortified, well-guided zeal,
Of saving truth the relish wont to feel,
Whose province, heaven, all his endeavour shares,
Who mixes with no secular affairs,
Oft on his pastoral amount reflects,
By holiness, not riches, gains respects;
Who is all that he would have others be,
From wilful sin, though not from frailty, free;
Who still keeps Jesus in his heart and head,
Who strives in steps of our Arch-priest to tread,
Who can himself and all the world deny,
Lives pilgrim here, but denizen on high.

Selections from the Poetical Works of Bishop Ken,
Hamilton Adams, 1857, pages 47–8

In his episcopal role, Ken gave advice and instruction to his clergy. He expected a serious keeping of Lent, an observance which tended to lose some of its previous solemnity until its revival in the nineteenth century by the followers of the Oxford Movement. His mention of 'poor Protestant strangers' refers to the Huguenots who fled from France after the revocation of the Edict of Nantes in 1685.

Remember that to keep such a fast as God has chosen, it is not enough for you to afflict your own soul, but you must also according to your ability, 'deal your bread to the hungry': and the rather, because we have not only usual objects of charity to relieve, but many poor Protestant strangers are now fled hither for sanctuary, whom as brethren, as members of Christ, we should take in and cherish. That you may perform the office of a publick intercessor the more assiduously, I beg of you to say daily in your closet, or in your family, or rather in both, all this time of abstinence, the 51st Psalm, and the other prayers which follow it in the Commination. I could wish also that you would frequently read and meditate on the Lamentations of Jeremy, which holy Gregory Nazienzen was wont to do, and the reading of which melted him into the like lamentations as affected the prophet himself when he penned them. But your greatest zeal must be spent for the publick prayers, in the constant and devout use of which, the publick safety, both of Church and State, is highly concerned: be sure then to offer up to God every day the Morning and Evening Prayer, offer it up in your family at least, or rather as far as your circumstances may possibly permit, offer it up in the Church, especially if you live in a great town, and say over the Litany every morning during the whole of Lent. This I might enjoin you to do, on your canonical obedience, 'but for love's sake I rather beseech you', and I cannot recommend to you a more devout and comprehensive form of penitent and public intercession than this or more proper for the season.

The Prose Works of Thomas Ken, Rivington, 1838, pages 476–7

The pastoral office is not fulfilled only by works of mercy, important though these are. In the words of the Ordinal, the priest must be ready 'with all faithful diligence, to banish and drive all erroneous and strange doctrines contrary to God's word; and to use both publick and private monitions and exhortations, as well to the sick as to the whole'. The charge given by Bishop Simon Patrick (p. 97) to the clergy of Chichester in 1692 might seem intimidating to the present-day incumbent, but it is a duty which should still not be neglected. In the last paragraph Patrick reminds his clergy of the special privilege of belonging to the Church of England.

In particular, you ought to warn your people of the heavy judgements of God which the sins of the land give us just cause to apprehend; and that the rather since God has spared us so long, whilst he has visited so many nations round about us in so terrible a manner, and has given us so great a measure of the light of the gospel, and so long a course of temporal as well as spiritual blessings.

And frequently set forth to them the heinousness of such sins as you find do most abound among them, whether they be the crying ones related to in the acts of parliament lately sent you, or others. You ought to represent to them the high contempt done to God when men make their bodies, which ought to be temples for God to dwell in by his Spirit, the members of a harlot; and the indignity done their own natures when by the excesses of drinking a man has changed himself into a beast.

You ought to show them what a horrible affront it is to Almighty God to profane his holy name by rash and vain swearing, and what a dreadful thing it is to swear falsely, even in common discourse, but much more when it is before a judge.

You ought to set often before your people the great wickedness of lying and slander, of falsehood and injustice, and of all cheating and oppression, and that in all cases of wrong done their neighbours there is no repentance that is acceptable to God, but that which is accompanied with restitution or reparation, as far as the party can possibly make it.

You are often to represent to your people the indispensable necessity of true holiness, without which no man can see God, and without which, their believing a true faith, and their being of a true church, cannot serve them in any stead. For we are assured from the word of God, that not only idolaters, but fornicators and adulterers, thieves, covetous persons, drunkards, revilers and extortioners, cannot enter into the kingdom of God.

Put them often in mind of the importance of the word-reformed churches, which imports, that as our doctrine and worship are by the blessing of God reformed, so our lives ought also to be reformed; otherwise all the advantages that we have of light and truth beyond other churches will rise up in judgement against us if we do not live suitably to them.

The Works of Simon Patrick, ed. A. Taylor, Oxford University Press, 1858, vol. 9, pages 338–9

The Office for the Visitation of the Sick in the Book of Common Prayer seems harsh and judgemental to the modern mind, with its implication that illness may well be the result of sin and its is likely to be terminal – the latter was probably true for much of the past. But offered with pastoral concern it brought comfort to generations. Jeremy Taylor (p. 36) advised that it was not only for the dying and that even in days of primitive medicine people did recover. It is a fact to this day that some people, often not frequent churchgoers, regard the coming of a priest to a sick person as a dangerous last resort.

Let the Minister of religion be sent to, not only against the agony of death, but be advised within the whole conduct of the sickness; for in sickness indefinitely, and therefore *in every sickness,* and therefore in such which are not mortal, which end in health, which have no agony, or final temptations, St James gives the advice and the sick man being bound to require them, is also tied to do it, when he can know them, and his own necessity. It is a very great evil both in the matter of prudence and piety, that they fear the Priest as they fear the Embalmer; or the Sexton's spade; and love not to converse with him, unless he can converse with no man else; and think his office so much to relate to the other world, that he is not to be treated with, while we hope to live in this; and indeed that our religion be taken care of, only when we die; and the event is this, (of which I have seen some sad experience) that the man is deadly sick, and his reason is useless, and he is laid to sleep, and his life is in the confines of the grave, so that he can do nothing towards the trimming of his lamp; and the Curate shall say a few prayers by him, and talk to a dead man, and the man is not in a condition to be helped; but in a condition to need it hugely. He cannot be called upon to confess his sins; and he is not able to remember them, and he cannot understand an advice, nor hear a free discourse, nor be altered from a passion, nor cured of his fear, nor comforted upon any grounds of reason or religion, and no man can tell what is likely to be his fate; or if he does, he cannot prophesy good things concerning him, but evil; Let the spiritual man come when the sick man can be conversed withal, and instructed; when he can take medicine and amend; when he understands, or can be taught to understand the case of his soul, and the rules of his conscience; and then his advice may turn into advantage; it cannot otherwise be useful.

The intercourses of the Minister with the sick man have so much variety in them that they are not to be transacted at once: and therefore they do not well that send once to see the good man with sorrow, and hear him pray, and thank him and dismiss him civilly, and desire to see his face no more; to dress a soul for funeral is not a work to be dispatched at one meeting. At once he needs a comfort, and anon something to make him willing to die; and by and by he is tempted to impatience, and that needs a special cure, and it is a great work to make his confessions well, and with advantages; and it may be the man is careless and indifferent, and then he needs to understand the evil of his sin, and the danger of his person: and his cases of conscience may be so many and so intricate, that he is not quickly to be reduced to peace; and one time the holy man must pray, and another time he must exhort; a third time administer the holy Sacrament; and he that ought to watch all the periods and little portions of his life, lest he should be surprised and overcome, had need be watched when he is sick, and assisted, and called upon, and reminded of the several parts of his duty, in every instant of his temptation. This article was well provided for among the Easterlings [Eastern Orthodox Church]; for the Priests in their visitations of a sick person did abide in their attendance and ministry for seven days together. The want of this makes the visitations fruitless and the calling of the Clergy contemptible, while it is not suffered to imprint its proper effects upon them that need it in a lasting ministry.

Jeremy Taylor, *Holy Dying*, Clarendon Press, 1989, pages 177–8

One of the most famous and the most endearing of clerical diarists is James Woodforde (1740–1803), Rector of Weston Longeville, Norfolk, from 1774. His diary tells of his social life, with many details of his food and drink, but records also pastoral concern that belies the bad image of the careless eighteenth-century parson.

June 9 [1787] I went and read Prayers again this morning to Mrs Leggatt and administered also the H<oly> Sacrament to her – she was very weak indeed and but just alive. She was sensible and showed marks of great satisfaction after receiving the H<oly> Sacrament. She never received it before. Pray God bless her..

May 8 [1796] By particular desire of Billy Gunton, & which I promised him on Friday last, as this day to administer the H<oly> Sacrament to him, himself with his Mistress Mrs Michael Andrews, came to my House about 11 o'clock this Morning and I then had them into the Parlour and there administered the H<oly> Sacrament to them and which I hope will be attended with due effects both to him, Mrs Andrews & myself. I put on my Gown and Band on the Occasion. Mrs Andrews appeared to pay as much Attention to Billy Gunton, tho' her Servant, as if it was really her own Son – very good of her. It gave me great pleasure, tho' far from well, in doing what I did, as it will ever give me pleasure to do any thing in my power, that may give any satisfaction or ease to any person whatever, especially to the distressed..

James Woodforde, *The Diary of a Country Parson*, Oxford University Press, 1935, pages 304, 522

While the parish priest has sometimes been detached from his parishioners by what was regarded as his superior social status, he has also had to suffer from the snobbery of those who thought themselves above him. Anthony Trollope (1815–82), who depicted more fictional clergy than any other novelist, took a poor view of innovations like theological colleges, whereas previously all that was required had been a classics degree and a quick interview with the ordaining bishop. 'Literates' are clergy who are not university graduates.

There is, alas! a new order of things coming on us which threaten us with some changes, not for the better, in this respect. There are theological colleges here and there, and men and women talk of 'literates'. Who shall dare to say that it may not all be for the best? Who will venture to prophesy that there shall be less energetic teaching of God's word under the new order of things than under the old? But, as to the special man of whom we speak now, the English parish parson, with whom we all love to be on familiar terms – that he will be an altered man, and as a man less attractive, less urbane, less genial – in one significant word, less of a gentleman – that such will be the result of theological colleges and the institution of 'literates', no one who has thought of the subject will have any doubt. And in no capacity is a gentleman more required or more quickly recognised than in that of a parson [...]

But the adult parson of the parish in England – the clergyman who has reached, if I may so say, the full dominion of his quarter-deck – is still customarily a man from Oxford or from Cambridge, and it is of such a one that we speak here. He has probably been the younger son of a squire, or else his father has been a parson, as he is himself. Throughout his whole life he has lived in close communion with rural affairs, and has of them that exact knowledge which close communion only will give. He knows accurately, from lessons which he has learned unknowingly, the extent of the evil and the extent of the good which exists around him, and he adapts himself to the one and to the other. Against gross profligacy and loud sin he can inveigh boldly, and he can make men and women to shake in their shoes by telling them of the punishment which will follow such courses; but with the peccadilloes dear to the rustic mind he knows how to make compromises, and can put up with a little drunkenness, with occasional sabbath-breaking, with ordinary oaths, and with church somnolence. He does not expect much of poor human nature, and is thankful for moderate results. He is generally a man imbued with strong prejudice, thinking ill of all countries and all religions but his own; but in spite of his prejudices he is liberal, and though he thinks ill of men, he would not punish them for the ill that he thinks. He has something of bigotry in his heart, and would probably be willing, if the times served his purpose, to make all men members of the Church of England by Act of Parliament; but though he is a bigot, he is not a fanatic, and as long as men will belong to his Church, he is quite willing that the obligations of that Church shall sit lightly upon them.

Anthony Trollope, *Clergymen of the Church of England* (1866), Trollope Society,
no date, pages 59–62

Parish priests today face challenges and problems unknown to their predecessors. Yet there must be still the same care for souls and bodies, the same variety of ministry in sorrow and joy. Barney Milligan, an experienced parish priest in England, Canon of St Alban's and chaplain overseas, tells of duties far removed from those which George Herbert knew, yet witnessing to the continuity of pastoral care through the centuries.

There are also ideas which people hold which the parson has, if not to accept, at least to work with, when he rejects them himself or even regards them as superstitious. There can be a spiritual snobbery which runs counter to the very heart of true pastoral care, and which can make people feel very silly when they falteringly offer their views – perhaps on the baptism of dangerously ill babies, or on a very literal Bible interpretation. Availability means taking people as they are. It means answering calls on the doorstep, or from homes or hospitals or referrals. It means dealing efficiently with requests for baptism or marriage or funerals, and spending time with the people. It means calling on people on their birthdays or wedding anniversaries. It means sharing in the real life of the real people, because they are great, and because they have the potential of being even greater, and because you like them and enjoy their company and believe in them. And then, whether or not the priest 'does any good', he will undoubtedly be invigorated and refreshed, and his organisation and his prayers will he earthed. If others with administrative responsibilities – in education or medicine or business or in government service – had to spend as much time on the ground floor as we do, it would benefit greatly themselves and those they serve.

A day's work which contains so much variety and contrast is not a soft option. Compared with a civil servant or a doctor or a bus driver, it can sometimes feel very disjointed. There is no such thing as a typical day; only very rarely is a parson able to stick at one job. More often it is one or two hours' prayer, reflection, reading, or conducting a service; half an hour at the cemetery; half an hour at the pub; two hours at a factory or a hospital; three hours in the office – working on parish nuts and bolts or planning some new initiative in the community or having a staff meeting or seeing people who call, or more commonly several of these jobs; an hour visiting people in their homes; two hours at a meeting in the evening [. . .] There are almost bound to be several complete changes of mood. Wholehearted attention has to be given to people and issues which vary dramatically.

But what could appear to be – and sometimes feels – very draining can also be refreshing: an afternoon in the hospital usually puts the frustrations of administration in perspective. What can – and on some days does – feel unrelated is actually all part of a unified purpose. And if one has confidence in that purpose, and believes that the parish machine is worth administering efficiently and not just an archaism to be reluctantly 'propped up', then, although the job will be demanding, it will also be invigorating.

Barney Milligan, *The Priest and the World*, SPCK, 1974, pages 32–3

John Whale, journalist and writer, compiled a history of the incumbents of St Mary's Church, Barnes, where he was once churchwarden. In his closing words he suggests a pattern for future parochial ministry which is a long way from the 'squarson'.

What sort of figure, then, ought to be the pattern for late-twentieth-century parsons? When a sequel to this book comes to be written in a hundred years' time, who will deserve the writer's and the reader's admiration?

He – or she – will be a servant of God. As such, his rank among his own parishioners will have little interest for him. The standing which comes with wealth he will never have expected; but he will disclaim, too, any special status as the steward of a mystery. Wherever he can, in the church's affairs, he will discern the talent in members of his congregation and enable them to use it. He will know his own, and trust them. Even in the sphere of worship and doctrine he will press his own judgement only sparingly, and submit it from time to time to the unofficial audit of his congregation's approval. As a sign, he will at the outset voluntarily divest himself of the parson's freehold, his peculiar impregnability to dismissal: he will undertake to reopen the question of his future at set intervals. He will thus be, and be seen to be, as other men are; and the release from any implicit claim to superhuman capacities will do much for his usefulness and contentment.

But the chief expression of his love of God will be a love of truth. He will already be an educated man, able to follow an argument and to set it out intelligibly in the written and the spoken word. He will keep up his reading in theology and the related disciplines, laying the fruits of it constantly before his parishioners, so that they can keep or learn a faith which has point for the world they live in. He will give thanks for congregations and incumbents of the past, for the continuity of belief which has brought him to that place; but his eye will be on the believers of his own time. In all this, being human, he will fall short; yet even to attempt it will earn him an honourable place in his church's history.

John Whale, One Church, One Lord, SCM Press, 1979, pages 166–7

10

Prayer

Assist us mercifully, O Lord, in these our supplications and prayers

The imposition of a set and authorised liturgy after the Reformation might seem to give less importance to personal and unwritten prayers. The Book of Common Prayer provides some additional prayers and thanksgivings for particular occasions, including the admirable General Thanksgiving which first appeared in 1662, and some collects to be said after Ante-communion when there has been no full celebration. The 1928 Book allowed the officiant to offer these or others 'authorised by the bishop' after the Third Collect at Morning and Evening Prayer. In practice, the usage of adding other prayers at this point was accepted long before the *Alternative Service Book* gave more freedom, including lay intercessions at the Eucharist, and *Common Worship* has even more scope for private initiative. Within these rules, the daily offices and the communion service encouraged more personal lay participation than had the older orders. The obligation on the clergy to say Matins and Evensong daily added the rubric that the church bell should be rung to call people to worship. The services have clear instructions to congregations to join in the prayers at certain points, to make a collective confession and give responses to versicles.

There was certainly for a long time a distrust of extemporary prayer in public worship. In the sixteenth and seventeenth centuries it was opposition to 'prophesyings', free prayer in unauthorised gatherings not held in the parish church. In the eighteenth century it was a fear of 'enthusiasm', ecstatic utterances breaching the Anglican code of moderation, a charge often brought against the early Methodists. But some faithful members of the Church with an Evangelical persuasion were drawn to prayer meetings with extempore lay offerings.

Yet the practice of personal prayer grew after the Reformation.

Personal devotion and responsibility for spiritual progress had certainly not been neglected in the previous century. Various primers, short books of prayers and basic instruction for the laity, were widely used, but the emergent Church of England was influenced by two new forces. One was the increased call to personal piety and devotion, not to gain merit but as a proof and thanksgiving for salvation through faith. The other was the wider gift of the Renaissance in creating an increased sense of individuality, an acceptance of being a private person as well as a member of a community, both a liberation and a challenge. New books of prayer were printed to replace the old primers, now rejected because of their use of indulgenced prayers and dubious legends of the saints. In 1545 the King's Primer was issued, with the Litany in English composed in the previous year and various prayers in the new reformed mode. Another Primer in 1553 was more clearly an individual companion to the Second Book of Common Prayer. These new primers had some success, but the Prayer Book itself soon proved its worth for private as well as public devotion. The daily offices could be, and were, read in family gatherings or by individuals alone. Learning the collect for the week was a task imposed on children in some pious households which, however unwillingly undertaken, produced a store of prayers in personal memories for the rest of their lives. When the Prayer Book was proscribed under the Commonwealth, many took the risk of using it in their own homes.

Other books of prayers for personal use soon followed, works by Lancelot Andrewes, William Laud and John Cosin as well as other less prominent seventeenth-century Anglican divines. The practice of prayers throughout the day was recommended in this period, becoming rather less regarded in the next century until the Evangelical Movement brought some Anglicans into a habit of devotion which by then was more familiar among Nonconformists. Family prayers became more widespread, using the Book of Common Prayer, or one of the many books written for the purpose, usually supplemented by extemporary prayer for the needs of the day. One of the most popular, Henry Thornton's *Family Prayers*, is cited below. The language of the Book of Common Prayer and the Authorised Version, established as the English religious style (see Toon, p. 130) was generally used for such forms of worship, which were by no means confined to Evangelical or notably pious families. In 1804 Thomas Burgess, Bishop of St David's, a High

Churchman, required that priests in his diocese should promise 'to promote among my parishioners the duty of family prayer' and to promise that 'I will not fail to have daily prayer in my own family'.

The technique and methods of prayer received comparatively little attention among Anglicans. There was a certain distrust of the elaborate exercises typical of post-Tridentine Roman Catholicism, and prayers for private use were generally distinguished by the sense of reserve which was advised for preaching and religious discussions (see p. 139). Although the writers of the Oxford Movement were proponents of this attitude, their successors rediscovered the Roman practices which had hitherto been spurned or ignored. Anglo-Catholic piety had recourse to books of prayer derived from Roman Catholic practice; exercises like novenas, litanies of the saints and the Rosary supplanted in some quarters the more austere and direct expression of spirituality. Even systems and methods like the Ignatian Exercises came into favour. At the same time, the attraction to Orthodoxy, which had for long been admired by some Anglicans as an alternative form of catholic Christianity, drew attention to a type of prayer unfamiliar to most English speakers. John Mason Neale (1818–66) translated, from both Latin and Greek originals, hymns which became Anglican favourites such as 'Jerusalem the golden' and 'Christian dost thou see them'. William Bright (1824–1901), also a writer of hymns, translated a number of ancient collects into the English religious idiom which was familiar to his compatriots.

With so many and so various approaches across the centuries, it is difficult to define the nature of Anglican prayer. There has certainly been a sense of prayer as a natural activity, proper and necessary to believers, to be practised reverently but not distantly. Perhaps intimate converse controlled by solemnity is a possible description. It feels a strong sense of the nearness of God, notably expressed by seventeenth-century writers like Herbert, Vaughan and Traherne. It seeks to be informed, to be based on biblical revelation, but to blend the intellectual and the intuitive, to reach out and build upon what has already been made personal. It fears the cold and casual approach, the repetition of set forms without conscious faith and present application, a danger which has not always been avoided, and which has been noticed by both admirers and critics of the Church's formal liturgy. It is inseparable from the desire for personal holiness which is examined in Chapter 11.

Richard Hooker (p. 10), with characteristic appeal to reason, considers some of the essential qualities of prayer.

Of prayer there are two uses. It serveth as a mean to procure those things which God hath promised to grant when we ask; and it serveth as a mean to express our lawful desires also towards that, which whether we shall have or no, we know not, till we see the event. Things in themselves unholy or unseemly, we may not ask; we may whatsoever, being not forbidden, either Nature or Grace shall reasonably move us to wish as importing the good of men; albeit God himself have nowhere by promise assured us of that particular which our prayer craveth. To pray for that which is in itself, and of its own nature, apparently a thing impossible, were not convenient. Wherefore, though men do without offence wish daily that the affairs which with evil success are past, might have fallen out much better; yet to pray that they may have been any other than they are, this being a manifest impossibility in itself, the rules of Religion do not permit. Whereas contrariwise, when things of their own nature contingent and mutable, are by the secret determination of God appointed one way, though we the other way make our prayers, and consequently ask those things of God, which are by this supposition impossible, we notwithstanding do not hereby in prayer transgress our lawful bounds.

The Works of Richard Hooker, Clarendon Press, 1820, vol. 2, page 182

John Donne (p. 12), preaching on Candlemas Day in 1623, utters the thought which appears in many writers on the subject of prayer. It draws the individual soul closer to God, and develops the state of perpetual devotion.

That soul that is accustomed to direct herself to God, upon every occasion, that, as a flower at Sun-rising, conceives a sense of God, in every beam of his, and spreads and dilates itself towards him, in a thankfulness, in every small blessing that he sheds upon her; that soul, that as a flower at the Sun's declining, contracts and gathers in, and shuts up herself, as though she had received a blow, whensoever she hears her Saviour wounded by an oath, or blasphemy, or execration; that soul, who, whatsoever string be strucken in her, base or treble, her high or her low estate, is ever tuned toward God, that soul prays sometimes when it does not know that it prays.

John Donne, *Selected Prose*, ed. E. Simpson, Clarendon Press, 1967, page 224

In contrast, but not in contradiction, to the many attempts to analyse and direct the process of prayer, George Herbert (p. 79) in a sequence of poetic images draws both public and private prayer into the eternal presence of God. The poem itself can be a profound source of meditation.

Prayer, the Church's banquet, Angels' age,
God's breath in man returning to his birth,
The soul in paraphrase, heart in pilgrimage,
The Christian plummet sounding heaven and earth;
Engine against the Almighty, sinner's tower,
Reversed thunder, Christ-side-piercing spear,
The six-days world transposing in an hour,
A kind of tune which all things hear and fear;
Softness, and peace, and joy, and love, and bliss,
Exalted Manna, gladness of the best,
Heaven in ordinary, man well dressed,
The milky way, the bird of Paradise,
Church-bells beyond the stars heard, the soul's blood,
The land of spices; something understood.

George Herbert, 'Prayer', F. E. Hutchinson (ed.), *The Works of George Herbert*, Oxford University Press, 1941

Matthew Hale (1609–76) was Lord Chief Justice of England and wrote extensively on legal subjects. He was also a devout Anglican and a poet. He writes of prayer as a natural and essential response to God's revealed love.

The Angels, whose pure nature had no spot
Of sin or fault, and therefore needed not
An expiation; yet when set they were
The tidings of Christ, peace and joy to bear

Which this day dawned to Man, they fill the sky
With acclamations: Glory to God on high,
Peace on the earth, Good Will to Man; thus they
Rejoice to see the spring of others' joy.
And shall the Angels when the news they bring
Of bliss to Man, an heavenly Anthem sing,
And Man be silent? Man of whose only sake
Our blessed Lord did human nature take,
And stooped below the Angels, to install
And place Man in a state Angelical.
Dear Lord! our hearts are narrow, let thy love
Fill and enlarge their compass, and inspire
Their due returns, that as Thy love's extent
Did cause that strange and wonderful descent
Of Heaven to Earth, so it again may raise
Our Earth to Heaven, our Hearts to Thee in praise.

Matthew Hale, 'Christmas Day 1655', *The Works of
Matthew Hale*, R. White, 1805, vol. 2, page 607

*John Cosin (p. 45) tried to reconcile the Presbyterian delegates at the Savoy
Conference in those discussions, but was probably influenced by the excesses
of some of the Commonwealth sects in his cautious approach to personal
extempore prayer. He adduces several reasons why the approved prayers of
the Church are to be preferred.*

The first is, to continue and preserve the authority of the ancient laws,
and old godly canons of the Church, which were made and set forth for
this purpose, that men, before they set themselves to pray, might know
what to say, and avoid, as near as might be, all extemporal effusions of
irksome and indigested prayers, which they use to make that herein are
subject to no good order or form of words, but pray both what, and how,
and when they list. [...]

And let them consider, that, when Christ had bidden us enter into our
chamber and pray *privately*, presently He sets us a *form* to pray by, even
there in secret, St. Matt. vi. 6. 7. 9. By which passages, those prayers are
chiefly allowed and recommended unto us, (for all sudden and godly

ejaculations are not to be condemned,) which with good advice and meditation are framed beforehand by them that best know what belong thereunto: that so, through this means, the worthiest part of our Christian duty to God-ward might suffer no such scandal and disgrace as otherwise it is forced to do; and that when we speak to, or call upon the awful Majesty of Almighty God, we might be sure to speak in the grave and pious language of Christ's CHURCH, which hath evermore been guided by the Spirit of God, the Holy Ghost; and not to lose ourselves with confusion in any sudden, abrupt, or rude dictates, which are framed by private spirits, and ghosts of our own. In regard whereof, our very priests and deacons themselves are, for their private and daily prayers, enjoined to say the Morning and Evening Devotions of the Church; and when at any time they pray, or bid the prayers before their Sermons, there is a set form of words prescribed for them to use; that they also might know it is not so lawful for them to pray of their own heads, or suddenly to say what they please themselves.

John Cosin, *Works*, Parker, 1855, pages 89–90

A similar line was followed by Robert Sanderson (p. 42). He does not condemn extempore prayer but, addressing his clergy, warns against making it a matter of pride and emulation.

A thing I the rather note, because the fault is so frequent in practice, and yet very rarely observed, and more rarely reprehended. God hath endowed a man with good abilities and parts in some kind or other: I instance but in one gift only for example's sake, viz. an ability to enlarge himself in prayer readily, and with fit expressions upon any present occasion. Being in the ministry or other calling, he is careful to exercise his gift by praying with his family, praying with the sick, praying, with other company upon such other occasions as may fall out. He thinketh, and he thinketh well, that if he should do otherwise or less than he doth, he should not be able to discharge himself from the guilt of unfaithfulness, in not employing the talent he hath received to the best advantage, when the exercise of it might redound to the glory of the Giver. Hitherto he is in the right: so long as he maketh his gift a rule but to himself. But now if this man shall stretch out this rule unto all his brethren in the same calling, by imposing upon them a necessity of doing the like; if he shall expect or exact from them, that they should also be able to commend unto God the necessities of their families, or the state of a sick person, or the like, by extemporary prayer; but especially if he shall judge or censure them that dare not adventure so to do, of intrusion into or of unfaithfulness in their callings, he committeth a great fault, and well deserving a sharp reprehension.

Works of Robert Sanderson, Oxford University Press, 1854, vol. 2, page 96

Henry Hammond (p. 13), writing in 1694, includes the subject of prayer in a book of catechetical instruction. The catechist replies to the question, 'How many sorts of prayer are there?' The importance of the family is made clear, though the modern reader may find the emphasis at this point too patriarchal.

There is first, prayer of the heart, and of the tongue. Prayer of the tongue when the soul sighs out its desires unto God; and of the tongue added to that, which is then vocal prayer. Secondly, there is either public or private prayer. Public of two sorts. First, in the church; secondly in the family. In the church, or meeting together of all that will join us, called together by tolling of a bell. And this is very useful and necessary, for the public testimony of our piety; for the stirring up and inflaming of others; for the making of those common public requests wherein all that meet are concerned, as for all men, the whole Church, the rulers and magistrates of that community wherein we live, for pardon of sins, the gift of grace, preservation from danger, and all other things that as fellow-members of a Church or state we may stand in need of; for the prevailing with God, (the union of so many hearts being most likely to prevail, and the presence of some godly, to bring down mercies on those others whose prayers for themselves have no promise to be heard,) especially if performed by a consecrated person, whose office it is to draw nigh unto God, i.e. to offer up prayers &c. to Him, and to be the ambassador and messenger between God and man: God's ambassador to the people, in God's stead, beseeching them, to be reconciled; and the people's ambassador to God, to offer up our requests for grace, for pardon, for mercies to Him. Then in the family which is a lesser congregation, the master or father of which is to supply the place of the priest, and to provide the spiritual food for all that are under his power and charge, as well as their corporeal food, and to ask those things which in that relation of members of the same family are discerned to be most needful for all there present. Then for private prayer, that is of two sorts again; either of husband and wife together, who are as it were one flesh, and have many relations common to one another, and yet distinct and peculiar from all others; or of every man and woman single or private from all others, in the closet, or other place of retiredness.

Henry Hammond, *A Practical Catechism*, Parker, 1847, pages 222–3

Jeremy Taylor (p. 36) commends the practice of frequent short prayers in a busy day.

In the midst of the works of thy calling, often retire to God in short prayers and ejaculations; and those may make up the want of those larger portions of time, which, it may be, thou desirest for devotion, and in which thou thinkest other persons have advantage of thee; for so thou reconcilest the outward work and thy inward calling, the church and the commonwealth, the employment of the body and the interest of thy soul: for be sure that God is present at thy breathings and hearty sighings of prayer, as soon as at the longer offices of less busied persons; and thy time is as truly sanctified by a trade, and devout though shorter prayers, as by the longer offices of those whose time is not filled up with labour and useful business.

Jeremy Taylor, *Holy Living*, 'Rules for employing our time', page 7, *The Whole Works of the Right Rev. Jeremy Taylor*, ed. C. P. Eden, Longman, 1862

William Law (p. 121) describes the good effects of regular and frequent intercessory prayer.

A frequent intercession with God, earnestly beseeching Him to forgive the sins of all mankind, to bless them with His providence, enlighten them with His Spirit, and bring them to everlasting happiness, is the divinest exercise that the heart of man can be engaged in.

Be daily, therefore, on your knees, in a solemn deliberate performance of this devotion, praying for others in such forms, with such length, importunity, and earnestness, as you use for yourself; and you will find all little ill-natured passions die away, your heart grow great and generous, delighting in the common happiness of others, as you used only to delight in your own.

For he that daily prays to God, that all men may be happy in Heaven, takes the likeliest way to make him wish for, and delight in their happiness on earth. And it is hardly possible for you to beseech and entreat God to make any one happy in the highest enjoyments of His glory to all eternity, and yet be troubled to see him enjoy the much-smaller gifts of God in this short and low state of human life.

For how strange and unnatural would it be, to pray to God to grant health and a longer life to a sick man, and at the same time to envy him the poor pleasure of agreeable medicines!

Yet this would be no more strange or unnatural than to pray to God that your neighbour may enjoy the highest degrees of His mercy and favour, and yet at the same time envy him the little credit and figure he hath amongst his fellow-creatures.

When therefore you have once habituated your heart to a serious performance of this holy intercession, you have done a great deal to render it incapable of spite and envy, and to make it naturally delight in the happiness of all mankind.

This is the natural effect of a general intercession for all mankind. But the greatest benefits of it are then received, when it descends to such particular instances as our state and condition in life more particularly require of us.

William Law, *A Serious Call to a Devout and Holy Life* (1728), Epworth Press, 1961, page 212

Hannah More (1745–1833) began as a playwright and poet, in the literary circle associated with Samuel Johnson. She was later drawn into the Evangelical Movement, founded schools and other philanthropic enterprises for the poor, and wrote a large number of religious tracts. Here she reflects on 1 Thessalonians 5. 17: 'Pray without ceasing'. Isaac Barrow (1630–77) whom she quotes was a classical and mathematical scholar, Master of Trinity College, Cambridge. One of his pupils was Isaac Newton.

To pray incessantly, therefore appears to be in his [St Paul's] view of the subject, to keep the mind in an habitual disposition and propensity to devotion; for there is a sense in which we may be said to do that which we are *willing* to do, though there are intervals of the thought as well as intermissions of the act; 'as a traveller', says Dr. Barrow, 'may be said to be still on his journey, though he stops to take needful rest, and to transact necessary business'. If he pause, he does not turn out of the way; his pursuit is not diverted, though occasionally interrupted, and unavoidably delayed.

Constantly maintaining the disposition, then, and never neglecting the actual duty; never slighting the occasion which presents itself, nor violating the habit of stated devotion, may, we presume, be called 'to pray without ceasing'. The expression 'watching unto prayer' implies this vigilance in finding, and this zeal in laying hold on these occasions.

The success of prayer, though promised to all who offer it in perfect sincerity, is not so frequently promised to the cry of distress, to the impulse of fear, or the emergency of the moment, as to humble perseverance in devotion; it is to patient waiting, to assiduous solicitation, to unwearied importunity, that God has declared that He will lend His ear, that He will give the communication of His Spirit, that He will grant the return of our requests. Nothing but this holy perseverance can keep up in our minds an humble sense of our dependence. It is not by a mere casual petition, however passionate, but by habitual application, that devout affections are excited and maintained, that our converse with heaven is carried on. It is by no other means that we can be assured, with Saint Paul, that 'we are risen with Christ' but this obvious one, that we thus seek the things which are above; that the heart is renovated, that the mind is lifted above this low scene of things; that the spirit breathes in a purer atmosphere; that the whole man is enlightened, and strengthened, and purified; and that the more frequently, so the more nearly, he approaches to the throne of God. He will find also that prayer not only expresses but elicits the Divine grace.

Works of Hannah More, Cassell, 1830, vol. 11, pages 369–71

Hannah More was writing at a time when family prayers were coming into frequent practice. One of the most popular such book of prayers was written by Henry Thornton (p. 148) with morning and evening prayers for each day through a month. This is an extract from the prayer for Thursday evening in the first week. It is typical of such prayers in its use of the formal religious style of language, its biblical references and echoes of the Book of Common Prayer, and its petition for personal holiness.

Remember not against us the transgressions either of this day or of our former lives; but be Thou pleased to receive us into Thy favour, and to adopt us into Thy family, as members of Christ, as children of God, and heirs of the kingdom of heaven. And vouchsafe unto us the gift of Thy holy Spirit, that we may be enabled to love Thee with all our hearts; and faithfully to perform Thy righteous will. We beseech Thee to renew us in the spirit of our minds. Help us to put off the old man, which is corrupt according to the flesh; and to put on the new man, which is created after Thine own image in righteousness and true holiness. Deliver us from blindness and hardness of heart; from love of this present world; as well as from coldness and indolence in Thy service. May Thy Blessed Spirit produce in us a deep and sincere repentance; and make us fruitful in every good word and work.

We also pray Thee to enable us to put our whole confidence in Thee. May we commit all our concerns into Thy merciful hands, who art ever ready to protect those who truly love and serve Thee. May Thy watchful providence defend us by night and by days in adversity and in prosperity, in sickness and in health; and, whenever the awful hour of our death shall draw near, may we find our consolations in Christ abound.

Henry Thornton, *Family Prayers* (1834), Hatchards, 1869, pages 39–40

Thornton's work remained popular through the nineteenth century. Family prayers, at least in the Church of England, favoured books of this kind, with the head of the household conducting them. The hazard of extempore prayer and free participation was amusingly remembered by George Russell (1853–1919).

After the chapter, my father read one of 'Thornton's Family Prayers', and, indeed, the use of that book was a distinctive sign of true Evangelicalism. Some friends of ours tried extempore prayers, and one worthy baronet went so far as to invite contributions from the servants. As long as only the butler and housekeeper voiced the aspirations of their fellows, all was decorous; but one fine day an insubordinate kitchenmaid took up her parable, saying, 'And we pray for Sir Thomas and her Ladyship too. Oh, may they have new hearts given to them!' The bare idea that there was room for such renovation caused a prompt return to the lively oracles of Henry Thornton.

G. W. E. Russell, *The Household of Faith*, Hodder & Stoughton, 1902, page 24

Henry Venn (1725–97), Fellow of Queens' College, Cambridge and later a parish clergyman, was one of the founders of the evangelical Clapham Sect. Perhaps with an eye to the growth of Unitarianism, he emphasises the need for prayer through Christ.

It is essential to acceptable prayer, that it be offered up in the *name of Christ*, if not immediately addressed to himself. We commit a capital offence when we overlook him. If any man, dare to think thus with himself – The mercy of God is sufficient encouragement to me to pray: I esteem it a disparagement of his goodness to apply to him by a Mediator. I need no one to intercede for me; nor will I be beholden to anything more than my own good qualities and fitness for pardon, to make my peace with God and procure for me the benefit of eternal happiness. Prayer offered up to God upon such principles by any man is as great a *wickedness* as if he blessed an idol.

It is an audacious censure of the divine constitution in the method of saving sinners and rebels. It is, as far as lies in man's power, to pull down the Son of God from his throne, and thrust him out of that highest office of unspeakable, benevolence and glory which he discharges in heaven. It is to treat even the revelation of God with scorn; since the most conspicuous doctrine in the Bible is that Jesus Christ, is the one Mediator between God and man, an advocate with the Father, and a propitiation for sin through faith in his blood, that God might be just, and yet be justifier of all who believe in Jesus.

There is an absolute need, therefore, that in all our approaches to God, we honour the Son, even as we honour the Father by solemnly expressing our dependence on his sacrifice, righteousness, and intercession, as the only means of enjoying the love of God.

Henry Venn, *The Complete Duty of Man* (1763), Longman, 1836, pages 338–9

In his Anglican days, John Henry Newman (p. 16) warned against excessive emotion in prayer and recommended set forms as a safeguard.

Granting there are times when a thankful or a wounded heart bursts through all Forms of prayer, yet these are not frequent. To be excited is not the *ordinary* state of the mind, but the extraordinary, the now and then state. Nay, more than this, it *ought not* to be the common state of the mind; and if we are encouraging, within us this excitement, this unceasing rush and alternation of feeling, and think that this, and this only, is being in earnest in religion, we are harming our minds, and (in one sense) I may even say grieving the peaceful Spirit of God, who would silently and tranquilly work His Divine work in our heads. This, then, is an especial *use* of Forms of prayer, *when* we are in earnest, as we ought always to be; viz. to keep us from self-willed earnestness, to still emotion, to calm us, to remind us what and where we are, to lead us to a purer and serener temper, and to that deep unruffled love of God and man, which is really the fulfilling of the law, and the perfection of human nature.

Then, again, as to the usefulness of Forms, if we are *not* in earnest, this also is true or not, as we may take it. For there are degrees of earnestness. Let us recollect, the power of praying, being a habit, must be acquired, like all other habits, by practice. In order at length to pray well, we must begin by praying ill, since ill is all we can do. Is not this plain? Who, in the case of any other work, would wait till he could do it perfectly, before he tried it? The idea is absurd. Yet these who object to Forms of prayer on the ground just mentioned, fall into this strange error. If, indeed, we could pray and praise God like the Angels, we might have no need of Forms of prayer; but Forms are to teach those who pray poorly to pray better. They are helps to our devotion, as teaching us what to pray for and how, as St. John and our Lord taught their disciples; and, doubtless, even the *best* of us prays but poorly, and *needs* the help of them. However, the persons I speak of, think that prayer is nothing else but the bursting forth of strong feeling, not the action of a habit, but an emotion, and, therefore, *of course* to such men the very notion of *learning* to pray seems absurd. But this indulgence of emotion is in truth founded on a mistake, as I have already said.

J. H. Newman, *Parochial and Plain Sermons* (1834–42), Rivington, 1875,
vol. 1, pages 263–4

Samuel Wilberforce (1805–73), Bishop of Oxford, was the son of the abolitionist William Wilberforce (p. 15). Although his eloquence and his capacity for getting the support of influential people earned him the sobriquet 'Soapy Sam' he was in fact one of the best of the Victorian bishops. He encouraged new developments in the Church, including the appointment of overseas bishops.

What, then, is prayer? it is the conscious drawing near of the soul of a sinful, weak, ignorant, self-willed creature to its holy, loving, all-wise, and almighty Creator. It is the coming of a creature who has a will, and who knows that he has it; who knows that he cannot help willing and choosing, and that, whatever his words may say, or whatever part of him may feel, or whatever he may desire to feel, yet that he, the true creature, is governed by that will of his and that he cannot, at last, choose what it will not; that he may be crushed by force from without, but that by no such force can his will be altered: it is the coming of such a creature as this to God. And it cannot, therefore, be his coming with the *form of* request, and the real meaning, 'Do as Thou wilt in spite of me and my prayers': this cannot be prayer. But neither can it be the drawing near with this request, 'I know what is best for me, and therefore I ask this of Thee whether Thou wilt or not'. This, surely, were no real prayer; this were to put down the Creator from His throne, and to put our own blind and wavering fancy on it in His stead.

If, therefore, neither of these be prayer, what must it be? It must be the approach of one conscious of possessing a will, to the Supreme Will, with this true supplication. 'I have these desires; I cannot still them; and they combine together into the voice of my soul. They grow up into my will, and I cannot choose against my will. Yet I would not set it up against Thy will. Give me the good after which my soul longs; give me the true good, and not the seeming good; all good is in Thee. It is after this that I am inarticulately craving. These desires of good, Thou must satisfy them, and therefore I come to Thee. This will of mine, it is now uncertain, varying, wayward, blind, and passionate. Lord, make it like Thy will. Make it straight, firm, and right.' Now in all this there is a real prayer. This may be the prayer of one who is yet far from having secured the peace and blessedness of a will which is in true harmony with the Will of God. It may be the cry against himself of one deeply conscious of much remaining rebellion – the one true note amidst abounding discords – the reaching out of a withered arm; such an one may truly long for his own straightening, and may thus ask it sincerely of God: and in some measure there must be this character about all real prayer.

And this may be present even in the most particular supplication; even when we go to ask of God some special temporal boon; when we beg of Him the life of some child, the turning aside of some calamity, the averting of some darkness, the gift of some desired object; yet still in the soul of the true child of God there is the calming undersong; this more than a merely negative resigning itself to God; this earnest craving after a straightened, quickened will: even in the trembling of the needle, in the midst of all these desires, still his inmost soul may point to its one right aim; there may be still the one highest longing to find in God the true good, which, with such an apparent reality, seems to be now present in this or that particular object of desire.

Samuel Wilberforce, *Sermons*, London, 1844, pages 153–5

The Anglican distrust of emotional prayer has continued. Edwyn Bevan (1870–1943), Fellow of New College, Oxford, cautioned against abuse of the evangelical notion of fervent 'wrestling in prayer'.

It is probably a mistake in prayer, as in other parts of the religious life, to try to work up emotion. We know to how large an extent emotion is bound to fluctuate according to all sorts of physical processes in our bodies and our environment, while the harmony of our wills with God's might be continuous, but for our own fault. Emotion is a normal part of the religious life, but we had best let it come spontaneously, and, when it comes to bear us in the right direction, thank God for the wind that fills our sails.

This bears on the subject of 'agonising' or 'wrestling' in prayer. I take it that by this phrase is meant prayer accompanied by desire raised to the degree of pain, a consciousness of some obstruction without the removal of which we cannot find ease. I think Christian experience from the New Testament times downwards would lead us to believe that prayer will sometimes take this form in the lives nearest to the spirit of Christ. Perhaps one might find that this particular kind of emotion is aroused when a man of Christ-like temper comes into contact with some form of moral evil. A man, for instance, might normally pray for his son with a placid and happy confidence, but might meet the evil of sin in a form of new horror, if his son were exposed to some special temptation, still more if he yielded to it. It is likely that in such a case his prayer might acquire a new quality of struggle and pain.

It would no doubt be a mistake to suppose that prayer must always have this quality, in order to be effectual, or that one ought to try to create the emotion deliberately when it was not there. But it would, I think, be no less a mistake on the other side to suppose that the quality of struggle and pain when it arises naturally from contact with some fresh manifestation of the evil in the world, should be considered to denote a deficiency of faith. Only in such a case, it must be remembered that the story of Jacob's wrestling with the Divine Stranger, or the parable of the importunate widow, cannot be so pressed in their details as to imply that we have to overcome by the vehemence of desire an unwillingness in God. We wrestle indeed *with God* in so far as the urgent desire is lifted up continuously to Him, and yet the desire, in the case supposed, accords with His own will and comes from Him. The Divine Will 'conquers, being conquered'.

Edwyn Bevan, 'Petition', in *Concerning Prayer*, Macmillan, 1916, pages 204–5

C. P. Hankey was Vicar of St Mary's-the-Less, Cambridge. He asserts that private prayer needs to be rooted in corporate prayer and disciplined through public worship.

The standard type of Christian prayer is common prayer: that is what the Lord taught us not only in the Liturgy, but also in the 'Our Father'. We are to learn how to pray by ourselves by having learned first how to take part in corporate prayer, for it is in that act that we discover how to pray as members of the Body of Christ. If we try to reverse this process – thinking of prayer as being primarily our private communion with God – we shall hardly keep from thinking of common prayer as the gathering of a number of people to say their private prayers together, a thing very difficult to achieve and of doubtful utility.

The objections to corporate prayer which are commonly met with to-day are due in large measure to a reversal of this process. It is indeed difficult to offer private prayers in public. The presence of other people, the necessity for making the concerted movements of the service – these and many other necessaries of common worship distract the individual in his private devotion. One reason for the popularity of Low Mass in Western Europe is the opportunity it provides for undisturbed private prayer. The solemn Eucharist, in which as many as possible, both clergy and laity, have a specific part to perform in the service, and everything is used for worship which can be used for that purpose, is often appreci-ated as an act of congregational worship to be preferred to sung Mattins as the leisurely and not too exacting devotion of the later hours of Sunday morning. But although this whole, corporate, dramatic act is the least inadequate form of worship, not so much because of its dignity as because it is most clearly the act of the whole Christian people, yet many devout church-people express a preference for making their communion at a Low Mass, in spite of its inadequacies and sacer-dotalisms. In effect they are saying 'Since corporate prayer is at times unavoidable, let it be as little distracting as possible; that is what matters most'. This suggests that the task of living in communion and fellowship with one's fellow-men is not particularly difficult or important, and that the final vision of God is to be like a private view of an exhibition of pictures.

It is precisely these difficulties and distractions of common prayer which make it so valuable, and which help to keep Christians within the stream of the catholic and apostolic life. The stuff of religion is not the refined desires and delicate movements of the soul reaching out after spiritual experience as though it were disembodied, but the common things of life – its 'bread and wineness' and the bodies which the Apostle besought his brethren to offer as a living sacrifice, and our human environment which is largely a physical environment. It is out of this stuff that our prayer is made.

We are to learn, then, how to make prayer in private by having learnt
first how to join in common prayer: we do not learn how to take our part
in common prayer by learning first how to pray as individuals. Common
prayer provides the visible setting of the earthly Church and its earthli-
ness, which we have to make ourselves remember when we are praying by
ourselves. That is why the churchman finds corporate prayer so great a
means of grace; but when we use prayer as a means of self-perfection-
praying, in order to make ourselves better – we find common prayer tire-
some. We have forgotten then that 'being made better' is a by-product of
prayer, not its purpose.

C. P. Hankey, in A. C. Hebert (ed.), *The Parish Communion*, SPCK, 1937, pages 152–3

*James Montgomery (1771–1854) wrote a number of hymns which are still
popular, as well as more secular poetry. This piece reminds us that verse can
express devotion in simple and easily remembered language as well as in
deeper and more complex poetry like that of Herbert quoted above.*

Prayer is the soul's sincere desire,
Uttered or unexpressed;
The motion of a hidden fire
That trembles in the breast.

Prayer is the burden of a sigh,
The falling of a tear,
The upward glancing of an eye
When none but God is near.

Prayer is the simplest form of speech
That infant lips can try;
Prayer the sublimest strains that reach
The Majesty on high.

Prayer is the contrite sinner's voice,
Returning from his ways,
While angels in their songs rejoice,
And cry, 'Behold, he prays!'

Prayer is the Christian's vital breath,
The Christian's native air,
His watchword at the gates of death:
He enters heaven with prayer.

The saints in prayer appear as one
In word, and deed, and mind,
While with the Father and the Son
Sweet fellowship they find.

O thou by whom we come to God,
The Life, the Truth, the Way,
The path of prayer thyself hast trod:
Lord, teach us how to pray.

New English Hymnal, Canterbury Press,
1986, no. 442

11

Personal holiness

True holiness and righteousness all the days of our life

At the present time committed members of the Church of England may regret the loss of her prominent place in the life of the country, the decline in church attendance and the growth of secularisation. For many years after the consolidation of the Established Church following the Restoration in 1660, the complaint was often that her official status, with conformity as much a social as a religious observance, was leading to a lack of personal commitment to the demands of the Christian life. As so often, the extent of the problem may have been exaggerated by those who felt strongly and could express their anxiety articulately and publicly. But there was certainly a need, and it is no less today than in the past, for trying to encourage a proper regard for reverence in services and spiritual formation in personal life. The importance of corporate worship, and grace received through the sacraments, is continually emphasised, but mere formal attendance is not enough.

Writers on personal devotion lay much weight on the need for proper preparation before receiving Holy Communion. Infrequent celebrations made it more reasonable to insist on such preparation. When the Tractarians and their successors brought eucharistic worship to the centre, they inherited the earnest devotion of those who had gone before and tried to ensure that it did not fall away among lay communicants. They tended to denigrate the eighteenth-century Church as having been lukewarm and casual. It was true that the outward act of receiving communion had been regarded as a test of orthodoxy and Anglican membership, and of loyal citizenship. It was required of holders of offices under the Crown until 1829. However, there were also notable examples of personal commitment. John Wesley and the 'Holy Club' at Oxford, and Charles Simeon who within three weeks of entering his

Cambridge college bought *The Whole Duty of Man* as a source of devotion to prepare for receiving Communion.

The essence of Anglican personal devotion, in respect of the Eucharist and in other ways, is a strong but moderate commitment. Spiritual writers tried on the one hand to avoid the pious but elaborate Roman Catholic devotional exercises which followed the Tridentine reforms. On the other hand, there was reaction against the lack of formality, and the refusal to admit any source of devotion but the Bible, which were associated with the Puritans and the many sects which sprang up during the Commonwealth. Although the extremes of Calvinism had been eschewed, the Calvinist sense of a constant awareness of faith, of assurance and recollection of one's personal salvation, remained. Most Anglican writers avoided the emphasis on human depravity, a legacy of St Augustine which weighed heavily on both Lutherans and Calvinists after the Reformation. It may fairly be said that Anglicans took their religion cheerfully. The sense of joy and wonder is characteristic of the seventeenth-century poets Herbert, Vaughan and Traherne and of many who came after them. It is a pleasant and laudable feature of the Church of England. Nevertheless, as the gloom of reflecting on total depravity can become stultifying, there is the opposite danger of being so light-hearted as to ignore the serious reality of sin and to worship in a spirit of complacent optimism. The Church of England has had to steer a middle course, to be a Church of the *via media,* in this as in many other ways

There has always been much attention to the importance of the family, of bringing up children instructed and nurtured in the faith, of ordering the household on Christian principles and being aware of its social as well as its personal obligations. A famous early example of this conviction is the community founded in 1625 by Nicholas Ferrar at Little Gidding in Huntingdonshire. Ferrar (1592–1637) was a Cambridge don and a Member of Parliament, who retired to lived in community with his own and other families, following a rule of austere life and regular prayer in the Anglican tradition, a discipline which was seldom observed again until the revival of the religious life in the nineteenth century. The community continued after the death of Ferrar until it was destroyed by a Parliamentarian force in 1646 during the Civil War.

Family life, daily work, the repetitive and seemingly unremarkable routine, have been commended as the sources of private devotion. The call to regard the sanctity of daily life is heard through the centuries of

Anglican devotion. It is not a unique possession: Brother Laurence in his kitchen practised and taught the presence of God in seventeenth-century Roman Catholicism, and he was not alone in his own confession or in the Protestant churches. But perhaps the vernacular liturgy, and the association of Church and State, have helped to lower the barriers between what is commonly thought spiritual and what is commonly thought secular. Seeking holiness in everyday activities and the world around us can bring the danger of losing transcendence, respect for the difference and majesty of God as well as the intimacy and the assurance. The Church of England has been equally rich in writers who have followed the Platonic and Augustinian tradition in which the things of this world are seen as a shadow or imperfect copy of the ultimate reality laid up in heaven. Devotion uses the familiar to try to look behind the veil and gain an apprehension of the divine. Jeremy Taylor among theologians, and Thomas Traherne among poets, are exemplars of this approach, which is not contradictory but complementary to the other.

'Godliness' was the ideal for devout members of the Church of England. After the religious controversies and conflicts of the seventeenth century, its negative counterpart came to be 'enthusiasm', a fear of any lively and public manifestation of religious zeal. It was a charge made against the early Methodists with their open-air revivalist preaching, and against Anglican Evangelicals who seemed to go beyond what was considered a decent moderation in their worship. It is a fear which has been a safeguard against the excesses which could lead to corporate schism and personal imbalance, but is has sometimes seemed to preclude fervent personal devotion. The great spiritual writers of the Church of England have generally recommended moderation as well as earnest faith. The doctrine of Reserve, considered in connection with preaching (p. 149) was applied also to private devotion.

The mainstream Evangelical stress has been not on 'enthusiasm' but on Bible study, serious reflection on sermons both read and heard, and private prayer for the individual and the family. The Book of Common Prayer has been greatly used, both as a direct source and as a model for extemporary prayer following its spirit and idiom. The Tractarians and their Puseyite successors were equally insistent on private prayer but commended other exercises on the Roman model – the rosary, novenas and litanies appeared in manuals of devotion for Anglo-Catholics, together with the practice of fasting and sacramental confession. These things once seemed to be badges of party and aroused suspicion and hostility from opponents. The Church of England's capacity for compromise and reconciliation has brought greater tolerance, and a willingness to explore the way to personal holiness through different traditions.

Serious preparation for receiving Holy Communion was enjoined from the earliest days of the new Prayer Book, although – or perhaps because – celebrations were less frequent than had been customary with the Latin Mass. The Book of Homilies *gives the call in vivid and forceful language; it might do no harm to read it occasionally to present-day congregations.*

Now come therefore, dearly beloved, without delay, and cheerfully enter into God's feasting house, and become partakers of the benefits provided and prepared for you. But see that ye come thither with your holyday garment; not like hypocrites, not of a custom and for manner's sake, not with loathsomeness, as though ye would rather not come than come, if ye were at your liberty. For God hateth and punisheth such counterfeit hypocrites; as appeareth by Christ's former parable. My friend, saith God, how camest thou in without a wedding-garment? And therefore commanded his servants to bind him hand and foot, and to cast him into utter darkness; where shall be weeping and wailing, and gnashing of teeth. To the intent that ye may avoid the like danger at God's hand, come to the church on the holy day, and come in your holy day garment; that is to say, come with a cheerful and a godly mind; come to seek God's glory and to be thankful unto him; come to be at one with thy neighbour, and to enter into friendship and charity with him. Consider that all thy doings stink before the face of God, if thou be not in charity with thy neighbour. Come with an heart sifted and cleansed from worldly and carnal affections and desires; shake off all vain thoughts, which may hinder thee from God's true service. The bird, when she fly, shaketh her wings. Shake and prepare thyself to fly higher than all the birds in the air; that, after thy duty duly done in this earthly temple and church, thou mayest fly up, and be received into the glorious temple of God in heaven, through Christ Jesus Lord: to whom, with the Father and the Holy Ghost be all glory and honour. Amen.

Sermons and Homilies Appointed to be read in Churches (1562), Prayer Book and
Homily Society, 1840, page 348

The same feeling of awe and solemnity is expressed in one of the splendid prayers of Lancelot Andrewes (p. 141). Reverence for the Eucharist was strongly urged in the Church of the early seventeenth century.

We then also, O sovereign Lord, in the presence of Thy holy mysteries, making mention of the salutary sufferings of Thy Christ, of His life-giving Cross, most precious death, three days' sepulture, resurrection from the dead, ascension into heaven, session at the right hand of Thee, the Father, His glorious and fearful return, beseech Thee, O Lord, that we, receiving in the pure testimony of our conscience, our portion of Thy sacred things, may be made one with the holy Body and Blood of Thy Christ; and receiving them not unworthily, may have Christ dwelling in our hearts, and may become a temple of Thy Holy Spirit. Yea, O our God! nor hold any of us guilty of Thy aweful and heavenly mysteries, nor infirm in soul or body from partaking of them unworthily. But grant us until our last and closing breath worthily to receive the hope of Thy holy things, for sanctification, enlightening, strengthening, a relief of the weight of my many sins, a preservative against all Satanic working, a riddance and hindrance of my evil conscience, a mortification of my passions, a keeping of Thy commandments, an increase of Thy divine grace; and a securing of Thy kingdom.

Lancelot Andrewes, *Sermons*, ed. J. P. Wilson Parker, 1841–3, pages 79–80

This poem by George Herbert (p. 79) has become a well known and loved hymn. It is a powerful meditation on the holiness of the little things as images of the divine, and the rewards of spiritual insight in daily living.

Teach me, my God and King,
In all things thee to see,
And what I do in any thing
To do it as for thee.

Not rudely, as a beast,
To rush into an action
But still to make thee prepossessed,
And give it his perfection.

A man that looks on glass,
On it may stay his eye;
Or if he pleaseth, through it pass,
And then the heaven espy.

All may of thee partake
Nothing can be so mean,
Which with this tincture (for thy sake)
Will not grow bright and clean.

A servant with this clause
Makes drudgery divine.
Who sweeps a room, as for thy laws,
Makes that and th' action fine.

This is the famous stone
That turneth all to gold:
For that which God doth touch and own
Cannot for less be told.

George Herbert, 'The Elixir', F. E. Hutchinson
(ed.), *The Works of George Herbert*,
Oxford University Press, 1941

A complementary aspect of Anglican personal devotion is given by Henry Vaughan (p. 35). The Christian finds God in the little things, as Herbert tells us, but also aspires to the divine transcendence.

Blest be the God of Harmony and Love!
   The God above!
   And holy Dove!
Whose interceding, spiritual groans
   Make restless moans
   For dust and stones;
For dust in every part,
But a hard, stony heart.

O how in this thy Quire of Souls I stand,
  Propped by thy hand,
  A heap of sand
Which busy thoughts, like winds, would scatter quite,
  And put to flight,
  But for thy might
Thy hand alone doth tame
Those blasts, and knit my frame;

So that both stones, and dust, and all of me
  Jointly agree
  To cry to thee;
And in this Music, by thy Martyrs' blood
  Sealed and made good,
  Present, O God,
The echo of these stones, –
My sighs, and groans!

Henry Vaughan, 'Church Service', H. F. Lyte (ed.), *Vaughan's
Sacred Poems*, Bell, 1890, pages 65–6

*Thomas Traherne (p. 35) wrote prose meditations as well as poems, express-
ing in both forms the sense of wonder which inspires the individual believer
to praise and adoration.*

As it becometh you to retain a Glorious sense of the World, because the
Earth and the Heavens and the Heaven of Heavens are the Magnificent
and Glorious Territories of GOD's Kingdom, so are you to remember
always the unsearchable Extent and illimited Greatness of your own
Soul; the Length and Breadth and Depth and Height of your own
Understanding. Because it is the House of GOD, a Living Temple, and a
Glorious Throne of the Blessed Trinity, far more Magnificent and Great
than the Heavens: yea a Person that in Union and Communion with
GOD, is to see Eternity, to fill His Omnipresence, to Possess his Greatness, to Admire his Love, to receive his Gifts, to Enjoy the World, and to
live in His Image. Let all your Actions proceed from a sense of this
Greatness, let all your Affections extend to this Endless Wideness, let all

your Prayers be animated by this Spirit and let all your Praises arise and ascend from this fountain. For you are never your true self, till you live by your Soul more than by your Body, and you never live by your Soul, till you feel its incomparable Excellency, and rest satisfied and delighted in the Unsearchable Greatness of its Comprehension.

Thomas Traherne, *Poems, Centuries and Three Thanksgivings*, ed. A. Ridler, Oxford University Press, 1960, pages 256–7

What the poets saw in visions and images was practised by Nicholas Ferrar's community at Little Gidding (see above). The order of the day may seem alarmingly austere in our time, but it shows how the best of Anglican spirituality could be put into practice.

They rose at four; at five went to the oratory to prayers; at six said the psalms of the hour (for every hour had its appointed psalms), with some portion of the Gospel, till Mr Ferrar had finished his Concordance, when a chapter of that work was substituted in place of the portion of the Gospel. Then they sang a short hymn, repeated some passages of Scripture, and at half-past six went to church to matins. At seven said the psalms of the hour, sang the short hymn, and the children went to breakfast. Then the young people repaired to their respective places of instruction. The old gentlewoman [Nicholas Ferrar's mother] took her chair, inspecting her daughters and grandchildren as they sat at their books or other good employments in great silence, or at least avoiding all vain talking and jesting that was not convenient. No hour but had its business. Eight, nine, ten o'clock come, those hours had their several companies, that came and did as at former hours: psalms said and a head of the Concordance, the organs playing, the hymn sung at each hour, as the clock struck, that gave notice to all of the time passing. At ten, to the church to Litany every day of the week, as their bishop had given them leave. At eleven to dinner (after saying the hourly office). At which seasons were regular readings in rotation, from the Scripture, from the Book of Martyrs, and from short histories drawn up by Mr. Ferrar, and adapted to the purpose of moral instruction. Recreation was permitted till one; then the bell tolled for the boys to school, and those that had their turns came up into the great chamber again, to say their psalms and head of Concordance, sing a hymn and play on the organ whilst they sung. There old Mrs. Ferrar commonly sat till four o'clock, and, as before, each hour had its performance. Church at four for Evensong; supper at five, or sometimes six. Diversions till eight. Then prayers in the oratory, where a hymn was sung, the organs playing, and afterwards all retired to their respective apartments.

H. P. K. Skipton, *The Life and Times of Nicolas Ferrar*, Mowbray, 1907, pages 99–100

Edward Taylor (c. 1644–1729) was born in England and emigrated to Boston. While he may more properly be regarded as an American poet, his origin and his place in the Metaphysical style of Herbert and Vaughan entitles his inclusion.

What love is this of thine, that cannot be
In thine infinity, O Lord, confined,
Unless it in thy very person see
Infinity, and finity, conjoined?
What! Hath thy Godhead, as not satisfied,
Married our manhood, making it its bride?

Oh, matchless love! Filling Heaven to the brim!
O'er-running it; all running o'er beside
This world! Nay, overflowing hell, wherein
For thine elect there rose a mighty tide,
That there our veins might through thy person bleed
To quench those flames that else would on us feed!

Oh, that thy love might overflow my heart,
To fire the same with love! For love I would.
But oh, my straitened breast! My lifeless spark!
My fireless flame! What, chilly, love, and cold?
In measure small? In manner chilly? See!
Lord, blow the coal. Thy love inflame in me.

Edward Taylor, 'Preparatory Meditations before my Approach to the Lord's Supper', *The Poems of Edward Taylor*, ed. D. E. Stanford, Yale University Press, 1960

Jeremy Taylor (p. 36) gives a judicious account of the basic requirements for a holy life, in both worship and conduct. It is a typically Anglican blending of earnestness and restraint.

The man does certainly belong to God who believes and is baptized into all the articles of the Christian faith, and studies to improve his know-ledge in the matters of God, so as may best make him to live a holy life; he that, in obedience to Christ, worships God diligently, frequently, and constantly, with natural religion, that is of prayer, praises, and thanks-giving; he that takes all opportunities to remember Christ's death by a frequent sacrament, as it can be had, or else by inward acts of under-standing, will, and memory (which is the spiritual communion) supplies the want of the external rite; he that lives chastely; and is merciful; and despises the world, using it as a man, but never suffering it to rifle [damage] a duty and is just in his dealing, and diligent in his calling; he that is humble in his spirit. and obedient to government; and content in his fortune and employment; he that does his duty because he loves God; and especially if after all this he be afflicted, and patient, or prepared to suffer affliction for the cause of God: the man that hath these twelve signs of grace and predestination does as certainly belong to God, and is His son as surely, as he is His creature.

The Whole Works of the Right Rev. Jeremy Taylor, ed. C. P. Eden, Longman, 1862,
pages 2–3

Robert Nelson (p. 61) writes on a theme dear to many Anglican divines: the need to combine Church observances and personal devotion to fulfil a holy life.

[On holy days] we should constantly attend the *Public Worship*, and par-take of the Blessed *Sacrament,* if it be administered. In private we should enlarge our *Devotions,* and suffer the Affairs of the World to interrupt us as little as may be. We should particularly express our Rejoicing by *Love and Charity* to our Poor Neighbours. If we commemorate any *Mystery* of our *Redemption* or Article of our Faith, we ought to confirm our belief of it by considering all those Reasons upon which it is built, that we may be able to give a good Account of the Hope that is in us. We should from our Hearts offer to God the *Sacrifice of Thanksgiving*, and resolve to perform all those Duties which result from the Belief of such an Article. If we commemorate any *Saint*, we should consider the Virtues for which he was most eminent, and by what steps he arrived at so great Perfection; and then examine ourselves how far we are defective in our Duty, and earnestly beg God's Pardon for our past Failings, and his Grace to enable us to conform our Lives for the time to come to those admirable Examples that are set before us.

Robert Nelson, *Companion for the Festivals and Fasts of the Church of England*,
1704, page 9

Daniel Waterland (p. 59) explains that proper preparation for Holy Communion is essential, but that there must be individual variations on the basic discipline.

As to the length of time to be taken up in preparing, there is no one certain rule to be given, which can suit all cases or circumstances: only, when a man has completely adjusted his accounts with God, (be it sooner, or be it later) then is he fit to come, and not till then. There is an habitual, and there is an actual preparation. The habitual preparation is a good life; and the further we are advanced in it, the less need there is of any actual preparation besides: but because men are too apt to flatter and deceive their own hearts, and to speak peace to themselves without sufficient grounds for so doing; therefore some actual preparation, self-examination, etc. is generally necessary even to those who may be habitually good, if it be only to give them a well grounded assurance that they really are so. However, the better men are, the less actual preparation may suffice, and the shorter warning will be needful. Some therefore may receive as often as they have opportunity, though it were ever so sudden or unexpected; and they may turn it to good account by their pious care and recollection in their closets afterwards. Others may have a great deal to consider of beforehand, many offences to correct, many disorders to set right, much to do and much to undo, before they presume to come to God's altar.

Daniel Waterland, *The Doctrine of the Eucharist*, Clarendon Press, 1896, page 405

Samuel Johnson (1707–84), well known for his great Dictionary and for literary work in several genres, was a devout member of the Church of England and composed a number of memorable prayers. Many of them, like the following, are a supplication for personal holiness.

O Lord, my Maker and Protector, Who hast graciously sent me into this world, to work out my salvation, enable me to drive from me all such unquiet and perplexing thoughts as may mislead or hinder me in the practice of those duties which Thou hast required. When I behold the works of Thy hands and consider the course of Thy providence, give me Grace always to remember that Thy thoughts are not my thoughts, nor Thy ways my ways. And while it shall please Thee to continue me in this world where much is to be done and little to be known, teach me by Thy Holy Spirit to withdraw my mind from unprofitable and dangerous enquiries, from difficulties vainly curious, and doubts impossible to be solved. Let me rejoice in the light which Thou hast imparted, let me serve Thee with active zeal, and humble confidence, and wait with patient expectation for the time in which the soul which Thou receivest, shall be satisfied with knowledge. Grant this, O Lord, for Jesus Christ's sake.

Samuel Johnson, *Prayers*, SCM Press, 1947, page 45

Thomas Browne (p. 12) urges a calm acceptance of life, with charity towards others: a typically quiet Anglican piety.

Guide not the Hand of God, nor order the Finger of the Almighty unto thy will and pleasure; but sit quiet in the soft showers of Providence, and Favourable distributions in this World, either to thyself or others. And since not only Judgements have their Errands, but Mercies their Commissions; snatch not at every Favour, nor think thyself passed by, if they fall upon thy Neighbour. Rake not up envious displacences at things successful unto others, which the wise Disposer of all thinks not fit for thyself. Reconcile the events of things unto both beings, that is, of this World and the next, so will there not seem so many Riddles in Providence, nor various inequalities in the dispensation of things below. If thou doest not anoint thy Face, yet put not on sackcloth at the felicities of others. Repining at the Good draws on rejoicing at the evils of others, and so falls into that inhumane vice, for which so few Languages have a name. The blessed Spirits above rejoice at our happiness below; but to be glad at the evils of one another is beyond the malignity of Hell, and falls not on evil Spirits, who, though they rejoice at our unhappiness, takes no pleasure at the afflictions of their own Society of their fellow Natures. Degenerous Heads! who must be fain to learn from such Examples, and to be Taught from the School of Hell.

Religio Medici and Other Writings of Sir Thomas Browne, Dent, 1925, page 267

William Law (p. 121) demands a more severe Christian discipline and deals sternly with possible objections.

When you look into the writings and lives of the first Christians, you see the same spirit that you see in the Scriptures. All is reality, life, and action. Watching and prayers, self-denial and mortification, was the common business of their lives.

From that time to this, there has been no person like them, eminent for piety, who has not, like them, been eminent for self-denial and mortification. This is the only royal way that leads to a kingdom.

But how far are you from this way of life, or rather how contrary to it, if, instead of imitating their austerity and mortification, you cannot so much as renounce so poor an indulgence, as to be able to rise to your prayers! If self-denials and bodily sufferings, if watchings and fastings, will be marks of glory at the day of judgement, where must we hide our heads, that have slumbered away our time in sloth and softness?

You perhaps now find some pretences to excuse yourselves from that severity of fasting and self-denial, which the first Christians practised. You fancy that human nature is grown weaker, and that the difference of climates may make it not possible for you to observe their methods of self-denial and austerity in these colder countries.

But all this is but pretence: for the change is not in the outward state of things, but in the inward state of our minds. When there is the same spirit in us that there was in the Apostles and primitive Christians, when we feel the weight of religion as they did, when we have their faith and hope, we shall take up our cross, and deny ourselves, and live in such methods of mortification as they did.

'Had St. Paul lived in a cold country, had he had a constitution made weak with a sickly stomach, and often infirmities, he would have done as he advised Timothy, he would have mixed a little wine with his water'. But still he would have lived in a state of self-denial and mortification. He would have given this same account of himself: 'I therefore so run, not as uncertainly; so fight I, not as one that beateth the air, but I keep under my body, and bring it into subjection: lest that by any means, when I have preached to others, I myself should be a castaway.'

After all, let it now be supposed that you imagine there is no necessity for you to be so sober and vigilant, so fearful of yourself, so watchful over your passions, so apprehensive of danger, so careful of your Salvation, as the Apostles were. Let it be supposed, that you imagine that you want less self-denial and mortification, to subdue your bodies, and purify your souls, than they wanted; that you need not have your loins girt, and your lamps burning, as they had; will you therefore live in a quite contrary state? Will you make your life as constant a source of softness and indulgence, as theirs was of strictness and self-denial?

William Law, *A Serious Call to a Devout and Holy Life* (1728), Epworth Press, 1961,
pages 123–4

This extract from a sermon by Newman (p. 16) given at the University Church in Oxford, is an eloquent statement of the quest for holiness which was one of the features of the Oxford Movement. Newman was one of the greatest men lost to the Church of England. There is some pleasure in knowing that these sermons were republished, with few alterations, long after his conversion.

Some one may ask, 'why is it that holiness is a necessary qualification for our being received into heaven? Why is it that the Bible enjoins on us so strictly to love, fear, and obey God, to be just, honest, meek, pure in heart, forgiving, heavenly-minded, self-denying, humble and resigned? Man is confessedly weak and corrupt; why then is he enjoined to be so religious, so unearthly? why is he required (in the strong language of Scripture) to become "a new creature"? Since he is by nature what he is, would it not be an act of greater mercy in God to save him altogether without this holiness, which it is so difficult, yet (as it appears) so necessary for him to possess?'

Now we have no right to ask this question. Surely it is quite enough for a sinner to know, that a way has been opened through God's grace for his salvation, without being informed why that way, and not another way, was chosen by Divine Wisdom. Eternal life is 'the gift of God.' Undoubtedly He may prescribe the terms on which He will give it; and if He has determined holiness to be the way of life, it is enough; it is not for us to inquire why He has so determined.

Yet the question may be asked reverently, and with a view to enlarge our insight into our own condition and prospects; and in that case the attempt to answer it will be profitable, if it be made soberly. I proceed, therefore, to state one of the reasons, assigned in Scripture, why present holiness is necessary . . . for future happiness.

To be holy is, in our Church's words, to have 'the true circumcision of the Spirit;' that is, to be separate from sin, to hate the works of the world, the flesh, and the devil; to take pleasure in keeping God's command-ments; to do things as He would have us do them; to live habitually as in the sight of the world to come, as if we had broken the ties of this life, and were dead already. Why cannot we be saved without possessing such a frame and temper of mind?

I answer as follows: That, even supposing a man of unholy life were suffered to enter heaven, *he would not be happy there*; so that it would be no mercy to permit him to enter.

J. H. Newman, *Tracts for the Times*, vol. 1, Parker, 1839, pages 1–2

W. Walsham How (1823–97) was the first Bishop of Wakefield when the diocese was created in 1888, and the author of hymns including 'For all the saints' and 'It is a thing most wonderful'. He urges the importance of frequent communion which was coming to be generally accepted by the end of the nineteenth century, with continual preparation by the practice of regularly recollecting the presence of God.

The life of faith is a life full of the presence of God. Faith is the eye of the soul, and that eye looks not at the things which are seen, but at the things which are not seen. It *realises* – makes *real* to us – the presence of God and of the world unseen. The thought of that world unseen is never far away, nor long away, in a life of faith. In a life of faith, then, it is not like going on a long journey, for which the soul is unprepared, when we seek the close presence of our Lord and our God in Holy Communion. It is only like going a little step nearer, for which the soul should be always ready.

It is a poor way of making a '*continual* remembrance of the Sacrifice of the Death of Christ' to live in daily forgetfulness of it, and to come to Holy Communion only two or three times in the year. I should not like to have to say every time I came, 'O God, I confess I have been too long without coming to this holy Sacrament; forgive me my neglect'. A life which cannot turn to Jesus at any time simply and naturally is a dangerous one. It is not a life of faith. So the best preparation is a Holy Life. One who is always ready will gladly come often.

But will not coming often make me feel less? May I not make it too common, and so come with less reverence? No, you will not find it so. It is found, as a rule, that those who come oftenest come most reverently, and love best to come. In the, Primitive Church the Lord's Supper was administered at least every Lord's Day. It would have seemed as strange to the early Christians to have a festival, such as Sunday always is, without Holy Communion, as to have a feast with nothing to eat. And certainly our Lord meant it to be a constant food for the souls of His people.

W. Walsham How, *Holy Communion*, SPCK, 1925, pages 5–6

The practice of sacramental confession was revived by the Tractarians and their successors and came to be regarded as a positive duty of Anglo-Catholics, but it had never been completely abandoned in earlier years. It is offered in the longer Exhortation before the Confession at Holy Communion, and in the Visitation of the Sick. John Jewel (p. 9) cautiously recommended it but did not see it as an exclusively priestly function.

We are required [. . .] to examine ourselves and confess our sins before God: who doth not so, he shall not find mercy and forgiveness of his sins. The other sort of confession, made unto men, I do not condemn. It may do much good if it be well used. St James commendeth it among the faithful: 'Acknowledge your faults one to another, and pray one for another, that ye may be healed' (James v). He speaketh not of priest or minister, but of every one of the faithful. Every Christian may do this help unto another, to take knowledge of the secret and inner grief of the heart, to look upon the wound which sin and wickedness hath made, and, by godly advice and earnest prayer for him, to recover his brother. This is a private exhortation, and as it were a catechising or instructing in the faith, and a means to lead us by familiar and special conference to examine our conscience, and to espy wherein we have offended God. The use and practice hereof is not only to be allowed, but most needful and requisite, if so the superstition, and necessity, and conscience, which many have fondly [foolishly] used and put therein, be taken away.

Works of Bishop Jewel, ed. J. Ayre, Parker Society, 1847, page 1133

John Cosin (p. 45) went a little further, making a distinction between what moral theology regards as venial and mortal sins.

The Church of England, howsoever it holdeth not Confession Absolution Sacramental that is made unto and received from a Priest to be so absolutely necessary, as without it there can be no remission of sins, and yet by this place it is manifest what she teacheth concerning the virtue and force of this sacred action. The Confession is commanded to be special. The Absolution is the same that the ancient Church and the present Church of Rome useth.[. . .] Our 'if he feel his conscience troubled' is no more than his *si inveniat peccata* [if he discovers sins]; for if he be not troubled with sin, what needs either Confession or Absolution? Venial sins that separate not from the grace of God need not so much to trouble a man's conscience; if he hath committed any mortal sin, then we require Confession of it to a Priest, who may give him, upon his true contrition and repentance, the benefit of Absolution, which takes effect according to his disposition that is absolved.

John Cosin, *Works*, Parker, 1855, vol. 5, pages 163–4

Vernon Staley, a member of the Anglican community at Clewer, was a prolific writer of devotional works at the end of the nineteenth century and the beginning of the twentieth. He invokes the authority of Cosin to support a stronger Anglo-Catholic approach to confession.

Contrition leads naturally to confession, or the truthful acknowledgement of sin. Confession is self-accusation, and the acknowledgement to

God of wrong doing. God demands confession as a condition of pardon. 'If we confess our sins, He is faithful and just to forgive us our sins.' A willingness to confess is an evidence of contrition. The most searching confession is that made privately before a priest [. . .]

The Church of England invites sinners, who cannot otherwise make their peace with God, to open their grief (i.e., to reveal the sin which causes the grief) before the priest, in order that they may secure 'the benefit of absolution'. Such confession is called by Bishop Cosin, *Sacramental Confession,* and is a blessed privilege open to all who heartily desire it. Our blessed Lord has given to his priests power and authority to absolve from all sins, and He surely means them to use this power. But before they can fully do so, it is needful that those seeking absolution should confess their sins. Thus we may be quite sure that private confession, as an outcome of real contrition, is a practice well pleasing to our Lord.

We must remember that, strictly speaking, to absolve is not to forgive; God alone forgives. To absolve is to unloose the bonds which sin has placed upon the soul, and to remove the bar to the receiving of grace. In raising Lazarus from the dead, our Lord pronounced the words, 'Loose him, and let him go'. This was the part of the people towards him whom Christ raised. And so God, who pardons the penitent, bids the priest in absolution to loose him and let him go.

Vernon Staley, *The Catholic Religion* (1893), Mowbray, 1904, pages 294–6

Edward King (p. 67) offers more specific advice on the question.

It is not easy to explain many of our religious acts so as to be satisfactory simply to the logical faculty. It may seem unreasonable to have an absolution in the daily office, and in the Holy Communion, and to repeat the Lord's Prayer, asking for forgiveness, so frequently in one Sunday morning service; and yet, when the moral and spiritual side of our nature is appealed to, these acts and prayers are found to have a real place, and to be not contradictory to our reason. With regard to the particular matter about which you ask, the following is the line of thought which has seemed to me most loyal to our Prayer Book, and most satisfactory to people's needs:

(a) Our Church does not make confession to a priest necessary.

(b) She instructs her children to guide themselves with God's help, by God's law, if they can; if they want help then to come to a priest.

(c) In sickness our Church urges confession to a priest, if there has been weighty cause.

(d) The Church of England bids her clergy teach what Holy Scripture teaches, and what the Fathers have gathered out of the same.

St Augustine and others would say, try and live on with only such daily faults as the Lord's Prayer will cover, but if you have fallen into the greater sins then you had better get the help of the priest through confession and absolution.

I know that many good people use confession who have not fallen into the greater acts of sin, but who have sinned in will, and, if they are real in such use of it, I think our Church allows it, and St Cyprian and St Gregory the Great speak of sins of thought, and Origen speaks of going to a priest in matters which are doubtful; but, on the whole, if we keep to the general line of the Church's teaching, I think the rest will be made clear as we want it.

Edward King, *Spiritual Letters*, Mowbray, 1910, pages 72, 74–5

At the time of the Great War early in the twentieth century Charles Gore (p. 19) set out the obligations of membership of the Church of England, restating the principles of its foundation and making clear, as his predecessors had done through the centuries, that neither public worship nor private devotion and discipline can stand alone.

When you come down the history of the church to the Church of England, as it was re-ordered at the Reformation, and read its Book of Common Prayer, you will see that it meant to maintain at a very high level the responsibility of membership. Those who are to be baptized are to recognise publicly before the congregation assembled their responsibility for renouncing what Christ forbids, for believing the common faith of the church, and for obeying the laws of discipleship. They are embarking, and that publicly, on a great adventure, and they must know what they are doing. If infants are to be baptized, then sponsors must be provided as sureties, to guarantee that the infants, as they grow to years of discretion, shall know the meaning of their religion. And they are to renew the vows of baptism through their own lips before they can be confirmed, by the laying-on of the bishop's hand, and so enter upon full membership in the strength of the Holy Spirit. The Lord's Supper or Holy Communion is the sacrament in which their membership is to be constantly renewed and reinvigorated, and it is to be guarded by the officers of the church from unworthy partaking. Those whose lives cause public scandal are to be warned or, if need be, excommunicated, or put out of fellowship, till they have shown themselves of a better mind, and 'been openly reconciled by penance', and so can be readmitted to fellowship. And private confession and absolution is provided for those whose conscience is troubled by secret sins. And the needs of the poor and sick are to be relieved by the alms of the whole community. And the law of indissoluble marriage is to set its consecration upon the home. And the sick and dying are to be dealt with as responsible members who must be brought to a right faith and penitence, and make their peace with God and man, that, if they die, the words of confident hope, such as belong rightly to the holy fellowship of the church, may be spoken over their graves.

All this is natural and right. Every union or society which exists for any worthy object must maintain a high sense of the responsibility of membership; and all its members must recognise that, if they fail to keep its obligatory rules, they must fall out of membership and lose its advantages. A nominal membership is the curse of any union. What trade union could last if a large percentage of its members never obeyed its rules or fulfilled its obligations?

Charles Gore, *The Religion of the Church*, Mowbray, 1916, pages 4–6

Martin Thornton, a priest of the Oratory of the Good Shepherd, gives good advice about eucharistic devotion, with a realistic assessment of human nature.

When the alarum goes off early in the Morning, a strong part of us really wants to get up unhurriedly and go to Mass; another part does not want to get up at all. Something tells us that duty comes before comfort and grace before nature, and another bit of nature backs this up by hinting that we shall enjoy sausages and bacon so much better when we get back; which seems subtly disconcerting and unworthy. We really are tired and we must keep up our strength, so perhaps a little more rest would be charitable towards our family and our firm. And so it goes on. It is all a jumble. But right conquers, after a fashion, and we get to Mass – a little hurriedly and without much preparation. During the Epistle we wonder if our unshaven chin is very noticeable, the Gospel is punctuated by a series of yawns, we are back in bed again for the Creed, and the bacon and sausage smell rather attractive during the offertory. We are not recollected, we are distracted. What we *should* do is to rise, shave and dress unhurriedly, walk to church in the presence of Christ alone, worship worthily, hear Mass prayerfully, communicate joyfully, and – in an Incarnational religion this is very important – enjoy sausage and bacon more than anyone has ever enjoyed it before: prayer must colour the *whole* of life, for that is what habitual recollection means. If this rather shows us up, if St Teresa's ideal seems glib and unattainable; then we are not to worry unduly, we are at least facing facts and so getting down to something practical and solid. And we may perhaps take heart from the fact that no less a man than St Paul knew the experience all too well.

Martin Thornton, *Christian Proficiency*, SPCK, 1959, page 61

The Oxford Movement restored a stronger sense of personal discipline and austerity, arousing hostility among its opponents but recalling many church people to a deeper sense of holiness. The balance between severity and gentleness has never been easy to maintain. Pusey both enjoined and practised a serious commitment.

And yet, after a few years, my brethren, if God, as we trust, continue to restore our Church as He is now doing, we shall think it strange, that members of a Church who, in her prayers, have besought God to be gracious unto them, as 'turning to Him in weeping, fasting, and praying', should not do that for which they beseech Him to be gracious – that they should ask Him to give them 'grace to use abstinence' and not seek to practise it – that they should plead to their Lord, that He fasted for them forty days and forty nights, and themselves fast not at all, with Him or for themselves. It will seem strange that what nature herself suggests, heathen have practised, Scripture directs, the Church enjoins, whereby Martyrs girded themselves to bear their last witness to their Lord, the whole white-robed army of Saints, (until such, as in these later years may, in their ignorance of its use and duty, have been brought through without it), subdued the flesh, deepened their penitence, humbled their souls, winged their prayers, died to the world that they might live to their Lord – members of a Church should acknowledge in words, in practice neglect.

E. B. Pusey, *Parochial Sermons*, vol. 1, Parker, 1860, page 187

12

Church and State

The Queen and all that are put in authority under her

The Reformation brought a new conception of national churches. The Middle Ages had been by no means free from disputes between individual monarchs and the central papal authority. But despite controversy abut money payments to Rome, the control of church properties and even the appointment of bishops, the idea of Christendom, with obedience however grudging, to the Pope, had held firm. In the sixteenth century the consensus was broken in countries which followed the new order. The principle of *cuius regio eius religio* – to each region its own religion – was accepted at the Peace of Augsburg in 1555. Even countries which remained Roman Catholic were more inclined to assert a degree of independence. In France the Gallican Articles of 1682 denied the authority of the Pope to rule in a number of temporal and civil matters and began a long period of uneasy relations with the papacy.

The relationship between the secular monarch and the religious establishment became a serious issue. In broad terms, Lutherans favoured the idea of the 'godly prince' with authority over spiritual as well as temporal matters within his realm. Calvinists wanted religious leaders to hold secular authority also and to impose church discipline on all citizens. To this end, Calvin established a theocracy in Geneva. For both Lutheran and Calvinist, civil obedience was part of a citizen's religious duty; and conversely sedition and treason were sins as well as crimes and were doubly to be condemned. Although the Church of England had some markedly Calvinist elements in its early years, it took a strong line about its relationship to the governing sovereign. By the Act of Uniformity the sovereign was the Supreme Head and Governor of the English Church. Offences against the rules of the Church could be punished in the criminal courts and there was no place for allegiance to any other authority in religion. Article 37 laid it down that 'The Bishop of

Rome hath no jurisdiction in this Realm of England'. On the other side, none of the more advanced Protestants could claim exemption from conformity to established ecclesiastical jurisdiction and order.

Some continuity with the medieval Church remained in matters of law. The ecclesiastical courts continued to sit, with authority over laity as well as clergy. The Consistory Courts kept some of their secular power until the middle of the nineteenth century. Charles Dickens put the eponymous hero of *David Copperfield* (1850) to work in Doctors' Commons, the association of ecclesiastical lawyers. His imaginary case shows the absurdity to which the system had declined and the resentment which it caused.

> We had an adjourned cause in the consistory that day – about excom-municating a baker who had been objecting in a vestry to a paving-rate – and as the evidence was just twice the length of Robinson Crusoe, according to a calculation I made, it was rather late in the day before we finished. However, we got him excommunicated for six weeks, and sentenced in no end of costs; and then the baker's proctor, and the judge, and the advocates on both sides (who were all nearly related), went out of town together. (Chapter 26)

In capital cases 'benefit of clergy' could be pleaded to escape execution by demonstration of basic literacy. The dramatist and actor Ben Jonson successfully pleaded benefit of clergy after killing a fellow-actor in a duel in 1598. Some serious offences were ruled to be 'without benefit of clergy'; the right was abolished in 1827. Church attendance was a legal duty, with fines or heavier penalties for absence. Such cases of 'recusancy' were regarded with suspicion of being caused by Roman Catholic allegiance or some other sedition dangerous to the State.

Bishops continued to sit in the House of Lords: the two archbishops and the Bishops of London, Winchester and Durham by right and twenty-one more in order of seniority of appointment, ranking high among the secular peerage. Bishops and Deans of Cathedrals continue to this day to be chosen by the Prime Minister's advice to the Crown, a matter which disturbs many, although in practice advice from within the Church is usually respected.

'State Services' were added to the Book of Common Prayer, strength-ening the link with the monarchy by commemorating the failure of the

Gunpowder Plot, the execution of Charles I and the Restoration of Charles II annually until they were removed in 1859. A service for the anniversary of the accession of the Sovereign is still newly authorised at the beginning of each reign. The Church of England generally has a leading role, though no longer a monopoly, in many official services, notably in the Coronation, and in national commemorations like Remembrance Sunday.

There has been a dark and regrettable aspect to the Establishment. Those who dissented, whether as Roman Catholic or Protestant Nonconformists, were subject to severe civil disabilities, even to the extent of being unable to be legally married except through the ministration and rite of the Church of England. Even more shamefully, reception of Holy Communion was imposed as sign of loyalty. The Test Act passed in 1673 required all holders of office under the Crown to receive the sacrament by the Church of England rite as well as taking oaths and declarations of loyalty. For a short period between 1711 and 1719 the Occasional Conformity Act imposed deprivation and other penalties on any person who took the Sacrament to obtain office and was later found to be attending a dissenting 'conventicle'. The universities of Oxford and Cambridge demanded subscription to the Articles by all their members until 1871. In practice the worst of the penal laws fell into disuse and Emancipation Acts relieved Protestant dissenters in 1828 and Roman Catholics in 1829, although the latter measure was passed only after considerable opposition, including the reluctance of George IV to give the royal assent.

Besides the overdue acceptance of other churches as equal partners in the State, there was a gradual weakening of the Anglican monopoly in other ways. Church rates, levied on all parishioners for the upkeep of the parish church, were abolished in 1868. Tithes were gradually abolished by successive pieces of legislation and ceased to have even a shadow by 1996. The Church of England, which had previously benefited from Establishment, now began also to suffer from it. The Parliament which met after the 1832 Reform Act was the first since the sixteenth century in which not all the members were Anglicans, although they were still able to legislate for the Church. Although there were many and deeper causes, the beginning of the Oxford Movement is taken to be Keble's Assize Sermon at Oxford in 1833, occasioned by the suppression of a number of Irish bishoprics. When he was in power as Prime Minister, Disraeli brought in the Public Worship Regulation Act in 1874 to proceed against some of the Anglo-Catholic usages which were considered unlawful. The result was the inhibition and even imprisonment of some good priests and a reaction which helped to secure acceptance for many ceremonial practices. Many churchpeople who had little sympathy with ritualism were outraged by use of the criminal courts in such proceedings, as they had earlier been by the decision of the Judicial Committee of the Privy Council in the Gorham case (p. 94).

The question of Establishment has been much debated in recent decades. The extended use of the word in the 1950s to include various other groups of traditional respect and influence may have helped to cause disquiet in some quarters. The Church of England sought more control over its own services, and the Worship and Doctrine Measure (1975) gave power to the General Synod to authorise new forms of worship. This freedom brought the *Alternative Service Book* (1980) and its replacement *Common Worship* (2000). Some Parliamentary control remains. When the Measure of the ordination of women as priests was passed by the General Synod in 1992 it had to go to the Ecclesiastical Committee of Parliament for ratification and for approval of provisions to protect those who held a conscientious opposition to the Measure.

Establishment has not consisted only of privilege over other churches, or of secular legislative interference. The idea may be unfashionable today, but it has also fostered a sense of national duty and loyalty. The Church of England has shown a desire to influence society for good, to encourage a social conscience, to use its power for general welfare. If the principle has too often been obscured in practice, there has remained a deep resistance to the idea of separation of Church and State, in terms of social action and justice as well as in the political Establishment. Formal societies and individual effort have done much to improve the condition of the poor and deprived. As some of the following extracts show, the emphasis on duties and responsibilities has not been entirely subordinated to the sense of privilege.

This is made clear in one of the sixteenth-century Homilies.

Let us therefore, good Christian people, try and examine our faith, what it is; let us not flatter ourselves, but look upon our works, and so judge of our faith what it is. Christ himself speaketh of this matter, and saith The tree is known by the fruit. Therefore let us do good works, and thereby declare our faith to be the lively Christian faith. Let us, by such virtues as ought to spring out of faith, shew our election to be sure and stable; as St. Peter teacheth, Endeavour yourselves to make your calling and election certain by good works. And also he saith, Minister or declare in your faith virtue, in virtue knowledge, in knowledge temperance, in temperance patience, in patience godliness, in godliness brotherly charity, in brotherly charity love. So shall we shew indeed that we have the very lively Christian faith; and may so both certify our conscience the better that we be in the right faith, and also by these means confirm other men. If these fruits do not follow, we do but mock with God, deceive ourselves, and also other men. Well may we bear the name of Christian men, but we do lack the true faith that doth belong thereunto for true faith doth ever bring forth good works; as St. James saith, Shew me thy faith by thy deeds.

Sermons and Homilies Appointed to be read in Churches (1562), Prayer Book and Homily Society, 1840, page 42

John Bramhall (1594–1663), Archbishop of Armagh, defended the Church of England against the many attacks made upon it during the troubled years of the Civil War and Commonwealth and later against the materialism and determinism which he found in the writings of Thomas Hobbes. When not engaged in polemics he was a moderate and irenical man. His comment on the relationship between Crown and Church is a classical Anglican statement for its time, and for long afterwards.

Neither do we draw or derive any *spiritual* jurisdiction from the crown; but either liberty and power to exercise, actually and lawfully, upon the subjects of the crown, that habitual jurisdiction which we received at our ordination; or the enlargement and dilatation of our jurisdiction objectively, by the prince's referring more causes to the cognisance of the Church than formerly it had; or, lastly, the increase of it subjectively, by their giving to ecclesiastical judges an external coercive power, which formerly they had not. To go yet one step higher; in cases that are indeed spiritual, or merely ecclesiastical, such as concern the doctrine of Faith, or administration of the Sacraments, or the ordaining or degrading of ecclesiastical persons, sovereign princes have (and have only) an 'architectonical' power, to see that clergymen do their duties in their proper places. But this power is always most properly exercised by the advice and ministry of ecclesiastical persons; and sometimes necessarily, as in the degradation of one in Holy Orders by ecclesiastical delegates. Therefore our law provides, that nothing shall be judged heresy with us *de novo,* but 'by the High Court of Parliament' (wherein our Bishops did always bear a part), 'with the assent' (that is more than advice) 'of the clergy in their Convocation'. In sum, we hold our benefices from the king, but our offices from Christ; the king doth nominate us, but Bishops do ordain us.

John Bramhall, *A Just Vindication of the Church of England* (1654), Parker, 1842, page 372

Herbert Thorndike (p. 123) was convinced the State should protect and enforce the rights of the Church. It was a line followed by the subsequent High Churchmen of the eighteenth and early nineteenth centuries, and by the Tractarians who were dismayed by what they regarded as State encroachments on Church rights. Perhaps with an eye to events during the Commonwealth, he points out that the Church authorities themselves may sometimes need correction in the name of traditional truth.

The secular power is bound to protect the ecclesiastical in determining all things which are not determined by our Lord and His Apostles, and to give force and effect to the acts of the same, but in matters already determined by them, as laws given to the Church, if by injury of time the practice become contrary to the law, the sovereign power being Christian and bound to protect Christianity, is bound to employ itself in giving strength, first, to that which is ordained by our Lord and His Apostles. By consequence, if those whom the power of the Church is trusted with shall hinder the restoring of such laws, it may and ought, by way of penalty to such persons, to suppress their power, that so it may be committed to such as are willing to submit to the superior ordinance of our Lord and His Apostles. A thing thoroughly proved, both by the right of secular powers in advancing Christianity with penalties, and in establishing the exercise of it, and in particular by all the examples of the pious kings of God's people, reducing the law into practice and suppressing the contrary thereof.

Theological Works of Herbert Thorndike, Parker, 1844, vol. 1, page 591

W. F. Hook (p. 18) defended the Establishment at a time when it was increasingly coming under attack, while regretting some of its effects on the freedom of the Church – a position still shared by many today, although the control has been considerably weakened. He has just described the ways in which the Established Church is beneficial to the general life of the nation.

It may be very true that, to a certain extent, much of this might be accomplished, even though the Church were not established. Religion would still have its influence. I will go even further and add that, so far as regards those who are Churchmen in deed and truth, the Church itself would be benefited by a separation from the State; for it would regain those undoubted rights from which, for the sake of harmony, she now recedes – the right, for instance, of legislating for herself, on all occasions, and of electing Bishops without the interference of the civil power. The question with the legislator is not whether the Church would do much good though unconnected with the State, but whether, by an alliance therewith, it cannot do more good: and the question with the Churchman is, whether, for placing in abeyance some of its spiritual rights, the Church does not receive compensation by the indirect influence it is enabled to exert. The Church may be less free, but is it not more efficient? The Church may be unduly controlled in the exercise of its authority over its own members, but does it not possess greater means of purifying society? – and to purify society, to act as the salt of the earth, is one of the purposes for which the Church was instituted. It is not, indeed, as Churchmen but as patriots that we deprecate the desecration of the State; that is to say, we deprecate it for the sake, not of those that are within the pale, but of those that are without; we deprecate it, not because the Church would be a less efficient minister of grace to the faithful, if, driven from her glorious cathedrals, she summoned her children around her in the upper room of a hired house, or the caves of the desert; but because she would be a less effectual preacher of morality to the unenlightened and the unbeliever, her voice would still be the voice of the charmer when heard, but it would not reach so far.

W. F. Hook, *The Church and its Ordinances*, Bentley, 1876, pages 124–5

Robert Southey (1774–1843) is best known as a poet of the Romantic Movement, associated with Wordsworth and Coleridge. He also wrote several prose works, including a long history of the Church in England, which he concludes with a triumphant – one might say triumphalist – defence of the Establishment.

From the time of the Revolution the Church of England has partaken of the stability and security of the State. Here therefore I terminate this compendious, but faithful, view of its rise, progress and political struggles. It has rescued us, first from heathenism, then from papal idolatry and superstition; it has saved us from temporal as well as spiritual despotism. We owe to it our moral and intellectual character as a nation; much of our private happiness, much of our public strength. Whatever should weaken it, would in the same degree injure the common weal; whatever should overthrow it, would in sure and immediate consequence bring down the goodly fabric of that Constitution, whereof it is a constituent and necessary part. If the friends of the Constitution understand this as clearly as its enemies, and act upon it as consistently and as actively, then will the Church and State be safe, and with them the liberty and the prosperity of our country.

Robert Southey, *The Book of the Church* (1837), John Murray, 1841, page 545

This optimistic view was shaken by the measures introduced by the House of Commons elected after the 1832 Reform Act. Benjamin Disraeli was no admirer of the Tractarians, but he could express something of the disquiet which they felt. A character in one of his novels puts the case.

'All ties between the State and the Church are abolished, except those which tend to its danger and degradation. What can be more anomalous than the present connection between State and Church? Every condition on which it was originally consented to has been cancelled. That original alliance was, in my view, an equal calamity for the nation and the Church; but at least, it was an intelligible compact. Parliament, then consisting only of members of the Established Church, was, on ecclesiastical matters, a lay synod, and might, in some points of view, be esteemed a necessary portion of Church government. But you have effaced this exclusive character of Parliament; you have determined that a communion with the Established Church shall no longer be part of the qualification for sitting in the House of Commons. There is no reason, so far as the constitution avails, why every member of the House of Commons should not be a dissenter. But the whole power of the country is concentrated in the House of Commons. [. . .] The only consequences of the present union of Church and State are, that, on the side of the State, there is perpetual interference in ecclesiastical government, and on the side of the Church a sedulous avoidance of all those principles on which alone Church government can be established, and by the influence of which alone can the Church of England again become universal.'

Benjamin Disraeli, *Coningsby*, 1844, book 7, chapter 2

Thomas Arnold (1785–1842) is still seen as the epitome of the Victorian headmaster and the spirit of the public schools. He was also a prominent churchman, liberal in his views and opposed to both Roman Catholicism and the Oxford Movement. He believed that the Church should have a leading part in the State as agent of social improvement.

When we look at the condition of our country; at the poverty and wretchedness of so large a portion of the working classes; at the intellectual and moral evils which certainly exist among the poor, but by no means amongst the poor only; and when we witness the many partial attempts to remedy those evils – attempts benevolent indeed and wise, so far as they go, but utterly unable to strike to the heart of the mischief; can any Christian doubt that here is the work for the church of Christ to do; that none else can do it; and that with the blessing of her Almighty Head she can? Looking upon the chaos around us, one power alone can reduce it into order, and fill it with light and life. And does he really apprehend the perfections and high calling of Christ's church, does he indeed fathom the depths of man's wants, or has he learnt to rise to the fullness of the stature of their divine remedy, who comes forward to preach to us the necessity of apostolic succession?

Thomas Arnold, *Christian Life, its course, its hindrances and its helps*, Fellowes, 1878, page li

Frederick Denison Maurice (1805–72) was one of the leaders of the Christian Socialist movement of the mid-Victorian period. He held chairs at King's College, London, and founded the Working Men's College in 1854. He made his political ideas known through lectures, prose works and fiction.

If the new and unwonted proclamation were to go forth, 'God has cared for you, you are indeed his children; his Son has redeemed you, his Spirit is striving with you; there is a fellowship larger, more irrespective of outward distinctions, more democratical, than any which you can create; but it is a fellowship of mutual love, not mutual selfishness, in which the chief of all is the servant of all' – may not one think that a result would follow as great as that which attended the preaching of any Franciscan friar in the twelfth century, or any Methodist preacher in the eighteenth? For these are true words, everlasting words and yet words which belong especially to our time; they are words which interpret and must be interpreted by that regular charity, that ministerial holiness, those sacraments, prayers and discipline, of which the Catholic speaks. They connect his words about repentance with those of the Evangelical, making it manifest, that nothing but an accursed nature and a depraved will could have robbed any of the blessings which God has bestowed upon us all. They translate into meaning and life all the liberal plans for the education of adults and children; they enable us to fulfil the notion, which statesmen have entertained, that the Church is to be the supporter of the existing orders, by making her a teacher and example to those orders respecting their duties and responsibilities; by removing the hatred which their forgetfulness of those duties and responsibilities is threatening to create in the minds of the lower classes.

F. D. Maurice, *The Kingdom of Christ*, Rivington, 1883, vol. 2, page 420

Henry Scott Holland (1847–1918) was a Canon of St Paul's Cathedral and then Regius Professor of Divinity at Oxford. He was a leading member of the Christian Social Union, which carried on some of the ideas of the earlier Christian Socialists. He makes a strong plea for members of the Church to recognise the duties as well as the privileges consequent on Establishment.

History will not ask whether, in nooks or corners of London, a few faithful met together to praise and worship God. It will ask, was the Church faithful to the big work to which she was summoned? As of old she encountered and won imperial Rome, and banded Vandalism, so now, did she once again rise to the new task? Did she run the course set before her? Did she seal to God the powers of the great cities? Did she enlarge herself to the measure of the new organisation? Did she learn and use the secret of combination? Did she discipline herself to the handling of vast masses? Had she the courage for this? Had she the largeness of heart? Had she confidence in herself? Had she the generous trust in others which alone could make it possible? Had she the inspiration of faith? Had she the splendour of love?

Or did she quail? Did she shrink up, creep, and fear? Was she poor, and thin, and niggardly, in her attempts? Was she weak and insufficient? Did she abandon the large hordes of crowded men to that ruin which she knew would be inevitable, unless Christ became their Master, unless Christian faith bonded them into that communion which alone hallows and endures? These are the questions to which we, in our generation, are asked to give answer.

It may not surely be that this National Church of ours will be content to ignore or falsify her claims to run level with the national life: she has responsibilities which it is criminal to decline, and these responsibilities compel her to make sure that her labours be no narrower in their scope than those of the entire nation. What England does, the Church of England must not be afraid to do; and England is now massing her works and population, as she never massed them before. The Church, then, must forward her energies with no stinting hand, with no captious or suspicious heart, if she is not to fail England in the critical hour.

Nor is it England only that she will fail: it is God – God the Father, Who summoned her to undertake: He it is Who moves (unseen, yet felt) this whole heaving world of men. His breath impels and shifts these massing multitudes: He shapes their destiny: He prepares their paths;

and yet they know Him not! They cannot know Him, until the Son, the Beloved, the only Righteous, stands before them in human flesh, in living Presence, to show them plainly of the Father.

Henry Scott Holland, Logic and Life, Longmans Green, 1892, pages 250–1

R. W. Dolling (1851–1902) was a priest with a strong sense of political as well as religious mission. He did great work in the deprived area of Landport in Portsmouth. In this extract from a sermon he declares the beliefs shared by many late-Victorian Anglicans who were seeking to influence social conditions.

I feel an interest in politics, and express that interest, first of all, because I am a Christian, and, secondly, because I am an Englishman. There was a day, you know, when in a large measure the Church of God exercised a mighty influence by speaking the truth upon political subjects. If you take, for instance, the Old Testament, you will find that in the Book of Psalms, which are, I suppose, the part of the Old Testament most read by modern Christians, the chief idea which underlies large parts of that wonderful collection is the right of the poor to be heard alike by God and man in all their needs and necessities, and to gain the redress of their wrongs. If you go farther into the Old Testament, and take the lives of God's prophets and their words, you will find that, as a rule, they were essentially political and social reformers, speaking with the authority of the voice of God and under the influence of a power which carried thorn into the palaces of kings and made their voice heard throughout the land of Israel, and even penetrated into the countries which were brought in contact with their own nation. You find these inspired men of God having one single purpose, and that was to preach of the God of Justice, a purpose the execution of which involved a most vigorous onslaught on every kind of oppression and on every species of wrong.

In fact, I suppose there has never been gathered together in any volume such magnificent statements of the rights of the weak and the helpless as you will find in almost every one of the writings of the prophets of the Old Testament.

Then you must remember that these are but the forerunners of Jesus Christ, that He is in Himself the gatherer up of all that the psalmists sung, of all that the prophets foretold, and therefore you may expect to

find in Him also the Champion of the weak and oppressed, and something more than that – the One who preached with a voice which is still
sounding throughout all the world the royalty of every single man, who
revealed to man His Divine origin, and showed not merely God's unceasing care for humanity, but God's desire that by his own actions, by
using the powers which He had given him, that man should be lifted up
even to the very highest of all ideals, that there should be no altitude of
virtue or intelligence that it should not be possible for man to attain to,
if he were but true to the power which God had placed in his soul.
Looking round on the world, Christ discovered that there were those
who had, as it were, absorbed or monopolised these human rights, and
rendered well-nigh impossible the development of man, and who had by
that very monopoly denied to him the possibility of his attainment to the
ideal which God had willed for him. Therefore the voice of Christ,
whether it speaks from Galilee or whether it speaks in the courts of the
temple, sounds and resounds to-day, and it shall never cease to re-echo
as long as the world has Christianity existing in its midst. It bids a man
not merely to be free in the sense in which human laws could give freedom – that is, to be free from the bondage or the oppression with which
the cruelty of others had bound him – but to be free in a much higher
and truer sense, that he may reach the stature which our Lord Himself
foresaw for him when He made him in the Divine Image. And if there be
in any country in which men live any custom, any privilege of others
which denies to men this opportunity, the Christian, be he priest or be
he layman, must never cease raising his voice until such restriction is
removed, until such privilege has been abolished, and the man is able in
the fullness of his Manhood to realise God's eternal Will for him.

C. F. Osborne, *The Life of Father Dolling*, Arnold, 1903, pages 131–2

*Herbert Hensley Henson (1853–1937), Bishop successively of Hereford and
Durham, took a liberal attitude towards biblical interpretation, which
made him a controversial figure. He was a strong supporter of Establishment until the rejection of the 1928 revised Prayer Book changed his
opinion, as this passage shows.*

The subordination of the Church to the State, involved in the existing
Establishment, may well bring the Church into great peril if it should fall

out in England, as in some Continental countries it has fallen out already, that the State should become hostile to the Church, and use its legal supremacy to the Church's undoing. Such a situation may at this moment appear to be remote and improbable, but the tendencies are in that direction, and events move quickly in these days. Considerations of prudence, however, do not go to the core of the case against the Establishment. It is no matter merely of prudence but of religious principle. Prudence does but require what duty plainly demands. Whether the State be, as generally in the past, friendly, or, as not improbably in the future, hostile, the subordination of the spiritual society to the secular power is intrinsically wrong, and, now that its reality has been demonstrated beyond all reasonable challenge, ought no longer to be acquiesced in [. . .] The issue of Disestablishment must be debated, and finally it must be decided, not as a matter of prudence, though assuredly it is that also, but essentially as the requirement of religious duty. We have to choose. 'Ye cannot serve God and Mammon.'

Herbert Hensley Henson, *Bishoprick Papers*, Oxford University Press, 1946, page 50

W. R. Inge (1860–1954), Dean of St Paul's, held robust and frequently controversial views on many things, ecclesiastical and secular. Writing just after the death of George V in 1936, he defended the Establishment of the Church on the social rather than political principle that it serves the whole nation. This, as we have seen, was the view of Hooker and others in the sixteenth century.

What do we mean when we speak of an established Church? Ever since Augustine of Canterbury (about AD 600) Church and State in England have been closely connected. Every member of the Church was a member of the State, and every member of the State was by right a member of the Church.

These are two aspects of an indivisible unity. To this day we pray for the King, 'over all persons and in all causes, ecclesiastical as well as civil, in these his dominions supreme'. The King symbolises the indivisible unity of the Christian State.

It will, of course, be said that this theory no longer corresponds with the facts, because we are not all Churchmen or even Christians. We are not all patriots either, except when we are deeply stirred; but at such times we rediscover our unity, both in civil and spiritual matters.

What would be the consequences if, as Bishop Creighton said, we repudiated the Christian basis of the State? What is the 'establishment' against which voices are raised, even by disgruntled Churchmen? The Crown never claimed spiritual jurisdiction, except for twenty years in the sixteenth century. It protected the rights and property of the Church, made them 'stable'. The parochial system was recognised and supported by the law of the land.

In every parish there was a person, or 'parson', to whose services every inhabitant of the district had a legal right. All have a right to worship in the parish church, to be baptised, married, and buried within its precincts. There are some districts where Free chapels or churches have had to be closed; the Anglican clergyman cannot run away if he wishes to do so.

W. R. Inge, *A Rustic Moralist*, Putnam, 1937, pages 83–4

A few years later Trevor Beeson, Vicar of St Mary's, Ware, believed that Establishment was not very relevant to the daily life of the Church, but could be a hindrance in the movement towards unity with other Churches. He wrote soon after the rejection by the General Synod of a plan for union with the Methodist Church. Like some earlier writers, he urges the social duty of a Church still linked with the State.

The Church of England's state links are no longer a serious problem in inter-church negotiations, but, as in the case of the proposed union with the Methodists, the establishment will have to go into the melting pot as soon as a new united church begins to emerge. At the present juncture, therefore, it would be a mistake for the Church of England to become deeply involved in a matter which, within the foreseeable future, will make very little difference to the ordering of its local life and which could provide yet another distraction from the main task in the parishes. This task requires it to sit very lightly on whatever privileges remain from the establishment, and to co-operate on equal terms with all those other Christians who are seeking to serve God and their fellow men. Equally urgent is the need to offer a Christian critique of contemporary society and, in particular, to show the church's concern for the underprivileged members of it. Without waiting for the repeal of Acts of Parliament, church leaders can shed the trappings and pomp which go with a privileged position in society. In all these ways the Church of England is free to demonstrate where its faith is really centred and so prepare for the day when it will have a new relationship with the English people. There is no reason why this new relationship should be any less creative than that of the past, provided that the church sees its primary role as service of the human race – whether gathered in village, town, national or international communities – and not the protection of its own rights and privileges.

Trevor Beeson, *The Church of England in Crisis*, Davies-Poynter, 1973, pages 112–13

David Nicholls (1936–96) was a priest and a scholar who wrote extensively on the relationship between politics and religion and lectured in politics at the University of the West Indies. His last years were as Vicar of Littlemore, the parish to which John Henry Newman retired before he entered the Roman Catholic Church.

If we reject the idea that politics is autonomous with respect to religion, then the outlook for a secular state is a bleak one. It is possible to maintain that in the present situation a free church in a free state is likely to spread the Christian faith more effectively than an established Church, and that the cause of Christianity will be damaged by a close association between Church and State – that politicians have a fatal propensity to corrupt anything that they touch. The Whig politician's argument for the established Church was neatly summarised by G. W. E. Russell. 'As long as the Church is Established we can kick the parsons; but once disestablish it, and begad! they'll kick us'. If we conclude that there is no ultimate autonomy of politics from religion, then the only way we can save the conception of a secular state is by maintaining that religion is more likely to flourish when there is a separation between Church and State, than when there is an established Church. For the Church to continue playing the part of an established Church, especially in present-day England, will be fatal for the cause of Christianity.

And so we return to the point that the Church must reconsider its role in contemporary society. It can no longer even *claim* to be the nation at prayer. The Church is not the religious side of the nation, nor can it play this part again in the foreseeable future. Many apostles of the Christian commonwealth idea come from Oxford and Cambridge, and from the public schools, where the chapel takes its place alongside the dining hall, the library and the playing fields as one side of the life of a total society. Dr. Thomas Arnold's vision of Britain as a public school writ large – a total community in which the Church is simply the nation seen from a particular angle – is untenable today. Yet there are still those in England who seem to think of the Church as a total community, an omni-competent body.

David Nicholls, *Church and State in Britain since 1820*, Routledge and Kegan Paul, 1967, pages 22–3

George Austin is a former Archdeacon of York and a well-known writer and broadcaster on religious affairs. He judiciously sums up the arguments in favour of continuing Establishment.

The privileged position of the Church of England as a national church by law established is one which gives it the responsibility of ministering, if required, to every citizen, without qualification. The Church needs the residual involvement with the State in order to preserve that duty against the iconoclastic tendencies of the General Synod. With disestablishment, it could be in grave danger.

In the same way, there is little justification for the requirement that clergy take an oath of allegiance to the monarch, nor for the monarch continuing to hold the title of 'Supreme Governor', since the political purpose of each has become an historical irrelevance. Nevertheless, for the monarch to be the chief lay person of the national church is an important symbolic reminder that, in a just society, secular and spiritual are inextricably linked. Of course to abandon the solemnity of the formal title of the monarch would not reduce the representative demands on that person but rather would deepen them. It would be a greater anomaly for an admitted and unreformed adulterer (let us say – hypothetically, of course) to be Chief Lay Person in a national church than it would be for him to be an impersonal and formal Supreme Governor.

In a similar way, the removal of the Lords Spiritual from Parliament would give a signal that society (through the State) had now no need of such an influence in the deliberations of Parliament. Yet at the same time to confine the Lords Spiritual to bishops of the Church of England cannot be defended in our ecumenical and multi-faith society. Reform of this would come with disestablishment, and ought to come without it.

George Austin, *Affairs of State*, Hodder & Stoughton, 1995, pages 97–8

13

Ecumenism

In unity of spirit, in the bond of peace, and in righteousness of life

The Christian Church has been troubled by disputes and divisions since its foundation. It is unrewarding to hope nostalgically for a return to 'the Church of the New Testament'. The New Testament writings show that the new churches, though united in preaching the Gospel of the Risen Christ, were already following traditions derived from different Apostles and their successors and had many quarrels within themselves. Doctrine and ecclesiology were worked out in the succeeding centuries after controversies which were usually acrimonious and sometimes physically violent. After years of dissension, the great schism between the Churches of the West and the East came in 1054. For a time in the fourteenth century rival Popes claimed universal jurisdiction from Rome and Avignon.

The reformed Church of England was born in a time of greater upheaval than any before. Europe was split between Roman Catholic and Protestant obedience, and the Protestant churches divided into more than one main grouping, with a number of smaller and usually short-lived sects. Anglicans therefore had to consider carefully their position relative not only to the papal jurisdiction which they had repudiated but also to other churches which had made the same break but taken their own distinctive courses. After a short period of formulating its structure and liturgy in the reign of Edward VI, the return to Roman obedience under Mary I, and the associated persecutions, created a climate of fear which lingered through the subsequent years of official authority over the religion of the country. The Elizabethan settlement was harassed by objections from those who wanted a more strongly Protestant Church, with a presbyterian instead of an episcopal model of government. Fear of Rome, now coupled with a political fear of Spain, caused the persecution and killing of some who were trying to re-establish the old order. A gesture towards Protestant ecumenism was made by the presence of some English delegates at the Synod of Dort (1618–19), a gathering of Calvinists which ended in a victory for strict Calvinist principles but did not directly affect the Church of England. The first decades of the seventeenth century, partly though by no means totally peaceful, ended with the triumph of a mainly hostile Parliament and eventually with the proscription of the Book of Common Prayer and the rejection of many faithful priests. In a different direction, some ten years later Richard Montagu (1572–1641), Bishop of Chichester and Norwich, wrote a tract, unpublished until recently, urging Catholic recusants to be reconciled with the Church of England and enumerating the points of contact between the two communions.

Such gestures, tentative though they were, did not come often. It is not surprising, even if to our present mind quite unjustifiable, that the eventual success of the Established Church was accompanied by legal suppression of both Roman and Protestant dissenters, to a degree ranging from civil disability to imprisonment. The search for identity as a Church of the Reformation claiming to be in the unbroken catholic tradition brought hostility rather than respect towards Christians of other confessions. Roman Catholics were feared and distrusted, Protestant dissenters were despised, any nonconformity was suspected of being seditious and disloyal. Richard Hooker, striving to define the distinguishing features of his church, took this view about the relation between church membership and citizenship. As often wiser and more clear-sighted than many of his contemporaries, he yet could accept Roman Catholics and even heretics as not totally severed from the universal Church.

Some few and grudging concessions were made to the Presbyterian deputation at the Savoy Conference which produced the revised Book of Common Prayer in 1662. There were proposals for further revisions in 1698 to accommodate the more Protestant climate in the late years of William III, but they were opposed by the Lower House of Convocation and never passed into law. Although most leading churchmen shared the popular and official line towards other churches, there were some serious Anglican thinkers who regretted the bitter divisions and showed more interest in other traditions. Early controversies lingered, but there were Anglican apologists like Jeremy Taylor who had something of the toleration which would at last lead towards ecumenism. The eighteenth-century Church, distrustful both of other denominations and of any signs of 'enthusiasm' in religion, was not generally inclined to be ecumenical. However, as the words of Wake and Wesley show, the spirit of tolerance was not entirely absent. William Wake, quoted below, looked calmly at the issues of authority with were to become prominent in Anglican–Roman dialogue in the second part of the twentieth century. The darker side was the continuing atavistic fear and hatred which culminated in the violent Gordon Riots in 1780 against an Act to give moderate relief to Roman Catholics.

The legislative Acts of 1828 and 1829, which brought relief and freedom of worship to Protestant and Roman dissenters respectively, did little to diminish popular hostility, particularly towards the latter. There was a closing of Anglican ranks as threats to the monopoly seemed to come from events like the election in 1832 of a House of Commons no longer confined to members of the Church of England, and the restoration of the Roman Catholic hierarchy in 1850.One strand in the complex roots of the Oxford Movement was the fear that the hard-gained supremacy of the Established Church was in danger: 'National Apostasy' was the theme of the sermon by John Keble in 1833 which is taken as the start of the Movement. At the same time, the threat from agnosticism and secularism, and what was seen by many as a threat from Darwinian evolution and the new discoveries of science, brought some even among the successors of the Tractarians to look with less bias towards other Christians. The idea of the Church of England as a 'bridge church' was discussed by Newman in his time as an Anglican, a way of drawing together the Roman and Orthodox communions which had been separated for eight hundred years. Later in the century, old wounds were opened by the failure of the overtures towards Rome which ended with the rejection of Anglican orders in the papal encyclical *Apostolicae Curae* (p. 51).

There was renewed interest in the Orthodox Church, an interest which went back much earlier, when the existence of another church with an unbroken succession but rejecting papal supremacy was seen as a model to support Anglican claims to authentic catholicity. A college for Greek students was founded at Oxford in the seventeenth century, but had little success and faded away. The Nonjurors made contact with the Russian Church but their separated status lacked authority to enter into serious talks. J. M. Neale, translator of early Latin and Greek hymns, was particularly interested in reunion with the East. He wrote a five-volume *History of the Holy Eastern Church,* and a novel, *Theodora Phranza* set at the time of the fall of Constantinople in 1453 with the intention of promoting interest in the Greek Church and the possibility of reunion. A more formal effort was made in 1840 by William Palmer, who visited Russia, met Orthodox bishops and published a *Harmony of Anglican Doctrines with the Doctrine of the Eastern Church.* He later became a Roman Catholic and did not pursue his project.

The Church of England was caught up in the ecumenical impetus of the twentieth century and was represented at the various conferences which brought about the World Council of Churches and similar initiatives. As disappointment over the reply of Leo XIII faded, more hopeful talks were held by the Anglican–Roman Catholic International Commission (ARCIC), which produced goodwill and better understanding but so far have been inconclusive in practice. In 1960 Pope John XXIII and Archbishop Geoffrey Fisher met, the first meeting of a Pope and an Archbishop of Canterbury since the Reformation; in 1966 Pope Paul VI and Archbishop Michael Ramsey met. In 1992 the Porvoo Agreement gave mutual recognition of orders and sacraments with the Lutheran Scandinavian Churches. In both directions, the emphasis in recent discussions has been on what unites and what divides the Churches at the present time, rather than a reprise of historical disagreements.

While organic unity is still not achieved, relations with other churches are better than at any time since the divisions of the sixteenth century. Local councils of churches, ecumenical projects and covenants, regular meetings by clergy of all denominations, have brought Christian love and co-operation in the things which can be done together. It is a powerful light of hope in the problems which still afflict all the churches.

Relationships within the Church of England, and with the rest of the Anglican Communion, are another matter and outside our present scope. An editorial in the *Church Times* on 22 October 2004, commenting on the Windsor Report, observed, 'We have often remarked on the charity and latitude shown by Anglicans to Christians in other denominations, in contrast with the intolerance they show to their fellow Anglicans.'

The attitude of Richard Hooker (p. 10) towards the Roman Catholic Church may seem grudging by modern standards, but it was advanced for its time.

The indisposition therefore of the Church of Rome to reform herself, must be no stay unto us from performing our duty to God; even as desire of retaining conformity with them could be no excuse if we did not perform that duty. Notwithstanding so far as lawfully we may, we have held and do hold fellowship with them. For even as the Apostle doth say of Israel, 'that they are in one respect enemies, but in another beloved of God; in like sort with Rome, we dare not communicate concerning sundry her gross and grievous abominations; yet touching those main parts of Christian truth wherein they constantly still persist, we gladly acknowledge them to be of the family of Jesus Christ; and our hearty prayer unto God Almighty is, 'that being conjoined so far forth with them, they may at the length (if it be his will) so Yield to frame and reform themselves, that no distraction remain in any thing, but that we *all may with one heart and one mouth glorify God the Father of our Lord and Saviour*, whose Church we are. As there are which make the Church of Rome utterly no Church at all, by reason of so many, so grievous errors in their doctrines; so we have them amongst us, who, under pretence of imagined corruptions in our discipline, do give even as hard a judgement of the Church of England itself. But whatsoever either the one sort or the other teach, we must acknowledge even Heretics themselves to be, though a maimed part, yet a part of the visible Church. If an Infidel should pursue to death an Heretic, professing Christianity only for Christian profession sake, could we deny unto him the honour of martyrdom? Yet this honour all men know to be proper unto the Church. Heretics therefore are not utterly cut off from the visible Church of Christ.

The Works of Richard Hooker, Clarendon Press, 1820, vol. 2, page 356 (Book 3, 1)

Jeremy Taylor (p. 36) took a wise and gracious attitude towards other Christians, a view not shared by many of his contemporaries, but looking towards the more ecumenical spirit which would eventually prevail.

It is a hard case that we should think of all Papists and Anabaptists and Sacramentaries to be fools and wicked persons. Certainly, among all these sects, there are very many wise men and good men as well as erring. And although some zeals are so hot and their eyes so inflamed with their ardours that they do not think their adversaries look like other men, yet certainly we find by the results of their discourses and the transactions of their affairs of civil society that they are men that speak and make syllogisms, and use reason, and read Scripture; and although they do no more understand all of it than we do, yet they endeavour to understand as much as concerns them, even all that they can, even all that concerns repentance from dead works and faith in our Lord Jesus Christ. And, therefore, methinks this also should be another consideration distinguishing the persons. For, if the persons be Christians in their lives and Christians in their profession, if they acknowledge the eternal Son of God for their Master and their Lord and live in all relations as becomes persons making such professions, why then should I hate such persons whom God loves, and who love God, who are partakers of Christ and Christ hath a title to them, who dwell in Christ, and Christ in them, because their understandings have not been brought up like mine, have not had the same masters, they have not met with the same books nor the same company, or have not the same interest, or are not so wise, or else are wiser; that is, for some reason or other, which I neither do understand nor ought to blame, have not the same opinions that I have, and do not determine their school-questions to the sense of my sect and interest?

Sacramentaries: Zwinglians and others who denied the Real Presence of Christ in the Holy Communion.

Jeremy Taylor, *Discourse of the Liberty of Prophesying, The Whole Works of the Right Rev. Jeremy Taylor*, ed. C. P. Eden, Longman, 1862

William Wake (1657–1737), Archbishop of Canterbury, became acquainted with the Church in France when he was chaplain to the English ambassador in Paris. He became sympathetic to the Gallican Church, which was Roman Catholic but claiming certain rights and privileges independently of the Pope. Wake had discussions with some of its representatives, but had no liking for the central Roman authority. He was also favourable towards Protestant nonconformists. He writes to William Beauvoir, who held the same chaplaincy which Wake had occupied.

The Church of England, as a national church, has all that power within herself over her own members, which is necessary to enable her to settle her doctrine, government, and discipline, according to the will of Christ and the edification of her members. We have no concern for other Christian churches more than that of charity, and to keep up the unity of the catholic church in the communion of saints. The Church of France, if it would once in good earnest throw off the pope's pretensions, has the same right and independence. She may establish a different worship, discipline, etc., and in some points continue to differ from us in doctrine too, and yet maintain a true communion with us, so long as there is nothing either in her worship or ours to hinder the members of each church to communicate with the other, as they have opportunity.

I make no doubt but that a plan might be framed to bring the Gallican Church to such a state, that we might each hold a true catholic unity and communion with one another, and yet each continue in many things to differ, as we see the Protestant churches do; nay, as both among them and us many learned men do differ in several very considerable points from each other. To frame a common confession of faith, or liturgy, or discipline for both churches is a project never to be accomplished. But to settle each so that the other shall declare it to be a sound part of the catholic church and communicate with one another as such: this may easily be done without much difficulty by them abroad, and I make no doubt but the best and wisest of our Church would be ready to give all due encouragement to it.

Norman Sykes, *William Wake*, Cambridge University Press, 1957, vol. 1, page 260

John Wesley (p. 81) spent some time in Dublin and came to know something of the Roman Catholic Church there. With his usual warmth of heart, he was able to feel a greater sympathy for their position than most of his Anglican contemporaries. In 'A Letter to a Roman Catholic' he urges that there is agreement on many basic articles of faith.

Are we not thus far agreed? Let us thank God for this, and receive it as a fresh token of his love. But if God still loveth us, we ought also to love one another. We ought, without this endless jangling about opinions, to provoke one another to love and to good works. Let the points wherein we differ stand aside: here are enough wherein we agree, enough to be the ground of every Christian temper and of every Christian action.

O brethren, let us not still fall out by the way. I hope to see *you* in heaven. And if I practise the religion above described, you dare not say I shall go to hell. You cannot think so. None can persuade you to it. Your own conscience tells you the contrary. Then if we cannot as yet *think alike* in all things, at least we may *love alike*. Herein we cannot possibly do amiss. For of one point none can doubt a moment: God is love; and he that dwelleth in love, dwelleth in God, and God in him.

In the name, then, and in the strength of God, let us resolve, first, not to hurt one another, to do nothing unkind or unfriendly to each other, nothing which we would not have done to ourselves. Rather let us endeavour after every instance of a kind, friendly and Christian behaviour towards each other.

Let us resolve, secondly, God being our helper, to speak nothing harsh or unkind of each other. The sure way to avoid this is to say all the good we can, both of and to one another; in all our conversation, either with or concerning each other, to use only the language of love; to speak with all softness and tenderness, with the most endearing expression which is consistent with truth and sincerity.

Let us, thirdly, resolve to harbour no unkind thought, no unfriendly temper towards each other. Let us lay the axe to the root of the tree, let us examine all that rises in our heart and suffer no disposition there which is contrary to tender affection. Then shall we easily refrain from unkind actions and words, when the very root of bitterness is cut up.

Let us, fourthly, endeavour to help each other on in whatever we are agreed leads to the Kingdom. So far as we can, let us always rejoice to strengthen each other's hands in God. Above all, let us each take heed unto himself (since each must give an account of himself to God) that he fall not short of the religion of love; that he be not condemned in that he himself approveth. O let you and me (whatever others do) press on to the prize of our high calling – that, being justified by faith, we may have peace with God through our Lord Jesus Christ; that we may rejoice in God through Jesus Christ, by whom we have received the atonement; that the love of God may be shed abroad in our hearts by the Holy Ghost which is given unto us.

The Works of the Rev John Wesley, Wesleyan Methodist Book Room, no date, vol. 10, pages 85–6

William Palmer (1803–85), Fellow of Worcester College, Oxford, supported the early work of the Tractarians, but became opposed to what he and others regarded as their Romeward tendency. Although unsympathetic to both Roman Catholic and Protestant Dissenters, he showed something of an ecumenical spirit in his assessment of the marks of the true Church, with criteria similar to those later set out in the 'Lambeth Quadrilateral'.

Amidst the existing diversities of religious doctrine, it will be found, that all those Churches which have not arisen from schism or voluntary separation from the universal Church, agree to a very great extent in their belief. In proof of this, it may be observed, that the three creeds, called the Apostles', the Nicene, and the Athanasian, are accepted and approved equally by the Greek or Oriental, the British, and the Roman Churches, as well as by the relics of the foreign reformation. The same doctrines which were universally received in the second century are still so in the nineteenth. All Churches believe, and with one mouth confess, one God, who created the world by his only begotten Son, our Lord Jesus Christ, who being co-eternal with the Father, and of equal glory, and power, and majesty, came down from heaven and became man for our salvation, and in his human nature suffered death on the cross, and ascended into heaven, making an eternal and all-sufficient atonement and intercession for us. All believe that the condition of man by nature is such, that he is unable without the aid of Divine grace to turn to God and become pleasing and acceptable to him; that to sinful man Divine grace is given by the free and unmerited mercy of God; and that he is enabled by the sanctifying influences of the eternal Spirit of God, the third person in the most blessed Trinity, to triumph over the sins and infirmities of his nature, and to become sanctified by faith and the love of God, bringing forth the fruits of obedience. All believe that we shall give an account of our works at the last judgement, when the righteous shall be rewarded with life eternal, and the wicked consigned to everlasting fire. The holy Scriptures of the Old and New Testament are universally acknowledged to be the word of God, given by inspiration of the Holy Ghost. The sacraments instituted by Christ are celebrated amongst all nations; and the same Christian ministry has descended by successive ordinations of bishops from the time of the apostles to the present day. Such is the substantial and real agreement in doctrine which exists between Churches which are in some respects dissentient from each other. Their differences turn chiefly on doctrines and practices not taught by our Lord, but which some men in later ages have imagined to be deducible from revelation, or to be allowable and justifiable. Questions as to the truth and lawfulness of such doctrines and practices divide the Christian Churches; but it will probably be found that no article of the faith, no doctrine clearly and distinctly revealed by our Lord, is denied by any of these Churches.

It may be added, that many even of the sectaries or schismatics, who have voluntarily forsaken the Church, still maintain the great mass of Christian doctrine, however destitute they may be of Christian charity.

William Palmer, *Ecclesiastical History*, Burns, 1841, pages 331–3

A. H. Stanton (1839–1913) was a saintly and much loved priest who never moved beyond a curacy at St Alban's, Holborn in London. His sermons still make good spiritual reading; in one of them he praises the comprehensiveness of Anglicanism, a quality valued by its members but unfortunately regarded by some of its opponents as weakness.

The Feast of the Nativity of our Blessed Lady is kept to-day, and this day is also set aside specially for prayer for the Unity of Christendom. Now, we each of us have our ideas of what Christian unity is, and there are those among us who are Anglicans who think that union in Christianity is centred in the Anglican Church. The difficulty, of course, in these cases, is always this, How possibly could a national Church be cosmopolitan? The thing is a contradiction in terms. The Church can be no more a territorial Church than the Church of Rome, the Church of England, or anything else. Now there is one thing for our position here which I should like to say, which to me is the best thing I can say of the position of Anglicans in the face of Christianity, and it is this, that our view of the Church is the largest. We include the Roman and the Eastern, so, practically speaking, our view is the widest and the largest of many views about Christianity.

A. H. Stanton, *Faithful Stewardship and other Sermons*, Hodder & Stoughton, 1916, page 52

A. J. Carlyle was a Fellow of University College, Oxford and later the incumbent of St Martin's Church, Oxford. He was an eccentric and loveable character. Osbert Lancaster recalled that in the 1920s, 'The exact age of Canon A. J. Carlyle was even then a matter for excited speculation; he was known to be the last of the Christian Socialists and the only surviving friend of F. D. Maurice.' Writing in 1902, Carlyle expressed the spirit of liberal Anglicanism which was moving towards the ecumenism of the twentieth century.

It is no doubt true that this repudiation of the absolute authority of the mediaeval Church, this interruption in the continuity of the development of the Christian society, has had its own lamentable consequences. The reaction against an exaggerated authority was so great that it has been often difficult to preserve the sense of authority in the religious societies. To this cause in part we may very well trace our deplorable divisions.

There is no Christian man who does not lament these unhappy divisions, who does not in some measure feel the terrible contrast between the ideal unity of the Church, of the one body of Christ, and the actual condition of Christendom. The East is separate from the West, and the West itself is rent and torn. We must feel that this condition of things is the result of great fault and sins in the past, and that the Christian man who does not strive with all his heart and might for the reunion of Christendom incurs a terrible responsibility. We cannot stand idle while those who are brothers in Christ are separated from each other, while the work of the Christian Church is hampered and thwarted by our divisions. For it is unhappily only too true that the divisions of Christendom are not only in themselves deplorable, but that they do constantly and disastrously hinder the work of God in the world. Where there should be mutual sympathy and co-operation, we find only too often jealousy, rancour, and strife.

There may have been a time when Christian men accepted the fact of these divisions as inevitable, and thought little of unnecessary separation. This is happily not the tendency of our time, but rather we can see on every hand the signs of a growing and deepening feeling for the necessity of reunion.

And we also, in our own time, have learned much of the importance of the continuity of life and order in the religious as well as in the secular society; we have learned that every violent break with the past, even when inevitable, tends to maim and narrow the life of society. It is not so long ago since we in the reformed countries, and not least in England, were anxious only to repudiate the mistakes and conceptions of the past; now we are all anxious to show that we too are the true heirs of the past.

A. J. Carlyle, 'The Church', in *Contentio Veritatis*, John Murray, 1902, pages 267–8

Arthur Middleton (p. 48) looks towards a possible realignment of the Churches in which old divisions will be forgotten in the discovery of a common catholicity and obedience to tradition. It may indeed be that the lines which have kept churches apart for so long will change direction and the distinction will be between what may loosely be called 'traditional' and 'liberal'.

In the face of an arbitrary liberalism that supplants true liberality and a facile comprehensiveness that too often lacks a theological coherence, what we are being called upon to save is the Apostolic Faith and Order of the Church for which Ignatius died. It will challenge the uncritical assumptions of much contemporary ecumenism and not be instantly popular, but in its appeal to Scripture and antiquity it will face it with something deeper. At the same time it will show us how theology can, and cannot, be influenced by the culture of the age. In other parts of the world there are other Christians in the face of this same liberalism in their own churches who share our concern. Is God leading us into a new kind of unity with such Christians, a faithful remnant in which the world will see what it wants to see, a reintegrated and holy Church, reflecting the oneness and unity of the Blessed Trinity, because it is rooted in the Apostolic Faith and Order? Herein lies the authentic note of a western Orthodoxy, Catholic Christianity, for the content and significance of the Christian experience enshrined in this Apostolic Faith and Order transcends all individual apprehensions and defies all final intellectual analysis. Its authority lies in its influence on the world of an insight more adequate than the world's own. It comes in all its saving power to identify with the world but as soon as the world attempts to accommodate and trim that Apostolic Faith and Order to its own limited insights it is lost and the world ends up shipwrecked. The Fathers in every age have known this, that the only way of salvation for a shipwrecked world is to be conformed to the Eucharistic self-giving of God. Let this be our ministry of reconciliation, the way for people of the tradition today.

Arthur Middleton, *The Peculiar Character of Anglicanism*, The Prayer Book Society, 1997, pages 30–1

The Lambeth Quadrilateral was offered again in a modified form, but with a strong insistence on the need for episcopacy, in a call for reunion by the Lambeth Conference in 1920.

The vision which rises before us is that of a Church genuinely Catholic, loyal to all Truth, and gathering into its fellowship all who profess and call themselves Christians, within whose visible unity all the treasures of faith and order, bequeathed as a heritage by the past to the present, shall be possessed in common and made serviceable to the whole Body of Christ. Within this unity Christian Communions now separated from one another would retain much that has long been distinctive in their methods of worship and service. It is through a rich diversity of life and devotion that the unity of the whole fellowship will be fulfilled [. . .]

We believe that the visible unity of the Church will be found to involve the wholehearted acceptance of:

The Holy Scriptures as the record of God's revelation of Himself to man, and as being the rule and ultimate standard of faith; and the Creed commonly called Nicene, as the sufficient statement of the Christian faith, and either it or the Apostles' Creed as the Baptismal confession of belief.

The divinely instituted sacraments of Baptism and the Holy Communion, as expressing for all the corporate life of the whole fellowship, in and with Christ.

A ministry acknowledged by every part of the Church as possessing not only the inward call of the Spirit but also the commission of Christ and the authority of the whole body.

May we not reasonably claim that the Episcopate is the one means of providing such a ministry? It is not that we call in question for a moment the spiritual reality of the ministries of those Communions who do not possess the Episcopate. On the contrary, we thankfully acknowledge that these ministries have been manifestly blessed and owned by the Holy Spirit as effective means of grace. But we submit that considerations alike of history and of present experience justify the claim which we make on behalf of the Episcopate. Moreover, we would urge that it is now and will prove to be in the future the best instrument for maintaining the unity and the continuity of the Church.

'A Letter to All Christian People'

The introduction to the Porvoo Agreement (see above) takes us back to the sixteenth-century claims to continuing catholicity but now reaches out in a way which would not have been found in the more insular Church of England of that time.

The faith, worship and spirituality of all our churches are rooted in the tradition of the apostolic Church. We stand in continuity with the Church of the patristic and medieval periods both directly and through the insights of the Reformation period. We each understand our own church to be part of the One, Holy, Catholic Church of Jesus Christ and truly participating in the one apostolic mission of the whole people of God. We share in the liturgical heritage of Western Christianity and also in the Reformation emphases upon justification by faith and upon word and sacrament as means of grace. All this is embodied in our confessional and liturgical documents and is increasingly recognised both as an essential bond between our churches and as a contribution to the wider ecumenical movement.

Despite geographical separation and a wide diversity of language, culture and historical development, the Anglican and Lutheran churches in Britain and Ireland and in the Nordic and Baltic countries have much in common, including much common history. Anglo-Saxon and Celtic missionaries played a significant part in the evangelisation of Northern Europe and founded some of the historic sees in the Nordic lands. The unbroken witness of successive bishops in the dioceses and the maintenance of pastoral and liturgical life in the cathedrals and churches of all our nations are an important manifestation of the continuity of Christian life across the ages, and of the unity between the churches in Britain and Ireland and in Northern Europe.

Each of our churches has played a significant role in the social and spiritual development of the nation in which it has been set. We have been conscious of our mission and ministry to all the people in our nations. Most of our churches have had a pastoral and sometimes a legal responsibility for the majority of the population of our countries. This task is today increasingly being carried out in co-operation with other churches.

Council for Christian Unity of the General Synod of the Church of England,
London, 1993

Poetry and hymnology may once again speak more forcefully than exposition. The need and the desire for reunion, if not the methodology, are here committed in a hymn of prayer.

O Thou, who at thy Eucharist didst pray
That all thy Church might be for ever one,
Grant us at every Eucharist to say
With longing heart and soul, 'Thy will be done.'
Oh, may we all one Bread, one Body be,
   One through this Sacrament of unity.

For all thy Church, O Lord, we intercede;
Make thou our sad divisions soon to cease;
Draw us the nearer each to each, we plead,
By drawing all to thee, O Prince of Peace:
Thus may we all one Bread, one Body be,
   One through this Sacrament of unity.

We pray thee too for wanderers from thy fold;
O bring them back, good Shepherd of the sheep,
Back to the faith which saints believed of old,
Back to the Church which still that faith doth keep.
Soon may we all one Bread, one Body be,
   One through this Sacrament of unity.

So, Lord, at length when sacraments shall cease,
May we be one with all thy Church above,
One with thy saints in one unbroken peace,
One with thy saints in one unbounded love:

More blessed still, in peace and love to be
One with the Trinity in Unity.

William Turton (1856–1938), *The New English
Hymnal*, Canterbury Press, 1986, no. 302

14

Postscript

Give us that due sense of all thy mercies

For centuries leading members of the Church of England have been lamenting its decline and prophesying its demise. Others have been confident about the present and optimistic about the future. A few examples of both attitudes may illustrate the capacity for accommodating different views which is often a virtue, and sometimes a weakness, in that same Church.

The suppression of Anglican order and worship during the Commonwealth was particularly distressing. Christopher Harvey (1597–1663) has not left a notable mark on English literature, although at one time his poems were published in the same volume as George Herbert's The Temple. *His lament over the Presbyterian attacks on episcopacy catches something of the feeling of members of the Church of England in those years.*

'The Bishop?' 'Yes, why not? What doth that name
Import that is unlawful or unfit?
To say the Overseer is the same
In substance, and no hurt, I hope, in it;
    But sure if men did not despise the thing,
    Such scorn upon the name they would not bring.

Some Priests – some presbyters I mean – would be
Each overseer of his several cure;
But one superior, to oversee
Them altogether, they will not endure:
    This the main difference is that I can see,
    Bishops they would not have, but they would be.

But who can show of old that ever any
Presbyteries without their bishops were?
Though bishops without presbyteries many
At first must needs be almost everywhere
    That presbyters from bishops first arose
    To assist them's probable, not these from those.

However; a true bishop I esteem
The highest officer the Church on earth
Can have, as proper to itself, and deem
A Church without one an imperfect birth
    If constituted so at first; and maim'd,
    If whom it had, it afterwards disclaimed.

All order first from unity ariseth,
And th' essence of it is subordination;
Whoever this contemns, and that despiseth.
May talk of, but intends not, reformation:
    'Tis not of God, of nature, or of art,
    T' ascribe to all what's proper to one part.

Complete Poems of Christopher Harvey, ed. Grosart,
privately printed, 1874, pages 40–1

In 1663 Thomas Ken (p. 103) wrote Ichabod or the Five Groans of the Church, *published in 1709 as* An Expostulation. *At a time when there was general rejoicing at the restoration of the Church of England after the Commonwealth suppression he found it to be at fault in respect of unsuitable ordinations, simony, non-residence, pluralities and profaneness. He begins with the voice of the Church lamenting her condition, in the idiom of the biblical book of Lamentations.*

O all you that pass by me, stand and see *if there be any sorrow like unto my sorrow*; if it hath been done to any Reformed or Protestant Church under heaven, as it is done unto me! O, now my wounds were ready to be closed, my ruins to be repaired, my desolations and wastes to be finished; when the barbarous was checked, the licentious was restrained, the usurpers were removed, the professed enemies of different interests and religion which persecuted me, were subdued, and I ready to settle

upon the eternal foundations of sound doctrine, of primitive government, of an holy and pure worship, of a decent and comely order, to
the amazement of the world, to the honour of religion, to the glory of
God, to the peace of the whole earth, and for good will among men.
Behold! my children are discontent, my government is complained of,
my ordinances are neglected, my ministers are despised, my peace is
disturbed, and my safety endangered.

The Prose Works of Thomas Ken, Rivington, 1838, page 3

*Augustus Toplady (1740–78) is best remembered for his hymn 'Rock of
Ages'. A parish priest in Devonshire, he was attracted to Wesley but
acquired extreme Calvinist principles and turned against him. In a 'Short
Address to the Clergy' he castigates the Church of his time for departing
from its early reformed purity. He is in a line descended from the 'Church
Puritans' of the sixteenth century. Like Ken, above, writing in a different
tradition of churchmanship, he believes that 'the glory is departed' – the
meaning of 'Ichabod'.*

Where shall we stop? We have already forsook the paths, trod by Moses
and the prophets, and by Christ and the apostles: paths in which our
own reformers also trod, our martyrs, our bishops, our clergy, our universities, and the whole body of this Protestant, of this once Calvinistic
nation. Our liturgy, our articles, and our homilies, it is true, still keep
possession of our church walls: but we pray, we subscribe, we assent one
way; we believe, we preach, we write another. In the desk, we are verbal
Calvinists: but no sooner do we ascend a few steps above the desk, than
we forget the grave character in which we appeared below, and tag the
performance with a few minutes entertainment, compiled from the frag-
ments bequeathed to us by Pelagius and Arminians; not to say by Arius,
Socinus, and by others still worse than they. Observe, I speak not of all
indiscriminately. We have many great and good men, some of whom
are, and some of whom are not Calvinists. But, that the glory is in a very
considerable degree, departed from our established Sion, is a truth
which cannot be contravened, a fact which must be lamented, and an
alarming symptom which ought to be publicly debated.

Works of Augustus Toplady, Baynes, 1825, vol. 2, page 347

*The Assize Sermon preached on 14 July 1833 by John Keble (p. 148) was
entitled 'National Apostasy'. The situation of the Church of England
seemed to Keble and his friends to be very perilous. His serious but confident
words are worth heeding at a time of later anxieties.*

Come what may, we have ill learned the lessons of our Church, if we permit our patriotism to decay, together with the protecting care of the
State. 'The powers that be are ordained of God', whether they foster the
true Church or no. Submission and order are still duties. They were so in
the days of pagan persecution; and the more of loyal and affectionate
feeling we endeavour to mingle with our obedience, the better.

   After all, the surest way to uphold or restore our endangered Church,
will be for each of her anxious children, in his own place and station, to
resign himself more thoroughly to his God and Saviour in those duties,
public and private, which are not immediately affected by the emergen-
cies of the moment: the daily and hourly duties, I mean, of piety, purity,
charity, justice. It will be a consolation understood by every thoughtful
Churchman, that let his occupation be, apparently, never so remote
from such great interests, it is in his power, by doing all as a Christian, to
credit and advance the cause he has most at heart; and what is more, to
draw down God's blessing upon it.

John Keble, *Sermons Academical and Occasional,* Parker, 1848, pages 146–7

In the first of the Tracts for the Times *(p. 62) Newman called his fellow-
clergy to stir themselves before the Church continued to decline. Similar
exhortations are being made from various directions today.*

I am but one of yourselves – a Presbyter; and therefore I conceal my
name, lest I should take too much on myself by speaking in my own
person. Yet speak I must; for the times are very evil, yet no one speaks
against them.

   Is not this so? Do not we 'look one upon another,' yet perform nothing? Do we not all confess the peril into which the Church is come, yet sit
still each in his own retirement, as if mountains and seas cut off brother
from brother? Therefore suffer me, while I try to draw you forth from
those pleasant retreats which it has been our blessedness hitherto to

enjoy, to contemplate the condition and prospects of our Holy Mother in a practical way; so that one and all may unlearn that idle habit, which has grown upon us, of owning the state of things to be bad, yet doing nothing to remedy it.

At the same time Thomas Arnold, Headmaster of Rugby School, Broad Churchman and opponent of the Tractarians, was equally pessimistic. He wrote: 'The church as it now stands no human power can save.'

Isaac Williams (p. 149) was unhappy about the lack of reverence and failure to acknowledge the authority of the Church as the interpreter of the Bible. His complaints can be matched in the sixteenth century and at the present time. Acceptance of the Old Testament Apocrypha has been divisive between Catholic and Protestant opinions since the Reformation.

The fearful extent to which this want of reverence in religion has gone, is, it is to be feared, very little considered or calculated upon. The degree to which all sense of the holiness of Churches is lost, is too evident; the efficacy of the Sacraments, the presence of God in them, and in His appointed ministerial ordinances is, it will be allowed, by no means duly acknowledged, and, indeed, less and less, men's eyes being not opened, they do not see with the patriarch, 'how dreadful is this place', 'the LORD was in this place, and I knew it not'. There is also another point in which all due fear of GOD'S awful presence is lost, very far beyond what many are aware of, and that is in regard for the Holy Scripture. Some indeed, who profess to uphold and value them, in order to do so, depreciate the Apocryphal books, and all others of less plenary inspiration; as if by so doing they were exalting the Scriptures. But in fact, they do but lower their own standard of what is holy; and then lower the Scriptures also to meet it. The effect also of setting aside the Catholic Church as the interpreter of Holy Scripture, as if it needed none, is of the same kind ; it incalculably lowers the reverence for Scripture, by making it subject to the individual judgement. From these things it follows, that although the Holy Scriptures are pronounced Divine (for no evil is done, but under a good name) they are treated as if they were not; as if human thought could grasp their systems, could limit their meanings, and say to that boundless ocean in which the Almighty walks, 'Hitherto shalt Thou come and no further'. If Holy Scripture contains within it the living Word, has a letter that killeth, and a Spirit that giveth life, with far different a temper ought we to regard it. By prayer, as the Fathers say, we should knock at the door, waiting till He that is within open to us; it should be approached as that which has a sort of Sacramental efficacy about it, and, therefore a savour of life, and also unto death; in short, as our SAVIOUR was of old, by them who would acknowledge Him as God, and receive His highest gifts.

Tracts for the Times, vol. 4, Rivington, 1840, page 119

Thomas Mozley, Fellow of Oriel College, Oxford and a Tractarian sympathiser, looked back to what he remembered as the position in 1833.

Every party, every interest, political or religious, in this country was pursuing its claim to universal acceptance, with the single exception of the Church of England, which was folding its robes to die with what dignity it could.

Thomas Mozley, *Reminiscences*, 1882

Mandell Creighton (p. 22), concerned about what seemed to be threats to the position of the Church of England at the beginning of the twentieth century, had some wise words which may be even more applicable at the beginning of the twenty-first.

I am aware that perfect peace and agreement cannot come at once, or indeed ever in this imperfect world; but those who are dealing with the highest interests of man may at least avoid conscious misrepresentation and appeals to prejudice. If controversy is inevitable, it should be about principles and not about petty details. We need not unduly regret a crisis which compels us to think more seriously and to weigh the tendency of our actions, not only as they appear in our own eyes, but in their relation to the religious life of our country as a whole.

Mandell Creighton, *The Church and the Nation*, Longmans, 1901, page 269

One of the many ways in which members of the Church of England may be divided is their attitude to synodical government. Some are enthusiastic about every gathering from Parochial Church Councils to the General Synod, and some are not. Towards the end of the twentieth century, the writer and broadcaster James Munson found no good in ecclesiastical bureaucracy. More recently, the General Synod has reduced the number of its sessions.

In our own day the Church of England, and increasingly the Roman Catholic Church, have followed the lead set by the Nonconformist or Free Church denominations. The Church of England now has its 'General Synod' which, to the delight of all activists, meets three times a year. Synodical government of the Church assumes, of course, that the Church needs to be 'governed'. It is an attempt to solve the dilemma brought about by the Church's assignment to the periphery of a secular society while still being under control of a Parliament only periodically Christian. Ecclesiastical self-government in the democratic mould, with lots of elections, committees, reports, debates and discussions is acceptable to the secular world. It may, however, only confirm the Church of England's peripheral existence.

William Oddie (ed.), *After the Deluge*, SPCK, 1987, page 162

The brighter view of things has had equally convinced exponents. Although Newman was despondent about the state of affairs in 1833 (p. 250), before he left the Church of England in 1845 he defended it in terms which may still stand as encouragement and challenge to its present-day members.

Now if there ever were a Church on whom the experiment has been tried whether it had life in it or not, the English is that one. For three centuries it has endured all vicissitudes of fortune. It has endured in trouble and prosperity, under seduction and under oppression. It has been practised upon by theorists, browbeaten by sophists, intimidated by princes, betrayed by false sons, laid waste by tyranny, corrupted by wealth, torn by schism, and persecuted by fanaticism. Revolutions have come upon it sharply and suddenly, to and fro, hot and cold, as if to try what it was made of. It has been a sort of battlefield on which opposite principles have been tried. No opinion, however extreme any way, but may be found, as the Romanists are not slow to reproach us, among its bishops and divines. Yet what has been its career upon the whole? Which way has it been moving through three hundred years? Where does it find itself at the end? Lutherans have tended to Rationalism; Calvinists have become Socinians; but what has it become? As far as its formularies are concerned, it may be said all along to have grown towards a more perfect Catholicism than that with which it started at the time of its estrangement; every act, every crisis, which marks its course, has been upward.

J. H. Newman, *The Via Media of the Anglican Church*, Longmans, 1845, page 155

John Keble was also despondent in 1833 (p. 250), but a little earlier had expressed a more positive view which he never abandoned and which many would still share.

Next to a sound rule of faith, there is nothing of so much consequence as a sober standard of feeling in matters of practical religion: and it is the peculiar happiness of the Church of England to possess, in her authorised formularies, an ample and secure provision for both.

John Keble, Preface, *The Christian Year* (1827), Oxford University Press, 1914

A. P. Stanley (1815–81), Professor of Ecclesiastical History at Oxford and then Dean of St Paul's, was a pupil of Thomas Arnold at Rugby and later wrote his biography. He angered some traditional churchmen by his liberal views, but here he shows himself a staunch and admiring member of the Church of England.

If there ever was a Church in which Ecclesiastical History might be expected to flourish, it is the English. Unlike almost all the other Churches of Europe, alone in its constitution, in its origin, in its formularies, it touches all the religious elements which have divided or united Christendom. He may be a true son of the Church of England, who is able to throw himself into the study of the first Four Councils to which the statutes of our constitution refer, or of the medieval times in which our cathedrals and parishes were born and nurtured. He also may be a true son of the same who is able to hail as fellow-workers the great reformers of Wittenburg, of Geneva, and of Zurich, whence flowed so strong an influence over at least half of our present formularies. But he is the truest son of all who, in the spirit of this union, feels himself free to sympathise with the several elements and principles of good which the Church of England has thus combined, who knows that the strength of a national Church, especially of the Church of a nation like ours, lies in the fact that it has never been surrendered exclusively to any one theological influence, and that the Christian faith which it has inherited from all is greater than the differences which it has inherited from each.

The Prayer Book as it stands is a long gallery of Ecclesiastical History, which, to be understood and enjoyed thoroughly, absolutely compels a knowledge of the greatest events and names of all periods of the Christian Church. To Ambrose we owe the present form of our *Te Deum*; Charlemagne breaks the silence of our Ordination prayers by the *Veni Creator Spiritus*. The Persecutions have given us one creed, and the Empire another. The name of the first great Patriarch of the Byzantine Church closes our daily service; the Litany is the bequest of the first great Patriarch of the Latin Church, amidst the terrors of the Roman pestilence. Our collects are the joint productions of the Fathers, the Popes, and the Reformers. Our Communion Service bears the traces of every fluctuation of the Reformation, through the two extremes of the reign of Edward to the conciliating policy of Elizabeth, and the reactionary zeal of the Restoration. The more comprehensive, the more free, the more impartial is our study of any or every branch of Ecclesiastical History, the more will it be in accordance with the spirit and with the letter of the Church of England.

A. P. Stanley, *Lectures on the History of the Eastern Church* (1861), Dent, 1907, pages 33–4

J. H. Shorthouse (1834–1903), a Quaker who became a firm Anglican, wrote several novels of which the most successful was John Inglesant *(1881). Very popular in its time, it tells of the progress of a young man in the time of Charles I and the Commonwealth who passes through many adventures before settling in the Church of England, which he here eulogises.*

The English Church, as established by the law of England, offers the supernatural to all who choose to come. It is like the Divine Being

Himself, whose sun shines alike on the evil and on the good. Upon the altars of the Church the divine presence hovers as surely, to those who believe it, as it does upon the splendid altars of Rome. Thanks to circumstances which the founders of our Church did not contemplate, the way is open; it is barred by no confession, no human priest. Shall we throw this aside? It has been won for us by the death and torture of men like ourselves in bodily frame, infinitely superior to some of us in self-denial and endurance. God knows – those who know my life know too well – that I am not worthy to be named with such men; nevertheless, though we cannot endure as they did – at least do not let us needlessly throw away what they have won. It is not even a question of religious freedom only; it is a question of learning and culture in every form. I am not blind to the peculiar dangers that beset the English Church. I fear that its position, standing, as it does, a mean between two extremes, will engender indifference and sloth; and that its freedom will prevent its preserving a disciplining and organising power, without which any community will suffer grievous damage; nevertheless, as a Church it is unique: if suffered to drop out of existence, nothing like it can ever take its place.

J. H. Shorthouse, *John Inglesant* (1881), Macmillan, 1883, pages 442–3

Opinions for and against the Book of Common Prayer as the ideal liturgy of the Church of England have been quoted. Some have thought that its virtues go beyond public worship and help to sustain the whole ethos of the Church.

It has always been clear that the Prayer Book and the Bible side by side should inspire all Anglican devotion. The Prayer Book is not a handbook of offices for the priesthood only; it is meant to be used, according to his capacity and his need, by every member of the Church. Though the obligation to say Mattins and Evensong daily rests only on the clergy, in the days which we have been considering it was by no means ignored by the laity. Some parts of those services, or some selections from the collects, together with passages from the Bible, formed the basis of those family prayers which, from the Reformation until comparatively recent times, were a regular feature of religious households. The ordinary Englishman was familiar with the Prayer Book at home as well as in Church. It was a part of the way of life which he took with him when he left his own country. Wherever English colonists, and particularly English ships, went, the Book of Common Prayer went also. Without it many a Sunday spent far from civilisation would have passed without prayer, and many a lonely grave would have been unhallowed if the Prayer Book had not provided such a service as a layman might read. The Prayer Book has well suited the genius of our English people.

This centrality of the Bible and the Prayer Book must be borne in mind if many of the classical books of Anglican devotion are to be properly assessed. What may seem deficiencies in breadth or feeling are accounted for by the fact that they do not attempt to do more than explain, or expand, what is to be found in the two books which are assumed to be in everybody's hands. Whatever lack of balance an author may be conscious of, he redresses by a reminder that the Prayer Book is the full expression of Anglican doctrine and devotion. The Protestant-minded accept its Catholicism, the Catholic-minded its Protestantism. The Book of Common Prayer was welcome to both wings and guaranteed that neither should triumph to the exclusion of the other

C. J. Stranks, *Anglican Devotion*, SCM Press, 1961, pages 275–6

Eric Milner-White (1884–1963), Dean of King's College, Cambridge where he instituted the popular Christmas Eve service of Nine Lessons and Carols, and later Dean of York, was very upbeat about the wide and beneficent influence of the Church of England.

The sacrament of the Church has not only survived, but has strengthened both its claim and function. If it has done this in England, it has done so throughout Christendom; for what is true of the triumph of Holy Spirit in one part of the field holds good for all. We do not pretend anything so absurd as that the English Church has – if the military metaphor be allowed – fought and won this battle alone; the old guard of Rome and the East lay behind; sharpshooters, pioneers, and allies, protestant, modernist, and independent, played essential if unorganised and sometimes embarrassing, parts in the forefront; but the brunt fell upon that Communion which, under the standard of the Catholic creeds and the discipline of Apostolic order, had the necessary freedom and mobility to march to the guns and make contact with the armies of science. The work of the Church of England through the scientific and critical revolution has been at least of an importance sufficient to justify at the bar of history her position in temporary separation from its fellow-communions of East and West. She has done for the Catholic Church that which Rome was not free to do, and which the East was too far from the centres of modern thinking to comprehend. It is not merely that Catholicism has not suffered by the new categories; new knowledge of the world has meant in every direction new understanding of God; criticism of the two Testaments – the fiercest effort of mind in history – has not only revealed the rocks on which they stand, but has given a re-interpretation of their place and meaning in religion which is well-nigh a new revelation; the concentration of study upon the figure of Christ has but lit up the unique majesty of His perfection and love. That such is now bound to be the result of the nineteenth-century renaissance in the religious sphere can scarcely be denied. A revolution of mind, in itself glorious and wonderful, has led to glorious revelation of God. The Church has lost nothing but what is good to lose; it has gained rich reality and outpouring of Holy Spirit.

Eric Milner-White, 'The Spirit and the Church in History', in E. G. Selwyn (ed.), *Essays Catholic and Critical*, SPCK, 1926, pages 338–9

David Hope, former Archbishop of York, suggests three distinctive marks of Anglicanism.

An abiding openness to be self-critical [. . .] worship and popular devotion continue to live side by side [. . .] a holy reticence in Anglicanism's soul which can be tantalising, not only for those on the inside.

David Hope in Geoffrey Rowell *et al.*, eds, *Love's Redeeming Work*, Oxford University Press, 2001, Afterword

Although our concern has been with the Church of England rather than the whole Anglican Communion, the claims made from the sixteenth century about Anglican identity and catholicity have become drawn into the wide range of churches in communion with the Archbishop of Canterbury.

William Jacob, Archdeacon of Charing Cross in the Diocese of London, makes this point succinctly.

The Anglican Communion illustrates the dynamic effectiveness of a church 'reformed according to the model of the primitive Church' in establishing itself as a communion of national churches, receptive to local language and culture in their liturgies and theology, with synodical processes, including bishops, clergy and laity, with a dispersed pattern of authority, and the Archbishop of Canterbury as *primes inter pares.* It has not been a smooth process. Many historic tensions are still present: between Church and state, between laity and bishops, about the nature of the teaching authority of the Church, about the nature of the church and theology, and about the nature and location of authority in the Church. These tensions have always existed within the Church. In the Anglican Communion they are contained within a community of dialogue, which, in my view, stands within the traditions of the Western Church, maintaining the traditions of the 'primitive Church'.

Stephen Platten (ed.), *Anglicanism and the Western Christian Tradition,*
Canterbury Press, 2003, page 206

We shall never please everybody, as the revisers of the Book of Common Prayer recognised.

Having thus endeavoured to discharge our duties in this weighty affair, as in the sight of God, and to approve our sincerity therein (so far as lay in us) to the consciences of all men; although we know it impossible (in such variety of apprehensions, humours and interests, as are in the world) to please all; nor can expect that men of factious, peevish, and perverse spirits should be satisfied with any thing that can be done in this kind by any other than themselves. Yet we have good hope, that what is here presented, and hath been by the Convocations of both Provinces with great diligence examined and approved, will be also well accepted and approved by all sober, peaceable, and truly conscientious Sons of the Church of England.

Preface to the Book of Common Prayer 1662

But the ultimate hope is not with the liturgists or the theologians.

O Lord, we beseech thee, let thy continual pity cleanse and defend thy Church; and, because it cannot continue in safety without thy succour, preserve it evermore by thy help and goodness; through Jesus Christ our Lord. Amen.

Collect for the Sixteenth Sunday after Trinity, Book of Common Prayer

Sources

Richard Allestree, *The Whole Duty of Man* (1657), 1700

The Alternative Service Book 1980, Clowes, CUP and SPCK, 1980

Lancelot Andrewes, *Sermons*, ed. J. P. Wilson Parker, 1841–3

Thomas Arnold, *Christian Life, its course, its hindrances and its helps*, Fellowes, 1878

George Austin, *Affairs of State*, Hodder & Stoughton, 1995

Lewis Bayly, *The Practice of Piety* (1611), London, 1820

(Edward Bradley), 'Cuthbert Bede', *The Adventures of Mr Verdant Green, an Oxford Freshman* (1857), Nelson, no date

Roger Beckwith, *Thomas Cranmer after Five Hundred Years*, The Prayer Book Society, 1989

Trevor Beeson, *The Church of England in Crisis*, Davies-Poynter, 1973

J. F. Bethune-Baker, *The Way of Modernism*, Cambridge University Press, 1927

Edwyn Bevan, 'Petition' in *Concerning Prayer*, Macmillan, 1916

William Beveridge, *Theological Works*, Parker, 1844

John Bishop, *The Ultimate Mystery*, John Bishop Charitable Trust, 1998

George Borrow, *Lavengro* (1851), John Murray, 1904

George Borrow, *The Romany Rye* (1857), John Murray, 1903

John Bramhall, *A Just Vindication of the Church of England* (1654), Parker, 1842

Religio Medici and Other Writings of Sir Thomas Browne, Dent, 1925

Gilbert Burnet, *A Discourse of the Pastoral Care*, (1692), London, 1766

A. J. Carlyle, 'The Church', in *Contentio Veritatis*, John Murray, 1902

The Works of William Chillingworth, Oxford University Press, 1838

S. T. Coleridge, *Collected Poems*, Oxford University Press, 1912

John Cosin, *Works*, Parker, 1855

Writings and Translations of Myles Coverdale, ed. G. Pearson, Parker Society, 1844

The Works of Thomas Cranmer, ed. G. E. Duffield, Sutton Courtenay Press, 1964

Mandell Creighton, *The Church and the Nation*, Longmans, 1901

F. L. Cross, *Darwell Stone*, Dacre Press, 1943

Evan Daniel, *The Prayer Book its History, Language and Contents*, Gardner, 1901

Gregory Dix, *The Shape of the Liturgy*, Dacre Press, 1945

John Donne, *Poetical Works*, Oxford University Press, 1979

John Donne, *Selected Prose*, ed. E. Simpson, Clarendon Press, 1967

D. L. Edwards, *Not Angels but Anglicans*, SCM Press, 1958

Henry Fielding, *The Adventures of Joseph Andrews*, 1742

Sue Flockton, *Why Not Ordain Women?*, Church Literature Association, 1977

Goldsmith's Complete Poetical Works, Oxford University Press, 1906

Charles Gore, *The Body of Christ*, John Murray (1901), 1931

Charles Gore, *The Mission of the Church*, John Murray, 1892

Charles Gore, *The Religion of the Church*, Mowbray, 1916

William Gresley, *Portrait of an English Churchman*, Rivington, 1840

The Works of Matthew Hale, R. White, 1805

The Miscellaneous Theological Works of Henry Hammond, Parker, 1849

Henry Hammond, *A Practical Catechism*, Parker, 1847

C. P. Hankey, in A. C. Hebert (ed.), *The Parish Communion*, SPCK 1937

Robert Hannaford, *A Church for the Twenty-first Century*, Gracewing, 1998

Complete Poems of Christopher Harvey, ed. Grosart, privately printed, 1874

M. V. G. Havergal, *Memorials of Frances Ridley Havergal*, Nisbet, 1880

Stewart Headlam, *The Laws of Eternal Life*, Verinder, 1888

A. G. Hebert, *Liturgy and Society*, Faber, 1935

Herbert Hensley Henson, *Bishoprick Papers*, Oxford University Press, 1946

The Works of George Herbert, ed. F. E. Hutchinson, Oxford University Press, 1941

Henry Scott Holland, *Logic and Life*, Longmans Green, 1892

W. F. Hook, *The Church and its Ordinances*, Bentley, 1876

The Works of Richard Hooker, Clarendon Press, 1820

W. Walsham How, *Holy Communion*, SPCK, 1925

W. R. Inge, *A Rustic Moralist*, Putnam, 1937

P. D. James, in M. Furlong (ed.), *Our Childhood's Pattern*, Mowbray, 1995

J. C. Jeafferson, *A Book about the Clergy*, Hurst and Blackett, 1870

John Jewel, *Apology* (1562), Religious Tract Society, no date

Works of Bishop Jewel, ed. J. Ayre, Parker Society, 1847

Samuel Johnson, *Prayers*, SCM Press, 1947

Benjamin Jowett, 'On the Interpretation of Scripture', in *Essays and Reviews*, Parker, 1860

John Keble, *The Christian Year* (1827), Oxford University Press, 1914

John Keble, *Sermons Academical and Occasional*, Parker, 1848

The Prose Works of Thomas Ken, Rivington, 1838

Selections from the Poetical Works of Bishop Ken, Hamilton Adams, 1857

Edward King, *Sermons and Addresses*, Longman, 1911

Edward King, *Spiritual Letters*, Mowbray, 1910

The Remains of Alexander Knox, 1836

Sermons by Hugh Latimer, Dent, 1906

Works of William Laud, Parker, 1847

William Law, *A Serious Call to a Devout and Holy Life* (1728), Epworth Press, 1961

H. P. Liddon, *Advent in St Paul's*, Longman (1888), 1896

W. Lock, 'The Church', in C. Gore (ed.), *Lux Mundi*, John Murray, 1904

H. L. Mansel, *Limits of Religious Thought*, Bampton Lectures, John Murray, 1859

A. J. Mason, *The Relation of Confirmation to Baptism*, Longmans Green, 1891

F. D. Maurice, *The Kingdom of Christ*, Rivington, 1883

Arthur Middleton, *Fathers and Anglicans*, Gracewing, 2001

Arthur Middleton, *Loving Learning and Desiring God*, Address to the Prayer Book Society, 2004

Arthur Middleton, *The Peculiar Character of Anglicanism*, The Prayer Book Society, 1997

Barney Milligan, *The Priest and the World*, SPCK, 1974

Works of Hannah More, Cassell, 1830

Thomas Mozley, *Reminiscences*, 1882

Peter Mullen (ed.), *The Real Common Worship*, Edgeways, 2000

Robert Nelson, *Companion for the Festivals and Fasts of the Church of England*, 1704

The New English Hymnal, Canterbury Press, 1986

J. H. Newman, *Essays Critical and Historical*, Pickering, 1871

J. H. Newman, *Parochial and Plain Sermons* (1834–42), Rivington, 1875

J. H. Newman, *Tracts for the Times*, vol. 1, Parker, 1839

J. H. Newman, *The Via Media of the Anglican Church*, Longmans, 1845

William Nicholson, *An Exposition of the Catechism* (1661), Parker, 1842

David Nicholls, *Church and State in Britain since 1820*, Routledge and Kegan Paul, 1967

William Oddie (ed.), *After the Deluge*, SPCK, 1987

C. F. Osborne, *The Life of Father Dolling*, Arnold, 1903

William Palmer, *Ecclesiastical History*, Burns, 1841

The Works of Simon Patrick, ed. A. Taylor, Oxford University Press, 1858

Michael Perham, *Celebrate the Christian Story*, SPCK, 1997

The Poems of Thomas Pestell, Oxford University Press, 1940

Stephen Platten (ed.), *Anglicanism and the Western Christian Tradition*, Canterbury Press, 2003

J. Purchas, *The Directorium Anglicanum*, 1858

E. B. Pusey, *Parochial Sermons*, vol. 1, Parker, 1860

E. B. Pusey, *The Real Presence of the Body and Blood of our Lord Jesus Christ the Doctrine of the English Church*, Parker, 1869

A. M. Ramsey, 'What is Anglican Theology?', *Theology*, vol. 48, 1945

J. A. T. Robinson, *Honest to God*, SCM Press, 1963

Christina Rossetti, Poems, Macmillan, 1904

Geoffrey Rowell, Kenneth Stevenson and Rowan Williams, eds, *Love's Redeeming Work*, Oxford University Press, 2001

G. W. E. Russell, *The Household of Faith*, Hodder & Stoughton, 1902

Works of Robert Sanderson, Oxford University Press, 1854

E. G. Selwyn (ed.), *Essays Catholic and Critical*, SPCK, 1926

Sermons and Homilies Appointed to be read in Churches (1562), Prayer Book and Homily Society, 1840

William Sherlock, *A Practical Discourse of Religious Assemblies* (1681), Burns, 1840

J. H. Shorthouse, *John Inglesant* (1881), Macmillan, 1883

P. N. Shuttleworth, *Not Tradition but Scripture*, Rivington, 1839

H. P. K. Skipton, *The Life and Times of Nicolas Ferrar*, Mowbray, 1907

Robert Southey, *The Book of the Church* (1837), John Murray, 1841

Vernon Staley, *The Catholic Religion* (1893), Mowbray, 1904

A. P. Stanley, *Lectures on the History of the Eastern Church* (1861), Dent, 1907

A. H. Stanton, *Faithful Stewardship and other Sermons*, Hodder & Stoughton, 1916

C. J. Stranks, *Anglican Devotion*, SCM Press, 1961

Norman Sykes, *William Wake*, Cambridge University Press, 1957

S. W. Sykes, 'The Genius of Anglicanism', in G. Rowell (ed.), *The English Religious Tradition and the Genius of Anglicanism*, Ikon, 1992

S. W. Sykes, *The Integrity of Anglicanism*, Mowbrays, 1978

The Poems of Edward Taylor, ed. D. E. Stanford, Yale University Press, 1960

Jeremy Taylor, *Holy Dying*, Clarendon Press, 1989

The Whole Works of the Right Rev. Jeremy Taylor, ed. C. P. Eden, Longman, 1862

William Temple, *Christus Veritas* (1924), Macmillan, 1949

Theological Works of Herbert Thorndike, Parker, 1844

Henry Thornton, *Family Prayers* (1834), Hatchards, 1869

Martin Thornton, *Christian Proficiency*, SPCK, 1959

John Tiller, 'Towards a theology of a local ordained ministry', in J. M. M. Francis and L. Francis (eds) *Tentmaking*, Gracewing, 1998

Peter Toon and Louis R. Tarsitano, *Neither Archaic nor Obsolete*, Edgeways Books, 2003

Works of Augustus Toplady, Baynes, 1825

Tracts for the Times, vol. 4, Rivington, 1840

Thomas Traherne, *Poems, Centuries and Three Thanksgivings*, ed. A. Ridler, Oxford Univeristy Press, 1960

Anthony Trollope, *Barchester Towers* (1857), Oxford University Press, 1998

Anthony Trollope, *Clergymen of the Church of England* (1866), Trollope Society, no date

Evelyn Underhill, *An Anthology of the Love of God*, Mowbray, 1953 (*The School of Charity*)

Vaughan's Sacred Poems, ed. H. F. Lyte, Bell, 1890

Henry Venn, *The Complete Duty of Man* (1763), Longman, 1836

Izaak Walton, *The Life of Mr George Herbert* (1670), Methuen, 1905

Daniel Waterland, *The Doctrine of the Eucharist*, Clarendon Press, 1896

The Works of the Rev John Wesley, Wesleyan Methodist Book Room, no date

B. F. Westcott, *Lessons from Work*, Macmillan, 1901

John Whale, *One Church, One Lord*, SCM Press, 1979

Samuel Wilberforce, *Sermons*, London, 1844

William Wilberforce, *A Practical View of the Prevailing Religious System etc.* (1797), SCM Press, 1958

A. T. P. Williams, *The Anglican Tradition in the Life of England*, SCM Press, 1947

Rowan Williams, *Anglican Identities*, Darton, Longman and Todd, 2004

The Works of Thomas Wilson, Parker, 1851

James Woodforde, *The Diary of a Country Parson*, Oxford University Press, 1935

William Wordsworth, *Poetical Works*, Oxford University Press, 1942

Charlotte M. Yonge, *Musings over the Christian Year*, London, 1871

Charlotte M. Yong, *The Castle Builders*, Mozley, 1854

Index of Authors